Making Changes

Family Voices on Living with Disabilities

Jan A. Spiegle
Richard A. van den Pol

Brookline Books • Cambridge, Massachusetts

Library of Congress Cataloging-in-Publication Data

Making changes: family voices on living with disabilities /
Jan Spiegle, Richard A. van den Pol, editors.
p. cm.
Includes bibliographical references and index.
ISBN 0-914797-93-X (pbk.) : $19.95
1. Handicapped children -- Family relationships. 2. Parents of handicapped children. 3. Parenting. 4. Hanicapped children -- Case studies 5. Handicapped children -- Care. I. Spiegle, Jan, 1952- II. Van den Pol, Richard Aart.
HQ773.6.C43 1993
306.874--dc20 93-23937
CIP

To purchase this book, order from:
BROOKLINE BOOKS
P.O. Box 1046, Cambridge, MA. 02238, Tel. 617-868-0360, Fax 617-868-1772

Discussions leading to preparation of this manuscript were supported in part by Grants #G008530084 and #G008730535 from the Early Education Program for Children with Disabilities, and Grants #H029J80029, #H024D00029 and H024D10024 from the Division of Personnel Preparation, Office of Special Education Programs, U.S. Department of Education. The opinions expressed herein do not necessarily reflect the position or policy of the U.S. Department of Education, and no official endorsement should be inferred.

Dedication

For Josh and Sharon and their families
and
To the memory of Gray Garwood, whose efforts
on behalf of children with special needs helped secure their future through a
free, appropriate, public education.

Webster's Ninth New Collegiate Dictionary (1986) defines "change" as "to give a different position, course, or direction to; to undergo transformation, transition, or substitution."

Today is not yesterday —
We ourselves change.
How then, can our works and thoughts,
if they are always to be fittest,
continue always the same?
Change, indeed, is always painful,
yet ever needful;
and if memory have its force and worth,
so also has hope.

— Thomas Carlyle

Table of Contents

FOREWORD • *Congressman Pat Williams, U.S. House of Representatives* .... **ix**

ACKNOWLEDGMENTS .... **xi**

PREFACE .... **xiii**

PROLOGUE .... **xix**

CHAPTER 1: Martha **1**
Insisting on the Positive Possibility • *Margaret Hansen* 1
Let Her Do It • *David Hansen* 5
Hope and the Ability to Dream • *Martha Hansen* 9

CHAPTER 2: Bruce **12**
Halloween and Hamburgers • *Jan Spiegle* 12
Twenty-Eight Years Later • *Bruce Blattner* 14

CHAPTER 3: Sammi **25**
Letter to a Friend • *Sue Wilson* 25
Sara's Lamp • *Sara Wilson* 31

CHAPTER 4: Jon **33**
Untold Diagnosis • *Mary Pielaet* 33

CHAPTER 5: Sara **42**
Daddy, Phone's Busy • *Bud Mariska* 42
It's OK Because She's Sara... • *Jan Spiegle-Mariska* 46
The Birthday Invitation • *Jan Spiegle-Mariska* 53

Sister of the Heart • *Jamie Mariska* 56
Skyriding • *Jan Spiegle-Mariska* 58

CHAPTER 6: Sean 60
Isn't Testosterone Wonderful? • *Fred McGlynn* 60
Dispensing More Than Drugs • *Kathy McGlynn & Byron Dodd* 65
Dear Mom and Dad • *Joel McGlynn* 70

CHAPTER 7: Lisa 71
Conversation on Butler Creek Road •
Lisa DeLand, Virginia DeLand, and Jan Spiegle 71
One Bite at a Time • *Virginia DeLand* 90

CHAPTER 8: Austin 96
The Decision for Out-of-Home Placement • *Delanie Baker* 96
Respite Care: A Most Necessary Choice • *Tane & Tim Walmsley* 106

CHAPTER 9: Miranda 109
On Miranda • *Anonymous* 109

CHAPTER 10: John 111
An Eye in the Storm • *Sally Freeman* 111

CHAPTER 11: The Health Care Providers 115
To Know Them as People • *Ethan B. Russo, M.D.* 115
Decisions and Objectivity • *Charles E. Bell, M.D., Bruce G. Hardy, M.D., Kathleen S. Rogers, M.D., & Scott Werner, M.D.* 122
Through the Door • *Scott Werner, M.D.* 125
Pharmacists Helping Families: An Unique and Untapped Resource •
Byron Dodd , R.Ph. & Kathy McGlynn 127

CHAPTER 12: The Teachers 135
Kids and Labels • *Jim Denny* 135
From a Classroom Teacher's Perspective • *Susan Harper-Whalen* 137
Feelings in a Manila Folder • *Sharon Richardson* 144

From a Sibling and Physical Therapist's Perspective •
Elizabeth A. Couch, R.P.T. *146*

CHAPTER 13: Nic **149**

From Provider to Consumer: An Involuntary Transition •
Rick van den Pol 149

CHAPTER 14: Marina and Katya **153**

And the Winner of the Rainbow Lottery is... • *Kate Carlyle* *153*

CHAPTER 15: Joshua **159**

"Are You Super Mom or What?" • *Jan Spiegle* *159*

Happily Ever After? • *Carly McClure* *161*

EPILOGUE **194**

APPENDIX 1: The Topical Index **195**

APPENDIX 2: The Instructor's Guide **197**

APPENDIX 3: The Support Group Discussion Guide **206**

INDEX **214**

Foreword

Congressman Pat Williams

Pat has long been an advocate for the educational rights of all children. His work in the United States Congress on behalf of all people with disabilities is exemplary and visionary.

People often ask me what influences members of Congress to offer and pass legislation. That is, folks want to know how legislation is encouraged, how do members of Congress come to recognize that the public wants a change in basic law? Of particular interest to people is how an important landmark piece of legislation comes to be.

There are many facets, many elements that go into the encouragement, development and eventual passage of legislation. I believe that the most important of those facets is the influence exerted by the American people. Americans constantly hear about the importance of "writing your congressman." Yes, cards, letters, phone calls, and personal visits are important, as is testimony given in hearings. But overlooked is the critical nature of the often unintended influence people have over those of us who legislate.

I have been influenced, directly and indirectly, in many ways—some of which were unrecognizable at the time. Let me share some of what influenced me to work for and secure the passage of Public Law 99–457, The Education of the Handicapped Act Amendments of 1986:

During my early years in grade school, I was intrigued by the other children I would occasionally see in the hallways. They were in something called the "Special Room." Why were they not in the regular classes I wondered? My passing "Hi" to those "special" children was always accompanied by a sense of mystery and frustration.

Both my wife, Carol, and I taught in public school classrooms in Montana. Some of the children we taught had disabilities of varying degrees. One cannot teach those children, and know their parents, without recognizing that with a little assistance these children can grow to full potential. And, conversely, one understands that without that extra assistance, those same children may well experience lives of deprivation.

As a young legislator, serving in the Montana Legislature during part of the decade of the sixties, I was often visited by personal friends who had children with disabilities. These friends impressed upon me the necessity of legislative attention for their children.

And there is another important influence. She was just hours old when I telephoned her father. Mother was fine, but the new baby girl had some problems, she had Down syndrome.

The child's father sounded anxious, disturbed, but also determined. . . symptoms I had also recognized in the parents of other children born into trouble.

I had heard of Down syndrome, of course. I wanted to know more, so I went to a medical dictionary. Some cases of Down syndrome have two cell lines, one normal and one with 47 chromosomes. Other children with Down syndrome have 47 chromosomes in all cell lines. In some, the additional chromosome 21 has been translocated. I read about not only the chromosomal variance, but the prognosis.

Her name is Keough. Her parents honored me by asking me to be her godfather.

And, of course, there were others. Christopher, whose family asked that I simply demonstrate my friendship for him by assisting in the passage of meaningful legislation to lend Christopher and all the Christophers and Keoughs a helping hand.

Thus, one is influenced; slowly, through the years, by people who often do not know that their actions and their presence are influencing someone who is, or may one day be, in a position to change public policy in a dramatic and meaningful way.

In 1986, former Senator Lowell Weicker and I determined that the federal government should provide incentives to states to serve all three-to-five-year-olds and develop a policy for early intervention for infants with disabilities. We knew that our determination and the determination of those who understood the need for this law would have to overcome our incredibly bad timing. Here we were trying to create another entitlement in the middle of a decade in which Americans seemed supportive of *reducing* federal intervention and spending. However, we had almost twenty years of research demonstrating the effectiveness, the cost savings, inherent in the early intervention and mandating of services for children from birth to five years of age.

The Senate acted first. Then our House Subcommittee on Select Education, which I chaired at the time, began to use what I believed was a "window of opportunity" for expanding possibilities for preschoolers with disabilities. It was a lengthy process lasting from June until almost year's end. The Congress listened to those of us in the House and Senate, but more importantly, they were moved by all those people who had been influencing members of Congress through the years.

P.L. 99–457 is an extraordinary piece of legislation. Under it the appropriation level for this effort was increased almost tenfold within three years.

Yes, the Congress did its job. But it was because some of us, many of us, had been influenced in very meaningful and thoughtful ways through the years.

My thanks to the editors for dedicating this book to the memory of Gray Garwood, who passed away at the age of 49. Gray was the Director of the Subcommittee on Select Education, which I chaired, and engineered the critical staff work that made this law possible.

Acknowledgments

Jan Spiegle

Jan is the mother of four daughters: Jamie, Jessica, Sara, and Hope. Sara has Down syndrome. Jan has worked as a family resource specialist for the CO-TEACH Preschool Programs, as an instructor at The University of Montana, and is currently the coordinator of Part H (Infant and Toddler) Services for the state of Montana.

There are many people without whom this book would not have been possible. Although I am the person through whom *Changes* came to be, its original concept was developed by our program director, Dr. Richard van den Pol, and parent/journalist/advocate, Susan Duffy.

Dr. Richard van den Pol has listened to me, advised me, and encouraged me in times of self-doubt. He has acted on what families have said (in research and in person) to make the programs he administers exceptional examples of how family\professional partnerships can function. His belief in "families as allies" has been a sustaining and empowering force in the lives of myriad families. Susan Duffy's ideas, friendship and encouragement have fortified me in times of difficulty and nurtured me in times of exhaustion. She has helped me to recognize the power that parents possess to make positive change happen for their children. The title of this book originated with her.

Congressman Pat Williams made time in what must be a formidable schedule to write the foreword for this book. I thank him for his leadership in matters of legislation and his understanding in matters of the spirit.

Vice President Ray Murray, former Dean John Pulliam and Dean Don Robson of the University of Montana have been supportive of this endeavor in many ways. Their professional expertise and personal interest have been a valuable asset.

I express my special appreciation to the staff with whom I worked at the CO-TEACH Preschool Programs. They helped me grow in my understanding and appreciation of the professionals who serve families like my own. They offered me an avenue to impact a small corner of the world and to find enormous personal growth and satisfaction in doing so.

The university students who are an integral part of the CO-TEACH Program became my friends, colleagues, and (sometimes most importantly) child care providers for my children. Without them, the hours to put this book together would not have been available to me. I take great personal joy in knowing that their lives will have positive impact on the children and families they go on to work with professionally.

Linda Kron, supervising teacher for CO-TEACH, has provided a nurturing and exciting classroom for all of my children at one time or another in the past five years. Moreover, she is an example of that elusive combination of professional expertise and personal tenderness, tempered with good humor. Much of the time I spent working on this book, my children were in Linda's classroom; that fact made it very comfortable for me to pursue this challenge. Lyn Wicks, Debbie Hansen, Jean Guidry, and Rhonda Alt listened to my frustrations and inspirations and got me out of every word processing predicament that I managed to create. They were "user friendly" co-workers. Particular appreciation is expressed to Beth Keeley for her conceptual and editorial contributions.

Jamie, Jessica, Sara, and Hope have taught me with infinite patience, what it means to be a mom. They have also taken out the garbage, kept their rooms clean, and fed the dog, the cats, the birds, and the snake while I worked on this book. I wouldn't know what to do without them. They, in turn, would not know what to do without their father, Bud, whose strength of spirit and perseverance give new meaning to the word "daddy."

To my new-found colleagues at the Developmental Disabilities Division of the Department of Social and Rehabilitative Services for the state of Montana, who were not part of my life while this book was being written, I still offer my thanks and respect. Framers of policy for the state of Montana, their mission statement embodies all of what *Changes* is about and serves to focus all of us on the work that must yet be done: "Through leadership, we plan, implement, evaluate and strengthen systems that assure opportunities for a good life for each Montanan who is at risk of having or has a developmental disability."

To those parents, professionals and families who shared feelings with me that were sometimes not easy to share, in the hope that they would make the path easier for those who walk after us, my respect and sincere thanks.

And my very special thanks to my new husband, David, for simply "being there."

Preface

Jan Spiegle

In April of 1984, four parents from Missoula, Montana — Susan Duffy, Jeannie Murphy, Kathy McGlynn, and I — attended a conference on early childhood education for children with disabilities in Billings, Montana. We presented a sectional on various aspects of parenting a child with special needs. The sectional was a great success and the content of our presentation was published in written form as a booklet entitled *Acceptance Is Only the First Battle*. Since its original publication, the booklet has continued to be one of the most requested among the materials available from The CO-TEACH Preschool Programs. Judging from the requests we've received, there appears to be an ongoing need within families and among professionals for written materials which address the issues involved in parenting and offering professional services to our children. In response to that need, we have assembled this sequel to the *Acceptance* booklet. (As the reader can see, it has evolved way past the "booklet" stage!)

The theme of change was chosen because it seemed to naturally follow our first theme of acceptance. Once families and professionals can determine and accept the disabilities a person may have, they can move forward to serving the needs of that individual. In meeting those needs effectively, parents and professionals almost always find that change of one sort or another is necessary:

- The parents of a child who is medically fragile may have to drastically alter their lifestyle in order to accommodate the constant care required by their child.
- Siblings of a child with disabilities may be asked to make many changes and even some sacrifices in their own lives to fulfill the needs of their brother or sister.
- The medical professionals charged with the care of a child or adult with a disability may have to accommodate needs that are very different from

those of their typical patients.

- Educational professionals serving developmental needs effectively will adapt their service model to fit each child and family that they serve.
- Persons who deal daily with complications of their own disability will (usually by trial and error) change their lifestyle to accommodate the fundamental complexities of their condition.

Thus, those of us whose lives are touched in any way by a child or adult with disabilities have probably made changes in the way we do our jobs and live our lives. Some of those changes are made of necessity; others are made because in the process of doing our jobs and living our lives, we recognize that changing what we do, or the way we do it, may greatly enhance the quality of life for a person with disabilities and his family. Those changes can also lessen the stress that is an inherent part of dealing with the everyday needs of people with disabilities.

All these changes, made of necessity or choice, alter the lives of people with life challenges and have great impact on those who are close to them. Given society's historical treatment of people who are "special," it is a sign of great progress that such options are now available to all of us.

The purpose of this project was to provide a resource book based on real-life experience for families and professionals who deal daily with disability issues. During the course of gathering, reading, and pondering the manuscripts, a second purpose emerged as equally important — that of helping families and professionals to understand and accept the varying emotions and attitudes which often govern our responses to the world in which we live and work with people who have disabilities.

When I set out to help assemble a follow-up to the *Acceptance* booklet, my thoughts were not very focused. The authors of the chapters provided that focus. Again and again, I listened as parents and professionals told of their experiences. Through it all there ran common threads. Foremost was the broad-based belief among our contributors that "acceptance" is not only an issue for families to come to terms with when a child who has a disability becomes part of their lives; it is also an issue which must be dealt with by the professionals who serve such individuals. The acceptance of these persons as *human beings first* (with all the basic emotional responses and needs common to our species) is, from any perspective, the key to effectively addressing their needs. Our hope is that these chapters will help professionals and parents understand these issues — that reading so many stories that come from the heart will allow each of us to make changes of our own toward this basic consideration: people with disabilities are people just like everyone else. That seems obvious, I know. But as you read *Changes*, consider how often the human factor gets lost in the system of service delivery. From the voices of those who have lived with disability, many commonalities are uncovered:

- There is the sense that when we take the time to listen, we are taught by people with disabilities that we are not custodians of their lives, nor should we be.
- There is the feeling that allowing choices to be made and risks to be taken (which are inherently a part of each "typical" person's existence) enhances human dignity and empowers each individual with a sense of self-possession and empowerment.
- There is the notion that persons with special challenges and their families can best tell us what it is they want and require from those professionals who serve their needs.
- There is living proof that, as the German philosopher Friedrich Nietzsche wrote, "that which does not kill us makes us stronger."

GETTING MORE OUT OF *CHANGES* — HOW TO UTILIZE THE BOOK'S STRUCTURE

The text of *Changes* is followed by a Topical Index, a Support Group Discussion Guide, and an Instructor's Guide. Those sections were written to assist those who may choose to share their reading of the book with others, to use the book as a starting point for a thorough examination of disability issues, or simply to focus their reading on a specific topical interest.

Support group members may find that focusing their shared reading around a theme chosen from the Topical Index will enhance their ability to respond openly to specific subject matter. Since many of the chapters offer a straightforward and sometimes painfully honest assessment of personal impact, there is the sense that sharing similar stories, reactions, and feelings may be facilitated by first sharing personal responses to *Changes*.

The Support Group Discussion Guide focuses the reader on particular family-focused topics; it will be useful in orienting and enhancing the sharing of parents, siblings, and other family members who choose to read the book as a common experience. The questions focus on the personal impact that parenting or living with a child with a disbility may have on individual family members and on family integrity, themes close to the heart of all families impacted by disability.

High school teachers or college instructors who use the book as a case study text may find the Topical Index useful for thematic reading assignments. The Instructor's Guide provides both fact-based and philosophy-based questions for discussion or contemplation, all keyed to the themes from the Topical Index. Each topical theme is paired with a Reflective Writing Assignment which requires not only commitment of ideas to paper, but earnest self-examination in the process.

The Instructor's Guide augments and reinforces the basic life-centered learning that is available through reading *Changes*. Strengthening and expanding on traditional textbook learning, the book's case study approach has much to offer professionals in training or those working professionals who seek a more genuine or deeper understanding of the individuals with whom they work and their families. For those who have never dealt "up close and personal" with disability impact and issues, the Guide provides a thematic structure through which the student is steered toward self-examination and closer inspection of the nature of the profession they have chosen.

Through the Index, individual readers will also be able to access topics which are of the most interest to them. The questions from both Guides may be helpful, even to the individual reader who wishes to ruminate about, or simply examine more closely, her reaction to the book and its themes.

Much like a painting that may be viewed by separate people from unique angles, or by a touring group at an art museum, *Changes* will mean something different to each of its readers, and to each group that experiences it collectively. For some it will validate things they already knew; for others it will widen the lenses through which our impressions of life are formed and substantiated.

We hope that all of those who read *Changes* will consider the wonderful progress we, as a society, have made towards understanding people with exceptional life challenges and towards integrating them into the world that belongs to all of us. Also, we hope you will consider how much work is left to be done.

We all (families, professionals, and persons with disabilities) stand together at the threshold of a vision which includes optimal service delivery to people with disabilities and their families; it also includes meeting their fundamental human need to be valued: for the strides in growth and knowledge that they make; for sharing their talents and strengths with our society; for their courage and perseverance; and for striving always towards greater dignity and independence. *Changes* is a touching and enlightening mosaic of many lives. Some articles were written under a pseudonym to allow their writers more freedom and anonymity in telling their stories. All the selections, however, tell of the experiences of real-life people and the events which have shaped their lives.

Prologue

Jan Spiegle

In some ways, I think I have been working on this book since I was five years old. That year (1957) my parents enrolled me in a private kindergarten which was held in the basement of a retired teacher's home. There was a tree fort and a wonderful jungle gym in Mrs. Van Ness's back yard which her husband was continually modifying to her specifications. To get there I walked about four blocks.

Mrs. Van Ness was a motherly, soft-spoken, gray-haired lady who was a natural at teaching small children. She taught us to be kind to one another, to share, to put things away, to stand in line without pushing, and to listen to one another. She taught us those things by modeling them herself. She often stood in line with us (we took turns leading because, she said, "I run a democratic classroom!"). If we interrupted her, she assumed what we had to say was important and she listened. If there was a more appropriate time to voice our thoughts, she gently told us so. She never appeared annoyed or impatient at our interruptions or frequent mistakes. We were encouraged to pat each other on the back when we did a good job. In her red-brick "classroom," I remember little in the way of tears and unhappiness and lots in the way of hugs and praise.

In class with us that year was a little boy named Josh. I remember that he was sort of "funny looking." He had big ears and he was clumsy. Since he was the son of my mother's best friend, and because he lived nearby, we walked to and from school together. The arrangement seemed logical to me; I never gave it a second thought. I know now that it was a situation created by my mom and Josh's mom to ensure that he got to and from school safely.

To me, Josh was just one of the kids. It wasn't until much later in my life that I realized he was educationally challenged, though I missed him when I started first grade and he wasn't there. I don't remember kids teasing him (but, then, Mrs. Van Ness never allowed teasing of any kind). I don't remember feeling funny about walking to school with him. I do remember Mrs. Van Ness praising me nearly every day for all the help I gave Josh. Her praise made me feel warm and glowing though I didn't see anything special about walking to school with a friend. Josh did seem sort of frail to me (he was sick a lot), and his art projects were awfully messy by my five-year-old standards. He was a boy, I concluded, and boys were just more messy. Basically, he was just one of my friends. I liked him because he often asked to hold my hand and he was always clearly happy to see me.

Later, in my elementary years, when I realized that Josh lived in our school district, but did not go to school, I quizzed my mom. Why did he get to stay home when I had to go to school? Mom explained that the schools were not set up for "kids like Josh." "He's smart," she said, "but it takes him longer to learn and he needs more help." She pointed out that my class had thirty kids that year and that the teacher had her hands full. Still, it seemed very unfair to me that just because he didn't learn things quickly, he got out of going to school. Even from my lopsided vantage point, something was amiss.

Then there was Sharon. She was the daughter of some friends of my parents who had moved to Utah when I was very young. We visited them and were guests in their home the summer I was twelve. Sharon was about thirty years old at the time and spoke only one intelligible word — "button." She had a button collection and would rip buttons off your clothes if you got close enough (I steered clear). She would also watch the detective show Peter Gunn, and try to warn the hero about the thug behind the door who inevitably cold-cocked him in every episode.

Sharon was cared for by her mother and grandmother. During our stay, I remember a stormy argument between her mom and dad. We kids had been outside playing cops and robbers in a tomato field when I scraped my neck on some barbed wire. I returned to the house for band aids, and walked in unnoticed. Before they saw me, I heard Sharon's mom scream, "She'll go to a home over my dead body."

I knew by then that there were places where people like Josh and Sharon were "put away." What I wondered at the time was not why they didn't put Sharon away, but why they didn't just teach her to behave better and to say more than "button." I reasoned that if she could learn to say "button," she must be able to learn other words. (It disgusted and embarrassed me that the only way she had to tell them she had to use the bathroom was to "hold herself" like a little kid.) I kept these thoughts to myself, though I did openly feel sorry for her brother and sister, who had to put up with Sharon every day and with parents who always seemed to be very angry with *everyone*.

Sadly, when Sharon's mom and grandma died several years later, she was placed in a state institution. I remember her dad coming to visit my folks (I was in college at the time). As I made coffee and snacks in the kitchen for them, I remember hearing the anguish in his voice as he spoke of having to "put her somewhere." I remember, too, the way my usually stoic father looked misty around the eyes as I poured his coffee. Sharon died shortly thereafter.

It wasn't until many years later, when I had borne my own child with Down syndrome, that I remembered those scenes from my youth. I was astonished at the clarity with which they returned to mind. Now, when I think of Sharon, I think of lost potential and the life she might have led had she been born thirty years later. I also think of Josh who, because of his family's love and his mother's insistence that he could learn (with the knowledge from her own eighth grade education, she taught him how to read and write at home), now works productively in a workshop in my home town. I am awed at the love and fortitude their parents must have had to do what they did — keep their children at home when most certainly there were well-meaning professionals and family members urging them to "do the right thing." I am fortunate to have had glimpses of what life was like for such families many years ago. By comparison, the path I have followed since the birth of my daughter has been infinitely easier. That's not to say it has been easy — just easier.

CHAPTER 1: MARTHA

Insisting on the Positive Possibility

Margaret Hansen

Margaret is the mother of four children. Her daughter, Martha, has Werdig-Hoffman's Disease, a congenital degenerative neuromuscular disorder. Margaret has worked as a parent coordinator at a school for children with disabilities.

This is a happy story about a family which was told, in 1961, that their youngest daughter would live for one more year, would suffer great physical loss during that time, and eventually die in her weakness. The name of the disease is not the important part. What is of value is the process our family developed, lacking much information or instruction, to deal with what we were told.

Naturally, at first, we cried and carried on. After that, we thought it over and decided that mourning before the fact was a great waste; we had better appreciate what we had for as long as we had it!

Our family consisted of two boys and two girls, six years between the oldest and the youngest. They were (and are) a happy, bright, fun-loving bunch; each one a precious gift. That, in fact, turned out to be the key — to view each child as a unique gift. Having a family was a privilege, we decided, one we would appreciate.

So, this is the story of what we did. It is a story about attitudes and choices. It probably has some element of use for any family who faces disability. We made mistakes, as all families will. Each member of any family that faces this kind of life challenge will come to his or her own conclusions. This story is intended solely to be the point of view of a wife and mother.

We were one of the families who first benefited from antibiotics, for without them our fragile child would have died of pneumonia before we even had a complete diagnosis. She lived through that threatening time, surviving a major weakening of her body. Thankfully, we did not lose her. In fact, she has gone on to accomplish more than we could have dreamed, and believe me, we dreamed big!

First, we came to understand that doctors often must give the "worst case" scenario; they do have a duty to inform their patients completely. We, however, have the right to choose to interpret that information as a challenge or to let it overwhelm us into total tragedy.

We had always had one goal for our children; we worked toward giving them the guidance and encouragement that would produce independent, responsible adults. As Martha's challenge arose in our lives, we decided that we would keep that goal in place for all four children. We were not going to hand over our girl without a fight! We especially were not going to sacrifice our other three wonderful children to the specter of what was "supposed to happen."

So we began, before support groups, before "networking" or any social services help, to seek our own path. One wonderful neurologist warned us not to spoil her, a great family doctor gave us unbelievable help, and we went about keeping everything as normal as possible. We did nothing that would give the impresssion of having "given in" to the prognosis.

The kids were great. They just naturally thought of games that Martha could play. When she was too weak to eat at the dinner table, we "picnicked" in her room. We did not "referee" the children, wanting them to figure our their own solutions to their internal power struggles. We wanted them to be friends after they were grown, and that meant not allowing ourselves to be put in between them for manipulation's sake. This meant some physical damage (nothing too serious), but they all learned along the way to handle the problems that arose. Early on, I decided that I would prefer my children have these independence skills in place rather than placate them as children and end up with functionally "disabled" adults. I guess I am somewhat of a tough cookie in that regard. Today, they still all love each other.

We went all out for the joy and delight of each individual. If we won, we knew we all would win; there would be no regret for having missed the attention needed by one of the healthy children because we were grieving ahead of the fact for the weak one. I wish I could say that the other children never lost out for Martha's needs; instead, I can say that they were extremely generous when, unavoidably, her needs took precedence over their own.

Several decisions we made were right. Most of them took a great deal of courage:

- We left the association that had been funding Martha's medical care because they insisted on our using their doctors who did not specialize in Martha's condition. This was financially taxing for our family, but we felt we had to think of her health and her future in a more positive way; these doctors saw only defeat.

- We declined an invitation for Martha to be a poster child. For us, it would have been too great an acceptance of the prognosis and it would have set her apart from our other children.

- We went into debt to put in a swimming pool to benefit the whole family and to give Martha therapy. It was something special for all of us, a fun family environment.

- We took Martha out of a special education school when she was unacceptably grouped with children whose disabilities were very different than her own. We talked the principal of our local grammar school into allowing Martha to attend there when she was physically able. (Remember, this was 1967, when mainstreaming was not a word I, or anyone else, had ever heard.) This school district had an outstanding home schooling program which carried Martha until she could go to college (that's a whole other story!).

- We encouraged Martha to believe that she could go to college, as we did all our other children. We received criticism for this stance. We had come to believe that a goal missed is not sad. But, not taking the risk of being successful is tragic. And regret always lasts longer than dismay.

- (This one I write about with caution.) Our supportive family doctor discouraged us from putting Martha on oxygen when her lungs began to weaken. He said that she would be bound by carrying that tank with her for the rest of her life. Today, she does have funny shaped lungs, but she learned to compensate and she lives more freely than she might have, encumbered only by her wheelchair.

- We decided to go for a spinal fusion for her at the age of eight, when her back gave out. We were told that this was the "expected development" for her condition and that there was no hope. We asked if she could live at all without the surgery, and when the answer was "no", we went ahead, gambling on the positive possibility instead of the negative definite.

- We always opted for hope. Each birthday Martha celebrated was a joyous occasion; we had fooled them again! While we have great respect for the medical profession, we had to determine how much of our lives we were willing to let them take over. We were careful without being care-worn.

- While there were no formal support groups for comfort, we had good, helping friends. We did not identify ourselves as part of any disability group; we were not elite, we were simply content to be ourselves. This is not to be construed as a slam at support groups and special education programs. Instead, it is an encouragement to each family to think out what they hope and want for their child. Getting on the slide of predicted behavior and limited potential is a downward spiral. Because of each family's close observations of their child and the simple nature of family love, their contribution to goal planning is both the most knowledgeable and the most appropriate.

If I were to step on my personal soapbox, my speech would focus on the individuality of each person. It is vital to look at each child as unique. A medical diagnosis says nothing about the intrinsic value of a child, or about the wonderful personality complex that makes up a cherished member of the family. We are not talking "sadly" here. We are not talking "burden". More work, almost certainly, but much more reward. We are talking about breaking out of the pre-shaped cast of what a family is or should be. Our family was given the opportunity for a new and better life experience because we actively searched for all the possibilities. We did not let ourselves get bogged down waiting for doom.

Today, all four of our children are independent and responsible adults; they have the tools necessary for living and the opportunity to design their own lives. Martha was recently accepted by a graduate program where she will pursue her doctorate in special education. We are grateful to them, all four, for the part each plays in our family. Each one has chosen a different career and interests, but all have used the ability to hope to foster the pursuit of their dreams. Daring to succeed, they insist on the positive possibility.

Let Her Do It

David J. Hansen

David is the father of three children, and the pastor of two small churches in rural Montana. He is Margaret Hansen's son and Martha Hansen's brother.

I grew up in a home with a sibling who has a disability. I was six years old in 1959 when my mother brought Martha home. Nothing seemed unusual at the time; two years earlier my mother had brought home a brother. Tom and I already had a sister, Mary, who was a mere fifteen months younger than I. When Martha was a year old I began to hear talk about her being "behind a little bit." It was declared in optimistic fashion, but I recall something in my mother's voice that gave the pronouncements an ominous sound. By the time Martha was two years old, they knew that something was wrong. Martha and Mom went on a long trip, to Washington, D.C., to have Martha looked at by doctors. They diagnosed Werdig-Hoffman disease, an extremely serious neuromuscular disorder. To us kids the name of the problem meant nothing. But when Mom and Martha returned, our whole world changed: we were no longer a normal family.

It is hard to remember how critical it was in the early sixties for families to appear normal. We liked tract housing, and television gave us a homogenized view of family life that stressed the necessity of being normal. We lived in the generation after the war, after the depression, with antibiotics and polio vaccine. It appeared that success would be the norm for our generation. And since success would be the norm, the converse seemed true as well: success surely depended on being a part of the norm. So when my parents unveiled Martha's wheelchair, with the cowboys embossed in the brown Naugahyde seat and back, I felt two feelings. I felt sorry for Martha, but I also felt sorry for myself and for our family. We were no longer normal; from now on we would stick out in a department store and at church. I think my parents felt the same. Martha's first wheelchair was an overwhelming symbol to us; we cried for her and we cried for us. Of course, as children we had no concept of the many hardships caring for her would bring. All I knew was we were no longer normal; we lived in a world where everyone was being dealt aces — but us.

We all knew that we were in for a long haul, and nobody we knew was facing anything like it. I, at least, felt alone for our family. Those first trips to the store and the church with Martha's wheelchair in tow were devastating for me. I was desperately embarrassed; not ashamed of her, but ashamed that we weren't "normal" anymore. Resolving the abnormality of it was, for me, the first transition. It was also the easiest; as the sixties progressed, normalcy became less important. It was going to be okay to be different. It wasn't long before I was very, very proud to have Martha around and it became a badge of honor to push her around in public. Somehow our parents had the grace to understand that it was important for us to run when we pushed her, to take her at breakneck speeds through stores and the hallowed halls of churches. I guess that made us normal. Her wheelchair became a toy to us. Soon we kids were taking turns tooling around the house in it, becoming experts at wheelchair "wheelies."

Early on, Martha encountered complications. The doctors talked about her dying young . . . real young, like in a few years. Martha was in diapers a lot longer than most children and she had a terrible kidney infection when she was about three or four. Her urine had an intense odor that smelled like death to me. She coughed and coughed and coughed. She cried a lot and went to doctors a lot. All of this made me sad. I remember being awake in bed, late at night, hearing my parents cry about Martha's condition, and I cried a lot too. I remember intensely the feeling of being around other children in grade school and realizing that they had no idea of what I was feeling about Martha, about death, about the fragility of life. This feeling continued into high school. I didn't feel envious of their naivete, and I didn't feel sorry for myself, thinking that someone should have tried to reach out and understand me; my assumption was that no one had any idea of what my situation was. I felt like my world was incomprehensible to anyone else. It's important to remember that in the early sixties children with disabilities were never in public school, and many were institutionalized, so I really didn't know anyone of any age, or any family, that had our problem or anything like it.

During my grade school years I began to live my life inside my head. I had a natural predisposition to this, to extreme inwardness, but our family situation certainly intensified my journey inward. My inwardness became a coping mechanism which I am only now, as an adult, attempting to replace with a balanced outward life.

In fact, as a result of my early transitions in living around sickness and sorrow, now, as an adult, I feel drawn to people with pain and heartache, and I really do try to connect with their loneliness. I don't know if I attempt to do this to help them, or to help me; I know that when someone shares their heartache with me, I feel less alone; they can't see the child in me smile for being understood. But it takes effort and risk to really connect with other people's pain; there is another side of me that doesn't want to be reminded by other people's pain of what it felt like to be me as a child.

Being normal in the sixties meant formica, melmac, copious amounts of television, and recreational activities. My parents always did their very best to shield us from the consequences of Martha's illness, but when they had to tell us that, because of Martha, we couldn't do something that other kids of other families did, they were forthright with us. Actually, we really did a lot of things together. We camped and fished and participated in scouting and sports. But, there were many times that we couldn't do things because of Martha and we knew it. They always explained things clearly and compassionately to us, they simply expected us to understand, and we did. I learned early to make sacrifices; this fit my identity of being different. It became part of my identity that I was different, and this because I gave up more than most.

My whole family assumed this identity. Each of us children, because of our unique place in the family, had our own sacrifices to make. These were reinforced by community members who admired us, prayed for us, pitied us, and thanked God in heaven that the*y didn't have to be like us.* I learned to despise the sickening smiles of people who talked about how strong we were, or how noble, or how courageous. I felt that they understood us the least. I, at least, never felt strong, noble or courageous; I just had to be different and I was willing to do what I had to do. I felt proud to be doing what I was doing, and I was proud of our family, of Martha and my parents. But back then no one ever remarked about being proud of our situation; how could you be proud of not being normal? Proud was a word reserved for normal, but above average. Not until much later, when all of us kids, including Martha, had graduated from college, and were launched on our successful careers did people talk about being proud. But now the word seems irrelevant to what we did. We didn't ask for the challenge, and taking credit seems inappropriate.

Like many postwar families, being normal meant going to church and we were no different. It is hard to say what real import it had to us in the early days, before Martha, and during her early years. But medical science could not help Martha, and as the seriousness of her situation became real to us, we realized, unlike most families at that time, that science and progress were not God (though He stayed a

Republican); we had to locate the real God. We found God not by going to crusades or by being born again, but by relying on Someone we just knew had to be there. We became very religious in time, and we eventually began to identify the God we relied on instinctively with a particular brand of Christian faith and a set of sub-cultural demands. I was a religious kid and I am a religious adult; I probably would have been religious in some way even if we hadn't had Martha, but praying for her made God real to me and still does.

Martha is still around. She has her Master's Degree in Special Education and teaches in a self-contained classroom for special education students in inner-city Fresno, California, getting around in her electric wheelchair. She is still in a fragile condition. But she lives on her own, hiring attendants to take care of her daily needs. Martha is pursuing her dreams methodically and courageously and with great faith.

The effects of being Martha's brother are far from over in my life. And we as a family have many transitions yet to come. They don't get easier, just different. The transition for me now, as an adult, is to give up being the "big brother who knows everything" and trust Martha's instincts to tell her how to meet her needs in all areas of her life. I have always been too conservative in my estimation of what she could accomplish, but in that I am not alone. Martha has spent her life surrounded by experts telling her what she could and couldn't do, and almost none of them were right; only Martha knows what she can do, and what she wants to do. The rest of us in her world just need to step aside and let her do it. For some reason, we the healthy tend to project our fears of failure onto people with challenges; perhaps we consider them a safe target for our greatest fears. Instead, our relationships with people who have disabilities should make us confront and evaluate our dreams, and stop fearing to pursue them. Growing up with a sibling who had disabilities was painful but rich. It continues to enrich me.

Hope and the Ability to Dream

Martha Hansen

Martha is a teacher of children with learning disabilities and holds a master's degree in special education. A genetic condition which causes muscular atrophy requires her to use a wheelchair. She is Margaret Hansen's daughter and David Hansen's sister.

When asked to contribute my experiences to this book, I spent an inordinate amount of time considering which portion of my life would be of interest. While many of the contributors to *Making Changes* were sharing how a certain person affected their lives, I needed to share how my situation has affected my life. This is actually a difficult task as I have always been the way I am. I was born with a genetic neuromuscular atrophy condition called Werdig-Hoffman which causes me to be in a wheelchair and have severely weakened muscles. The one change that has obviously taken place is that, over the years, I have gotten better. Now that I am a teacher in special education I can see that a transition from being a "client" to being a "professional" has occurred.

From childhood I rarely felt different from my other siblings. The primary difference that I was aware of was that I went to therapy and doctor's appointments rather frequently. My mother and I spent large amounts of time waiting for, talking to, and/or being treated by medical professionals. My father attended as many doctor's appointments as possible, but mostly my mother and I were the ones who continually heard all about my deficits and weaknesses, and how I probably would not get any better or even live much longer. There were periods of time when circumstances indicated the professionals were right. Yet, in both of our minds, we knew things were going to change, I was going to get better, a great deal better.

Other differences were often due to fatigue. If I was too tired to sit up at the dinner table, my family often had dinner in the bedroom that I shared with my older sister. I can recount numerous memories of similar experiences where my family rallied to make my weaknesses our strengths. Similarly, in my classroom today, I want my students to make positive experiences out of their not always positive circumstances. I continually try to be the affirming strength to my students that my family was to me.

Although I was in bed most of the time when I was younger, my parents allowed my brothers and sister and me to play on the rough side, racing around in my wheelchair, one brother pushing me while we chased each other, and teased each other unmercifully. These experiences are not only fond memories, but were necessary to the shaping of my person; as my brothers were always much bigger than me, so are most of my eighth grade male students. They, just like my brothers, enjoy standing over me in a somewhat menacing way. I let them know, just as I did my brothers, that their size is of no benefit to them in my classroom.

Early on, my parents radiated the philosophy that a person should certainly know of his or her weaknesses, but should emphasize his or her strengths. For instance, my mother was encouraged by therapists to teach me how to dress myself. After two hours of struggling on my parents' bed, I would finally manage to complete the task; I was ready to lie down for the remainder of the day due to fatigue. My mother decided (and we joke about this now) to tie my shoes for me and let me go play with my brothers and sister. In the same way, in my classroom, I see discouraged parents who feel that their child will be a failure because he or she cannot read or perform other academic tasks. I try to point out that all the children have strengths of their own; I try to let them know what those strengths can do for them in the future. I grew up thinking that to be strong and able to walk would be wonderful, but I knew *I would still have a future if I did not walk.* Similarly, I want my students and their parents to know that reading is important, but it is not a required factor for a productive, fulfilling life. In spite of a person's inability to successfully perform academic tasks, they can achieve personal goals.

Most of my grade school years I spent in bed. There were small periods of time when I attempted to attend school or go to physical therapy, but both of these activities drained my energy so that I could do nothing else. At an early time in my life, my parents set their minds to accomplishing that which was most important. To them it was more important to have energy to do positive activities than to drain it in defeating ones. To solve those problems, they had home teaching provided through the school district and though it was a financial strain, they had a swimming pool built. These difficult and expensive decisions allowed our family to use our energy in a more positive and efficient way.

By the time I was in high school my ability to stay upright in my chair during the day increased tremendously. I was involved in our church's youth group, went swimming three times a week, and still had school services provided in our home. Near the end of my junior year, my strength had increased so that about three days a week, I was able to participate in several high school classes. The solution to scheduling was easier in college, since I could schedule classes to fit my personal needs.

After three successful years at college, I began feeling that moving away from home to complete my education would be an important next step. Now, ten years later, through much effort, creative problem-solving, the devotion of friends, and tremendous amounts of family support, I have transitioned from living at home to living on my own, teaching a special day class for students with learning disabilities.

I believe one of the most important gifts my parents gave my brothers and sister and me was that of always having hope and the ability to dream. If there is any one thing I want to do for my students it is to help them learn how to consider their strengths and interests, develop goals for their future, and continue to change themselves until the goals are attained. That is, in fact, the ability to dream. And the ability to dream is what gives us hope.

CHAPTER 2: BRUCE

Halloween and Hamburgers

Jan Spiegle

Bruce Blattner has been my friend for twenty years, although for many of those years we have not seen or spoken to one another. Most of our contact took place during the years when we were both attending The University of Montana. At that time, Bruce was obtaining a graduate degree and I was an undergraduate student.

Having grown up in the same home town, I knew of Bruce and the car accident which left him confined to a wheelchair. We met on campus one day and he asked if I might be interested in driving his van to and from our home town during vacation breaks. At that time, there was no adaptive equipment available to allow Bruce to drive, so he was often in need of transportation assistance. Over the next three years he and I, and various other home town natives, made the one-hundred-mile journey in an old milk delivery truck that Bruce's father had converted into a wheelchair-accessible van. I remember much laughter and camaraderie on those journeys; young people were discussing their dreams and their plans for the future, and there was lots of guitar playing and fun.

As Bruce graduated and I went on to finish my degree, we lost track of one another. I have kept track of his accomplishments through mutual acquaintances and articles which frequently appear in our local newspaper telling of his work as an advocate for persons with disabilities. Most recently, he has been the originator and promoter of a project which has secured a 1.3 million dollar loan from the Department of Housing and Urban Development to provide a "state-of-the-art" housing development for twenty-seven persons with physical disabilities. His accomplishments in the fields of teaching, guidance and counseling, and advocacy (both for himself and for others) are an enabling force in the lives of his former students, his friends, and our community at large.

As with Josh and Sharon (see Prologue), the impact that Bruce had on my life and my attitude towards people with disabilities was not readily apparent during the time that we had close contact with one another. After my daughter was born, my memories of those times with Bruce became very vivid and important to me. I remembered an attractive young man who struggled mightily to simply be on campus to attend classes each day. I remembered the freight elevator in the Liberal

Arts Building which was frequently out of order; it was Bruce's only means of accessing the upper floors of a building where most of his courses were taught. I remembered laughing with him about how difficult it was for him to eat spaghetti; I remember him eating hamburgers by perching the burger on his clenched fist. I remember one Halloween costume party that he attended as a Roman gladiator.

The memory that seems most significant to me now is an image that comes to mind each time I think of Bruce and all he has accomplished in his life. The picture is of a vital young man whose eyes shone with pride and courage as he would tell me how much closer he was coming each quarter to attaining his graduate degree. I have seen that look many times in the last nine years, as my daughter has reached each milestone in her development. I saw it this morning as Sara turned to wave goodbye to me as she boarded the bus for school — all by herself.

Twenty-Eight Years Later

Bruce Blattner

Bruce is a teacher, guidance counselor, and advocate for persons with disabilities. He has spent the last twenty-eight years of his life in a wheelchair.

Wicker Wheelchairs, Little League, and Lori

In May of 1962, I was involved in a car accident that left me with C-5 Quadriplegia. That meant spending the remainder of my life in a wheelchair with no use of my legs and only limited use of my arms. Following the accident, I spent two years in hospitals, readying myself for the attempt at entering society again at the age of twenty-one. This manuscript deals with the lessons I have learned over the course of my life; they are lessons that taught me how to look at life (and disability) from a completely different viewpoint.

In 1950, I played Little League baseball in a small town in western Montana. After practice or a game, I would often head with my friends to the local magazine store for a bottle of pop, some bubble gum, and a "sneak preview" of the "girl" magazines. The owner of the magazine store was confined to a wicker-backed wooden wheelchair. He would discourage us from looking at the magazines by shooting marbles at us from behind the counter with a slingshot. We all knew he couldn't come down the aisle after us, but he sure was effective at bruising our bottoms with marbles!

This was the first contact I can remember having with a person who had a disability. I thought his disability to be overwhelming; although I felt compassion and sorrow, it was uncomfortable for me to be around him. My uneasiness was caused by a lack of knowledge. I didn't know what had happened to him or if I could catch it. And, because I was afraid to ask, my questions were left unanswered. *I missed the opportunity to know the man behind the counter.*

By the time I reached the seventh grade I was developing into a good athlete. I had lots of friends and my parents had become financially successful enough to buy their first home. I adjusted quickly to the new neighborhood, and was accepted by my new peer group. During this time, I met a neighbor girl named Lori. She was several years younger than most of the kids in our neighborhood and she had Down syndrome. Lori decided since I was friendly with her that I was her "boyfriend"; she would tag along around the neighborhood behind me. I felt very sorry for Lori because she was teased by the other kids. I always tried to talk to her and be friends with her. I didn't know at the time what was "wrong" with Lori, or (again) if I could catch it by being with her. My heart reached out to her, but there was a wall of ignorance that kept me from really developing a close relationship with her. I am happy that I was secure enough within myself that the heckling from the other children about Lori being my "girlfriend" didn't bother me. I am happy that I remained distantly friendly with her. But again my fears and ignorance kept me from discovering who Lori was; *I missed the chance to really get to know her.*

Don't let fear and/or lack of knowledge prevent you from growing as an individual. Ask questions and take advantage of the opportunity to learn about other people who may be different from you. Always bear in mind that people with disabilities are much more like you than they are different. People with disabilities that you may see "out" in society have, without a doubt, overcome many obstacles in their lives to be where they are. Very few of them, if any, would be offended by an honest question. Indeed, we would prefer it to the uncomfortable silences and stares we often meet. People with disabilities are much more a part of society today because of programs like Special Olympics, much increased media coverage, support groups, and laws which protect us from discrimination. These are important advances because they help us all to better understand one another and to communicate. But the ultimate form of "societal acceptance" and communication begins with *personal* friendship.

Changing Perspectives and Risk

Fighting for one's life when you are nineteen years old is all-consuming; being confined to a hospital for months on end caused me to become more introspective. The initial result of that introspection was the feeling that everything that was good in my life had been taken from me. I spent a great deal of time feeling sorry for myself, grieving for what I had lost.

Toward the end of the first year of my hospital stay, I was moved to a ward with four other young men with severe disabilities. One of these roommates was Jon Paul from Montreal. He spoke only French, so in addition to his disability, he was fighting a language barrier. Side by side for the next five months, Jon Paul and I became very close friends. We both learned a little about the other's language and, as best we could, tried to support and protect one another. It was the kind of relationship that could only develop from crisis, when total trust and total caring became essential for survival.

During the latter days of our friendship, Jon Paul developed a serious kidney infection and was battling a high fever and the associated delirium for days on end. In my fear and concern, I tried to bolster Jon Paul's spirit by telling him jokes and providing words of encouragement and comfort. After fifteen days, Jon Paul died.

My introspective look at life and disability fell apart when I felt Jon Paul's suffering. *His* loss hurt me even more than my own. It made me realize what my parents were going through. It took me outside my own grief; I was able to see that going on with life was possible.

With the loss of this close friend came much pain — and a lesson; it was much harder to helplessly watch Jon Paul suffer and die than it was to go through the same illness myself, as I would many times later in my own life. With this lesson comes *a perspective for the reader:* I know that if you truly love someone who is living with a disability while you are powerless to help, *yours* is the tougher burden.

Sexuality

An historical reference point is appropriate in discussing my sexuality. In 1962, when I was injured, the life expectancy of a person with quadriplegia was five years. Many people with quadriplegia never left the hospital setting; if they did, they most likely went home to "bed care." Without antibiotics and many other advancements in medical technology, people with quadriplegia simply did not have a future. Not surprisingly, but very unfortunately, it was thus assumed that there was no need to discuss school, careers, *or* sexuality.

During my two-year hospital stay, the subject of sexuality literally never came up. It was assumed by me and given unspoken credence by the doctors and staff that having quadriplegia meant being asexual, not an accurate assumption to make about *any* nineteen-year-old male. There was, in fact, a hospital policy governing the nursing students stating that any student nurse caught "fraternizing" with a patient from our ward (known as "Darvon Alley") would be immediately dismissed from school.

I was, at the time, particularly interested in one student nurse and I thought she was interested in me. After much deliberation, soul searching, and thought on my part, I found the courage one day (with my heart in my throat) to ask the nurse if she would like to meet me at a prearranged spot in the hospital some evening. She said "yes", and I excitedly put the plan into action.

During the months I had been in the hospital, an orderly who had become my friend had pushed my wheelchair throughout the three-block-long, seven-story facility. I had come to know the hospital well. The meeting place I selected for this (hopefully) romantic evening was the doctor's lounge on the seventh floor. It had floor to ceiling windows looking out over the city, a pool table, a couch and an old antique wooden and leather operating table. The room was used by doctors waiting to perform surgery or to see patients during the day. Through my hospital travels, I had found it to be locked and dark most evenings. In fact, my friend, the orderly, had a key and would play pool while I looked out over the lights of the city during some of our journeys. I thought it to be a perfect meeting place. It was romantic, off the beaten path and provided her with an element of safety from discovery. The date was set!

I hurriedly ate dinner, had the staff put me in my hospital wheelchair with my hospital gown and a blanket thrown across my lap. I didn't have my own wheelchair yet, and I had *no* clothes. (There hadn't been a need for clothes for over a year. I didn't get up for long, and when I did get up it was only to go to therapy.) New to the wheelchair, and barely able to push the chair by using the backs of my hands on knobs specially adapted for people with quadriplegia, I clumsily worked my way down the third floor hall to the elevator. The necessary key had been safely pinned to my blanket by my "orderly confidant."

I left for the date an hour and a half early, allowing myself time to get from one end of the hospital (where my room was) to about the middle of the hospital (where the lounge was). In addition, I was on the third floor and the lounge was on the seventh floor. After forty minutes of work, with scrapes and bruises on my hands from slipping off the knobs, I finally reached the service elevator. Already I had done more work than I had done since the accident, but then, I had incredible incentive!

Now I was faced with pushing the elevator button and getting the pedal of the wheelchair in the door before it closed. Without the use of my triceps, I would throw my arm against the elevator "up" button and occasionally get the door to open. But, I could not move into the elevator quickly enough to keep the door from closing; another half hour of sweat and frustration followed.

Finally, a nurse's aide pushing a cart full of hospital equipment needed to use the elevator. To my relief, she asked if she could help. "Yes," I said, "Seventh floor, please!"

I was now on the seventh floor and it was twenty minutes until rendezvous time. Excitement and anticipation overwhelmed me as I crudely maneuvered the last block to the lounge door.

When I got there, it was ten minutes after the time we were to meet. She was nowhere in sight. Had I missed her? Did she change her mind? Did she get caught? Had my elaborate plan failed? Had I somehow clumsily left a trail to follow? Then she came down the hall. Wonderful! She was coming down the hall! I tried to wipe the sweat from my face and the blood from my now swollen hands, saying to myself, "I hope at least my hair is straight."

We said our hellos and I guided her to the key. Once inside the lounge, she pushed my chair over by the couch and sat down. Unfortunately, I was sitting at least a foot higher than her couch seat. In vain, I attempted to put my arm around her. I threw my arm back over her head, but instead of falling on her shoulder it came back and landed in my lap. We made small talk while inside I cursed myself for my clumsiness. I *did* like this woman very much and wanted to hold her close, smell her neck and feel her warm body against mine.

Although I was not heavy (130 pounds), I was tall (six feet, four inches). My mind raced. I knew if I asked her to transfer me to the couch there would be a good chance that she couldn't get me back in the chair because the couch was lower than the wheelchair. But there *was* the antique operating table. It was higher than the wheelchair seat. I reasoned that if she could get me onto the table there would be no problem coming down into the wheelchair seat later. Also, if she *couldn't* get me up on the table, I would still be in the wheelchair. After some time, I blurted out my plan to her. To my great surprise she said, "Alright." I was flying now! I had her put my chair beside the table, grab both heels and put my feet up on the table. She then got behind me, wrapped her arms around my chest and attempted to pull my dead weight up onto the operating table. As she lifted, the chair slid out from under me and down I went. There was no way of getting me back into the chair.

As I lay there on the floor, I hoped the world would end. The feeling of "flying" had given way to despair and an inward cursing of my plan. She was afraid I was hurt. I assured her I was physically fine, or at least as well as I had been before. After some discussion and planning, we decided it was best for her to leave me, go back to the nurses' dormitory and call my orderly friend, telling him where I was and about the problem. She left the key for the orderly on a window sill outside in the lounge corridor.

I made it back to my room that night. The nurse and I remained friends and corresponded for some years after I returned to Montana. But the opportunity for another rendezvous never presented itself.

The issue of successful male\female relationships is difficult for all people. My generation of people with disabilities has had the opportunity to break ground in many ways for those who would come after us. Socially, the world is much more open to the "younger generation" of people with disabilities. Unfortunately, many people with disabilities continue to believe that our disability is a deterrent to entering into a loving relationship. It is my observation that the issue of forming intimate, lasting relationships is no less a problem today for people with disabilities than it was twenty-eight years ago.

Although becoming disabled changed my life and the way I felt about myself in very many ways, the basic human needs for love, companionship and closeness with another human being never changed a bit. The need for social relationships, a productive life, independence and love, are universal. Although it seems obvious, perhaps it bears repeating: people with disabilities are much more like people without disabilities than they are different. Yet, sadly, it seems to be our few differences that are made important, sometimes not just by society, but by people with disabilities themselves.

"Stay home where we can protect you"

After my two years in hospitals, I came back to Montana to live with my folks. I fiercely wanted to be independent. I started several small businesses that I ran out of my parents' home. After several years, I determined that I could not make enough money at these businesses to gain my independence. I decided instead to go to college, seeing a degree as my way to freedom.

My parents were strongly opposed to this idea. Their response to me was, "Why don't you stay home where we can protect you and provide for you? Why go out there and risk the chance of hurting yourself or failing?" My parents said what they felt out of love and the natural parental tendency to protect a child. Their attitude also grew out of the mindset of a time when people with quadriplegia were not expected to live very long or to do anything with their lives. Making the decision to pursue my career was one of the hardest things I've ever done. I could sense my parents' fear, and their protective love (which I was driven to defy) made the decision that much more difficult.

Fortunately, I was determined enough to override their objections. I went to school in a city one hundred miles away from home, obtaining several degrees, including a graduate degree. I became a counselor/teacher. My parents are both deceased now and I am able to continue living independently because of my education and willingness to risk. If I had not made this change of choice, if I had stayed with my parents, my life would, I know, be very different and not as full today.

If you are dealing with someone who has a disability, no matter how much you want to love and protect them, allow them the opportunity to grow through reasonable risk. Allow them to make choices, to succeed, and to fail. This autonomy is a part of every human being's life, and is no less important for those who have disabilities. Indeed, for us, it is probably even more important.

Who's the Expert?

During a recent stay in the hospital (I had broken my legs in a fall from my wheelchair), I experienced a great deal of pain and consumed large quantities of morphine and codeine. These drugs have the common side effect of producing constipation, as was the case with me. During this time, a well-meaning hospital professional was making suggestions as to how I could improve my bowel program. This professional made the assumption that I *needed* help with my program; she forgot to ask one very basic question — how my program worked under normal circumstances at home. My answer to her, had she asked, would have been that in the last twenty years I had suffered less than one unexpected bowel movement per year. She did ask me how often I did my program, and after my response, very seriously suggested that I should change my program to an every-other-day system which she said would "solve all my problems." I politely thanked her and told her I would consider her option.

I have tried many times to discuss this kind of situation with health care professionals and very often find them to be uncomfortable with my suggestions or unwilling to consider my solutions as the best way for *me* to accomplish whatever goal I'm working toward. My suggestion that there might be a more efficient or better way *for me* is usually met with resistance.

Many health care professionals would do well to remember that persons with disabilities, especially those who have lived with a disability for a number of years, by necessity, and through trial and error, learn systems that work well *for them*. Before suggesting lifestyle changes, the professional should strive to find out how well the person is functioning without their advice. To illustrate the difference a professional who is also a good listener can make, consider the following.

After living twenty years with my disability, I decided to see a doctor of rehabilitation to find out what medical advances might be helpful to me. I had not consulted a rehabilitation doctor in over fifteen years. My appointment consisted primarily of the doctor asking me questions about my lifestyle. He also checked my level of injury, went through range of motion and strength exercises and asked about bed sores and bowel and bladder programs. When he was finished he said that I seemed to him to be functioning quite well; he would not make any major changes in my approach at that time. He did offer suggestions about using a new kind of plastic bandage and some new kinds of antibiotics to treat bladder infection, if *I* would like to try them. This doctor had the skills of an active listener and knew that my having coped even somewhat successfully with my disability had indeed given me some insight into my own treatment.

It is my observation that medical professionals, while very good at treating recent trauma and very good at dealing with disability during the patient's first stages of recovery, are less successful at *learning from* more experienced people with disabilities. These people have developed successful care plans of their own outside of any medical setting. The following personal experience from my life is an example of how this attitude of "non-learning" and "non-listening" can cause problems both for the health care professional and the person with a disability.

About five years ago, I was confined to a Clinitron bed (a "state of the art" bed which displaces weight and pressure so that burn victims and people with bedsores may heal more quickly) to help heal a persistent bed sore. While in the hospital, it was necessary for the staff to change my external catheter on an every-other-day schedule. I brought my catheters from home, my adhesives and the necessary straps. I had chosen to use this particular catheter after having experimented with many kinds and styles over a three-year period. I had found this one to be far superior *for me*. In regular daily use I would experience a leaking catheter very infrequently.

When the hospital staff came in to change my catheter, even though I was very ill, I tried to explain to them how to change it so we would have no leaks. The orderly insisted that the hospital used "a new brand that was very successful." Since I was too sick to push the issue, I allowed them to use their brand. The catheter was leaking within half an hour. After three more unsuccessful tries, two nurses came in to attempt to use my brand. But they did not follow my directions for washing the area and making sure it was completely dry. This resulted in four more unsuccessful attempts. After spending most of the night changing wet beds and washing me, we still didn't have a leak-free catheter. At 7:00 a.m., I phoned the personal care attendant who worked with me at home. He came to the hospital, quickly changed the catheter, and I was dry for two days.

It is difficult, at best, for an experienced individual with disabilities who is ill to explain his or her care plan to a member of the hospital staff. It is asking too much that they have to explain everything to each and every individual who works with them, let alone have to argue with staff to get them to even consider the patient's home care methods. Keep in mind that, more often than not, people with disabilities have come to know what works best for them. Getting that information *once* from the person, recording it in the chart, and then sharing that information as each new staff member assumes care responsibilities would greatly help the patient and staff members move toward more effective, humane delivery of care.

A Note to Myself and Other People with Disabilities

During the winter of 1988, two friends and I had made plans to cruise the Mexican Riviera. I left for California with all my personal care supplies including a prescription for Cipro, an antibiotic used to treat bladder and kidney infections. I was saving the antibiotic for the cruise, hoping to avoid bladder and kidney problems aboard ship and in Mexico.

The day before the cruise I developed a urinary tract infection. I *knew* it was a urinary tract infection because I had suffered the symptoms of these infections a hundred times during my twenty-eight years of disability. Chills, periodic hot and cold flashes, heavy perspiration around the head and a general inability to get warm were my common symptoms. I spent the day drinking as much liquid as I could and sat in front of the gas stove and oven in our motel kitchenette. I was wearing a flannel shirt and wool sweater, yet the chills persisted. There was no urine flow, but I was sure that if I just kept drinking liquids, the urine would flow and I could stall the development of further infection. However, by 8:30 that evening there was still no flow, the chills were worse and I was becoming less sure of my ability to deal with this problem.

My two companions started looking for a hospital that would take a person with C-5 quadriplegia. After calling five hospitals, they found one that would treat a person with quadriplegia who had a urinary tract infection. We drove to the emergency room to await processing.

When they took my temperature and blood pressure in the emergency room, they prepared my friends for the worst. The problem was complete kidney failure; my blood pressure and temperature were very high. The emergency room doctor thought I was a "poor risk" to survive. My blood test showed I had already become "toxic," which meant the infection had entered my blood stream. At that point, I probably had only ten hours to live.

Fortunately, my solitary kidney (I had lost one as a result of the car accident) began functioning again in the emergency room. After ten days of antibiotics and close observation I was released from the hospital. The doctors told me I was very lucky to have come into the hospital when I did.

While we do indeed know a great deal about our own care and physical condition, we are not medical experts. We need to be constantly aware that the symptoms we experience may not necessarily always be caused by the problems we are used to handling. As we grow older, the problems themselves will probably change. We walk (or wheel) a very risky path if we try to treat the symptoms we incur without expert medical advice.

Reflections and Conclusions

There is definitely a stigma associated with having a disability in our society. I do believe that the amount of prejudice has decreased to some degree during the time I've been disabled. Possibly, that is because of the sheer number of people with disabilities who are living longer and who are no longer hidden in the "closet." I really don't pretend to know why things are getting better. But some very strong and persistent advocates and organizations have had great impact on legislation, education, accessibility issues, community acceptance and the opening of career choices to persons with a disability. In 1962, when my injury occurred, it would have been nearly impossible for me to become a teacher/counselor. Many states then still had laws preventing people with disabilities from teaching.

I have learned, from seeing the world as both a disabled and a non-disabled person, that I am much the same person inside, no matter how my "outsides" look or function. We all have very similar needs, aspirations and dreams. Life has given each of us a different load to carry. It is important to remember that the load we carry is not nearly as important as our attitude towards it. The fact that "there will always be greater or lesser among us" has absolutely nothing to do with individual successes or plans or dreams. As long as these life works are worthy and meaningful to the individual attempting to attain them, they are valid pursuits. Depending on who is walking and who is climbing, a walk across a room may indeed be a greater accomplishment than climbing Mount Everest.

Life is made up of successes and failures. I believe it is most fully lived *by anyone* when reasonable, realistic risks are taken. I have learned as much, if not more, from my failures as I have from my successes. *All* of life's experiences either teach us or kill us a little bit . . . and just maybe both.

CHAPTER 3: SAMMI

Letter to a Friend

Sue Wilson

Sue is the mother of two children, one of whom has multiple disabilities.

Dear Jan,

When you called and asked me to write about why we chose an alternative form of therapy for our daughter, I don't think you realized what a can of worms you were opening up. I'm afraid there will be a lot of anger and bitterness seeping through this letter, and not enough of the humor and love that have sustained us through the last seven years. I'll give it my best shot.

Our daughter was a twin. She was full term, while the other baby died in *utero*. Apparently, something went wrong during the first two weeks of pregnancy (as is often the case with twins). The baby we lost was anencephalic; she had no skull. Sammi has bilateral porencephaly; she's missing almost her entire occipital lobe and most of both parietal lobes of her brain. We were unaware of this at birth. She needed no help at delivery, her Apgar scores being 9 and 10. Other than being a "difficult baby," she seemed entirely normal to us. No seizures were evident. She was diagnosed at close to six months of age with the use of a CAT scan.

At the time of diagnosis, we were told that Sammi would never roll over, sit, walk, talk or feed herself. She might develop the mental capacity of a six-month-old. When we could no longer handle it, we should consider an alternate living situation for her. The neurologist was so afraid of giving us false hope, he left us no hope at all. I understand why he did what he did, but I don't condone it.

The push from professionals for complete acceptance of their prognosis was so great, we finally did so — for one month. During that time, I denied showing, doing, and saying many things to my daughter because, of course, she couldn't possibly understand or see them. At the end of a month, I woke up to the realization that my daughter would never do anything if our total acceptance of her prognosis (not diagnosis) continued. Our daughter's response to us before and after her diagnosis was too great, and her ability to make us understand what she needed and wanted was too strong, for her to have the low capabilities the doctors described. What we saw in our daughter's eyes was too great a motivator for us to accept the prognosis completely.

From that time on, we have always tried to trust our instincts. We weigh what professionals tell us against what our own daily knowledge of Sammi tells us, and if we are uncomfortable with something, we look for a different approach.

Since that time, we have approached our daughter with two philosophies, the first being "If it won't hurt her and might help her, try it." That philosophy is always tempered with the second which is, "Does the end justify the means?" We will not destroy our family in the pursuit of a goal that probably cannot be accomplished. We do not doctor hop or look for miracle cures.

We tried the accepted path of treatment for our daughter — neurologists, ophthalmologists, an early intervention program, and extra physical therapy. These were steps that had to be taken. Eventually, the time we spent on the road to and from appointments, and the waiting during appointments became so inhibitive, I found my older daughter eating most of her meals in the car. She seemed to know more about driving and therapy sessions than about playing with friends. It was becoming clear to me that we could never approach any semblance of normalcy within our family life if this regimen of therapy continued.

We had a wonderful home trainer through our early intervention program who was a licensed physical therapist. She taught me that I was the expert on our daughter. The one message I received from her over and over was, "The more therapy your daughter has, the better." As is common in families with special needs children, and by my own choice, the burden of that therapy fell on my shoulders. By the time Sammi was eighteen months old, she was losing ground, I was burning out, and our family was showing signs of severe wear and tear. There simply had to be another way.

A friend of mine had decided to use the home therapy approach. Because of its philosophy, this home-based therapy may afford families the opportunity to provide for a child's therapeutic needs within the context of everyday family life. Given training by qualified professionals, a family implements their program through the use of community volunteers. For three months I volunteered one hour a week to work with her son, learning how the therapy was carried out. After seeing the wonderful changes in him, I couldn't help but try it with our daughter. Guilt is a great motivator. I did not want to look back on our daughter's life and wonder "What if we had tried?" I knew by then that the "what ifs" and the "if onlys" could drive you crazy.

In May of 1983, we went to Seattle to receive our daughter's home program. Our home trainer from the early intervention program went over the program and could find nothing detrimental in it. She even videotaped a full therapy session.

At 22 months of age, our daughter began her alternative therapy program. We started with 68 volunteers, five hours a day, five days a week for three years. For the last three years, we have cut back to two hours a day, five days a week, because our daughter is attending school part time and we have fewer volunteers.

One of the major reasons for continuing our home program, other than the progress that our daughter has made, is that the burden no longer falls solely on my shoulders. *I am not alone.* We have the energy, imagination, and dedication of our volunteers. Some have been with us the full six years. If I run out of ideas for motivation, they will think of something new. They give me extra time for housework, laundry, and the hundred other things that need to be done to keep a family functioning. I can do those things without feeling guilty about time not spent doing therapy — because it is being done. Most importantly, they give me time to visit with my older daughter or help her do her homework. They have added a new dimension to our lives and have given us more than was ever asked.

In deciding to use a therapy approach with Sammi that was less than orthodox, I did battle with many professionals. I'm afraid it may sound as though I am lumping all professionals together. That is not my intent. There are many excellent people out there who do not deserve stereotyping. But by the time my daughter was two, I had developed a large chip on my shoulder concerning professionals and I'm afraid over the years, it has become a small log. I found myself continually having to defend a program that was working for our daughter, and continually having to explain that all the conventional therapy in the world was useless to us if (a) it didn't work for Sammi and\or (b) it tore our family apart to implement it.

I found, as the parent of a child with multiple disabilities, I was often stereotyped as "emotional," "unrealistic," or unaccepting of the extent of my daughter's disability. To overcome that stereotype, I felt I had to meet certain standards of behavior with professionals: I should not be emotional either by grieving openly or losing my temper; I had to prove that I never neglected my child's needs, and always went the extra mile to do what had to be done; I had to appear intelligent and well versed in the terminology; and, above all, I was to follow their directions and advice and never (God forbid) disagree completely with their approach.

I found myself in a double bind. I wanted and needed professional expertise and advice. But in choosing what appeared to me to be the most rational course of therapy, I was often labeled irrational, unrealistic, and unreliable. It was extremely difficult to make them see that we had to do what was best, not just for Sammi, but for all of us.

I have no problem saying my daughter has cerebral palsy, bilateral porencephaly, spastic quadriplegia, or that she is visually impaired. I *do* have trouble saying that she is mentally retarded. We have days, bad ones, when it seems definite to me that she is. But we have many more days of such clarity of response that I am positive she understands everything and that it is only her physical limitations which prevent her from normal response.

Perhaps what was and still is most frustrating for me is that most professionals look at what our child cannot do because of her disabilities, and not at what she *can* do in spite of them. Most are not aware of the condition her body and mind would be in if it were not for her home therapy program. It has taken unfailing, daily effort and many years of hard work and dedication by many people to keep her body from being contorted, to prevent constrictures, and retain range of motion in her joints. It has taken boundless energy, imagination, and love to continue the stimulation program so that our daughter can reach her maximum cognitive ability. Given our daughter's diagnosis and prognosis at six months of age, I am always amazed when professionals are not struck speechless by her good physical condition, if nothing else.

The situation has further frustrated us because instead of professionals having to prove she is severely mentally retarded, some of them act as though we are supposed to prove she is not. I have been questioned and re-questioned on my assessment of my daughter's potential. I always question myself, and am so afraid of reading too much into her responses, that I often read *too little*. How thoroughly unfair that people who do not know my daughter the way I do could make me doubt my own belief in her capabilities! How sad that I have to defend her potential.

At times, I feel I am walking a tightrope, trying desperately to balance all the aspects of my life. We question and weigh the effects of what we do with our daughter in relationship to the effects on the entire family. We have another (wonderfully typical) daughter as well, who will someday perhaps have a career and a family of her own. Without neglecting either child, we owe them both equally the chance to be brought up in a loving family. We try each day to find that elusive, happy medium that will bring us through all this, not unscathed, but whole (and with humor* and love intact). We are, I know, better people for having traveled this path.

Sincerely,
Sue

* P.S. Humor has been the most important tool that we have had. Believe it or not, we laugh a lot! Granted, the jokes are sometimes slightly warped. Although it seems obvious, it took us a while to learn that laughter can see you through rough spots. We know that there is a time to cry, but there also is a time when grief becomes debilitating. Overall, humor can make you much more productive. I have a new-found ability to find something good in something bad. Sometimes, you just have to look harder and wait longer.

Questions for Parents to Consider Before Starting a Home Therapy Program:

- Is it reputable from your point of view? I don't mean accepted by the professional community. I mean is it a viable form of therapy for you to undertake? If the program promises you a normal child if you do everything correctly, question it. We were told it would help our child and not hurt her. We checked with professionals to be sure that was true. It was our choice about "how much" and "how often," so we could tailor the program to our family's finances, needs and time constraints. We were given the information and not pressured.

- Can you financially afford it? Is the cost so inhibitive that you will need to go far into debt? Compare the cost with equal amounts of alternative therapies. In our case our home program cost for three months was equal to the cost for one week of equal time of accepted physical therapy.

- Can your family handle the program emotionally? It really has to be a family decision. The whole family needs to be involved in a home program in some way. I organize, run the therapy, and work with the volunteers. My husband is the handyman. He makes and repairs most of the equipment we need. Our older daughter helps decorate the therapy room, makes word cards for Sammi, and, in the beginning, was one of few people who were effective at motivating Sammi to do what we were asking of her.

- If it is at all possible, talk to someone who is doing or has done the same type of home program. Other people who have been in your shoes are perhaps the most valuable source of information you have.
- Do not disregard any information. Professionals have years of education and experience. They are a precious resource. Other parents of children with disabilities have valuable information because of their experience and their own research. Everyday people whom you may come in contact with are also good sources of information. Because they are detached and inexperienced, very often they can make an observation or a suggestion everyone else has overlooked. The key is to be flexible and listen.
- Weigh all your options. Make a list of pros and cons. Get as much information as you can, then make your decision. It has to be your own choice. Though it is not the right path for everyone, for our family it was right, and we would do it again.

Our home program required many volunteers; there are several things to remember if you will be going that route. Volunteers will be giving you their time, the most precious commodity any of us have. We ask our volunteers for one hour a week. Because they are giving us their services for free, there are certain responsibilities owed to them:

- Above all else, be organized and on time. Have your child ready at the scheduled time. Have the materials needed available and easily accessible.
- Make it clear in the beginning that if it is necessary to cancel a therapy session, you will give them as much advance notice as possible. Ask them to do the same for you.
- If you need more than one volunteer at a time, try to pair them with people with whom they will work well. Good rapport among the volunteers makes the "work" that much more productive and enjoyable.
- Always remember that your volunteers are people with personalities, lives and families of their own. Over time, they become friends with each other and with you. All deserve respect and a "thank you" at the end of each session.

Sara's Lamp

Sara Wilson

Sara is Sue Wilson's daughter and Sammi's sister, today a vibrant teenager, and one of the first authors to write for Changes. She wrote the following article when she was ten.

My name is Sara. I have a sister named Sammi who has lots of disabilities. What happened is my mom was going to have twins. My sister Sammi has her skull, but not the back part of her brain. My sister that died had no skull, but did have her brain. The part of Sammi's brain that is missing is the part that makes her see and talk and move. She can still move her arms and legs, but not as good as normal people can. Her vision when she was little was terrible, but gets better and better every year. She has glasses that are very thick. My sister can't talk, but she makes lots of different sounds. Some of them are pretty weird. I can understand them, because I have been around her all her life. The thing that she can say pretty good is my name. She can form her mouth to say "Hi," but she can't get the sound out. The way my sister screeches when she's happy is amazing. It can blow your ears out!

Anyone who meets my sister thinks she's a sweetie. My mom has gone to the school we go to and talked about her to lots of the classes. She says the kids need to know about people with disabilities, so they won't be afraid of them and won't be mean to my sister. Most of the kids at school are nice to my sister and don't make fun of her, but there are some that do. I've hit a boy two years older than me because he made fun of Sammi. It made me so mad and I felt so bad, because she can't help the way she is.

I love my sister all the time, and most of the time I like her. Don't get me wrong. My sister can still be a brat. If she gets mad at me, she'll bite me or ignore me when I try to talk to her. That really makes me mad.

From having a sister like Sammi, I learned not to make fun of anyone. I think that having her changed my whole life. Sometimes I am jealous because I think she gets more attention than me. If I had a wish, I would not like to wish for my sister to be normal, because I love her just the way she is. I do wish she could talk.

In my opinion, a kid or person with a disability can, in time, do anything they put their minds to. They may need special equipment to help them, but they can do anything.

In my last words, I want to say that if you see my sister and me around, go ahead and ask questions. I'd be happy to answer them. Try not to stare. It makes me uncomfortable and angry and it is very rude.

I would do anything for my sister. I would even die for her. I love her dearly. She's the lamp that lights up my life.

CHAPTER 4: JON

Untold Diagnosis

Mary Pielaet

Mary is the parent of three children, one of whom has cerebral palsy.

In August of 1986, I gave birth to identical twin boys. The boys were small, but in good health. While everyone even remotely acquainted with us was overjoyed for us, my husband and I were completely overwhelmed as changes we had anticipated for many months became reality.

Because of all the hidden dangers involved in having twins, we decided to have our boys by Caesarean section. My family doctor, who had been our physician and friend for over five years, was my attending physician during pregnancy and he assisted the obstetrician with delivery. He had never delivered or cared for twins; he was excited for us. At times it was hard to tell who was more excited — my husband or my doctor.

Though the boys were small (5 lbs. 8oz. and 4 lbs. 13 oz.), they needed no special care. Our doctor went on vacation and we brought our sons home when they were four days old.

There were small differences in our boys from the start. We did, however, leave their name bracelets on for a few weeks. I think that we used the bracelets more than we would like to admit, because after we had removed them, we would often disagree about who held who, or find them in the wrong beds. Even dressing them differently sometimes didn't help. Soon, however, we did learn the differences in their dispositions and voices.

My husband was laid off from his job a month before the boys were born. This was actually a blessing in disguise because we made a good team; he woke up to one baby and I to the other. I would not have made it through this time if it hadn't been for all his help and support.

One of our boys, Jon, was very strong. While on his stomach he would lift his head and move it from side to side getting comfortable. At bath time or changing time, he would become so rigid that we could not make him bend. He was always stiff, but when he became upset handling him was like handling a large brick.

At about three months, Andrew began holding his head up, something Jon had done since birth. Andrew also started rolling over. At five months, he sat up, and soon thereafter started crawling. At the same time, Jon still was not rolling from side to side, let alone sitting or crawling. We would prop him up in the corner of the chair to help him learn to sit, but this didn't seem to help much.

My husband and I were trying very hard not to compare our boys — but it was becoming increasingly difficult. We were so concerned about Jon, we propped pillows under his stomach to get him into a crawl position thinking maybe this would help, but he only got stiff and looked like a board lying across a pile of pillows. I had to hold Jon at all his feedings because he couldn't sit in a high chair; we had to unfist his hands in order to place toys in them.

We expressed our concerns to our doctor time after time. His reply was always that Jon was taking his own sweet time; Jon was just being lazy. Our family members said that if we hadn't had twins we probably wouldn't have noticed any differences.

Jon was seven months old when I took him to the doctor because his ribs on the left side were very prominent. They appeared ready to come through his chest. They weren't growing correctly, and his back seemed to be curving. I wondered, why couldn't my baby move as he should?

Again, our doctor said not to worry about Jon's bones; he would "be alright." He urged our patience and said that it was normal for one twin to develop more slowly than the other. With everyone telling us not to worry so much — that Jon was fine — my husband and I tried not to let each other know just how upset we really were. We would wait a little while longer, and we continued to prop him up.

At eight months, Jon could not do most three-month skills. He couldn't hold his own bottle, he couldn't feed himself crackers, he drooled constantly and choked on everything. Something was wrong with my son and *no one was listening to me.*

I had met a health department nurse a couple of years earlier and after talking it over with my husband, we called her. We expressed our concerns and set up a time for her to come over and evaluate Jon, using a basic screening test. We went over the usual family and pregnancy history, and told her our concerns at length. She listened, and after she had finished the evaluation of the boys, she told us that Jon did test low, but that her evaluation wasn't set up to find all the information we needed. Yes, she said, we had definite reason to be concerned. She told us about the Comprehensive Developmental Center (CDC), an agency which provides full evaluation and intervention services to children and their families in our area. This agency, she said, could help us figure out how to help him.

The nurse also showed us how to sit Jon in a cardboard box low enough that he had free use of his hands. Jon loved being upright in his box. We would fill his lap with toys. I believe that it was this trick that got Jon to open his right hand and reach for the toys. It didn't help him sit up, but he was using one of his hands now!

We finally knew that we really did have reason to worry, that our fears were justified, and we knew of a place that could perhaps help. However, we needed our doctor's referral — back to square one.

It took us three more months to convince our doctor that Jon needed the referral. Jon had never had any medical problems; he gained weight and grew at a normal rate. He had never even had a cold, but for those three months he was seen at the doctor's office once a week until finally he completely failed the Pediatric Developmental Questionnaire, which turned out to be the same evaluation test used by the nurse. Jon had not been able to complete half of the items on the test for the past nine or ten months, but this time as I looked at the sheet of parent response questions, I realized that it would be blank. Jon could not do any of the tasks on the questionnaire for his age level. After the doctor saw the blank page, he began asking questions. After I had said "no" to all the questions, the doctor began to try out the exercises on Jon. Then he asked to see both boys at the same time (to compare them), before he would make a final decision.

Finally, the doctor agreed that for some unexplained reason, something was wrong. Jon was eleven months old now, and still he could not roll over, hold his bottle, or sit up. The doctor gave us the referral to CDC.

We were placed on CDC's waiting list for four months; they were just too busy to see us before then. By this time, you would have thought we would have gotten used to waiting for answers. In actuality, we were getting really frazzled and frightened; the "not knowing" and waiting started taking apart our lives piece by piece, in a slow and agonizing way. During this time my husband and I never shared the personal pain we felt with each other. I think neither of us realized until much later how depressed and scared we were. We just led very separate lives (in the same house) during this time. Somehow, to voice our fears to each other out loud would have made them more real — and more possible.

By the end of the third month of waiting, I was losing my patience; our CDC family case manager (I'm sure she was tired of me by now) gave me the name of a physical therapist who might be able to see Jon before our evaluation date. Why hadn't I thought of physical therapy? Now maybe we were getting somewhere.

Jon's first appointment was set for the next day.

I learned that there are a lot of children with the same problem as Jon. I learned different ways of holding, changing, and positioning him. Now, I (sort of) understood why Jon couldn't do some physical tasks. It was because he overused some muscles and didn't use others. He didn't have a sense of balance. His ribs flared out because he could not use his stomach muscles properly. (By now they flared on both sides.) Most of the time I felt that it was I who was undergoing therapy; I learned so much. I will forever be grateful for the understanding and lessons I acquired during this time; it made a great difference in our ability to cope with Jon and the still unknown diagnosis.

We started physical therapy in late September; by early October our therapist sent our doctor a report on Jon's condition. She told him what was wrong with Jon, and made a request for hip x-rays. We needed the x-rays for therapy purposes.

In November, Jon was evaluated by CDC; he was 15 months old. CDC did not evaluate him on gross motor skills because he was already seeing a physical therapist. Nor was he evaluated by a doctor, because he had a regular doctor within the county.

The evaluation was long and stressful, for Jon and for me. I supported Jon while he sat in a chair for over two hours. During this time, I watched him fail about eight out of every ten tasks presented to him. At the end of the evaluation, and after a short meeting among the therapists, each therapist summarized his or her findings for me. Each had suggestions for me to try to help teach Jon how to complete certain tasks that he should have been doing, but wasn't. They said that each therapist would follow up with a full written report in a few days and that we and our physician would be getting a copy.

I received my copy approximately one week later. I agreed with most of the findings, and there were more suggestions on activities to do with Jon. The evaluation found Jon at least three months delayed in all areas. Because of Jon's delayed condition and his young age, we were placed a little farther up the waiting list for in-home early intervention services. I took my copy of Jon's evaluation report to our next physical therapy appointment. Our therapist went over it with me and made a copy for her own files.

Although I was happy to be finally getting some help, I was angry and hurt at the fact that Jon was found three months behind cognitively and socially. I felt that the evaluators expected too much out of this child who, when faced with a number of strangers, was expected to do tasks that either were impossible or uncomfortable for him.

Over the next three months, my marriage fell apart. My husband and I stopped communicating; he was depressed and I was so involved in making Jon "perfect" that we just lost track of each other.

Jon continued his therapy twice a week and he was still seeing the doctor twice a month. In November, he lost a lot of weight; I assumed it was caused by all the therapy and the therapist agreed. From that time on, dishes of cereal or other snacks graced our floors so that Jon could get to them whenever he wished. While this was great for Jon, Andrew was getting about twice the food he needed each day. And my floor was in constant need of vacuuming. Soon, I changed to feeding Jon high calorie puddings, and Andrew got yogurt. Not very fair, but it worked. Jon slowly regained his weight and Andrew stayed healthy.

At each doctor's appointment, our doctor would go through a ritual of questions: How was Jon doing with therapy? What exercises were we doing? Did I see any improvement? These were always followed by the one question which at first confused and later angered me: What did the CDC evaluation find? I would repeat the results each week, wondering all the time why he would ask. I knew he had received a copy of the evaluation report. Was he really too busy to read it? Was he expecting *them* to diagnose my son?

Around the first part of January, our therapist expressed the importance of a hip x-ray series again to me. Then she explained that for the past six weeks, she had tried to reach our doctor by phone. She left message after message and spoke with his nurse a number of times. But she never spoke with our doctor and he had not returned any of her calls. I began to get suspicious.

In light of what was now happening, I began to request at each appointment that our doctor order the hip x-rays. I had to explain why we needed them and how important they were in determining the course that Jon's therapy would take. Finally, he ordered them. Thankfully, they showed that what we were doing was working; Jon's hip joints were fine.

In January, I took the boys in for their 18-month checkup and immunizations. Again, the doctor finished by asking what the CDC evaluation findings were. Then he asked me if Jon would ever walk. I don't know quite how to explain what kind of shock wave went through my body and mind at that moment. I had never considered that my son might never walk. I was completely perplexed and anger started to well in my throat. But, somehow, I did not want to lose my control with this doctor. Putting my emotions on a back burner, I swallowed and calmly said,

"He should be walking by the time he's three or four." It is humorous to note, in retrospect, that I had absolutely no justification for my answer — but if he didn't know when or even *if* Jon would walk, I surely could trust my best instincts. It was apparent to me, finally, that I know much more about my child and his condition than this doctor ever would.

As soon as we were outside the building, I became filled with overwhelming fury. I don't remember the ride home, but I do remember that my family gave me lots of space for the few hours it took me to calm down. When I did, I called our therapist and asked which doctor worked well with her. Of course, she wanted to know what happened. I told her what he had asked me and how I had responded. Though we had never discussed it, she thought my prediction (about when Jon would walk) was fairly accurate. This reinforced my faith in maternal instinct.

The therapist gave me the names of three doctors. She told me to set up an appointment as soon as possible, and to let her know whom we were to see so that she could be in touch with them. She did, in fact, call the new doctor at home on the eve of the appointment and fill her in on Jon's condition.

This appointment was much the same as any first-time appointment. We covered pregnancy and family background and a few other questions. After a moment's thought, the doctor told me that Jon had spastic diplegic cerebral palsy. She told me which agencies to contact for assistance, which forms to fill out first, and what other kind of therapy Jon might benefit from.

I had heard of cerebral palsy, of course, but I really didn't know what it was. I came home and sat at the kitchen table; my husband came in and asked how it went. I told him the diagnosis and he went to the bookcase and pulled out our family medical guide. Finding the right page, he silently began to read. When he finished, it was my turn. There it was in black and white. The description fit Jon perfectly.

What should have been a devastating experience was actually quite the opposite, given how long we had waited and agonized over this moment, what we felt most of all was relief. *We finally knew what was wrong.* We were uplifted to know that there were things which could be done to help our son. We contacted the referred agencies and requested all the paperwork. At last the ball was rolling in the right direction.

We contacted friends and family. After 18 months, we finally knew what to tell them. My best friend completely fell apart. Each time I spoke to her for the next three days, she was crying. She felt that she had been filling me with false hope; that all the time, she had refused to see just how behind he was, and that she had somehow caused me more hurt. I felt that she was going through my grieving for me.

All I could think was that *knowing what was wrong with Jon didn't change him.* It didn't change the future. It only helped, because now we could get the help Jon needed. This thought helped me through the adjustment even though it didn't help my friend.

That same day, Andrew had a bad reaction to the immunization shot. He was running an extremely high temperature, and our new doctor was not on call. We had to settle for our original doctor meeting us at the emergency room. My husband went with me this time.

After we knew that Andrew was out of danger, I said to the doctor, "We took Jon to a different doctor today, and we found out what's wrong with him." He replied, "Oh, what's that?" "He has spastic diplegic cerebral palsy," I said. The doctor looked straight at me and said, "I knew he was spastic diplegic, but that doesn't mean cerebral palsy."

At this point, my husband spoke out (an action for which I will be eternally grateful). How could this man stand here and say these things to me? My husband informed the doctor that spastic diplegia does indeed mean cerebral palsy, and that if *we* could look it up at home in a medical guide, he surely should have known what was going on, especially after a year and a half. The doctor never said a word; he just turned and walked away. None of us has ever seen him again and within a week I had all our medical files pulled from his office.

I still have a lot of bitter feelings about this doctor. Why didn't he ever find the courage to tell us what was wrong? Why did he want everyone but himself to make the diagnosis? Was he protecting us? Himself? All I know is that he wasn't doing his job, and he did none of us any good. I've never blamed the doctor for Jon's condition. Perhaps he blames himself.

In February, we had a Magnetic Resonance Image (MRI) Scan done on Jon's brain. It came out completely normal. We also got a home trainer from CDC and started speech therapy shortly thereafter. In April, CDC re-evaluated Jon and found him still only three months behind. In most cases like ours, the child continues to become more delayed. Staying the same meant improvement for us because it had been six months since Jon's last evaluation.

My husband and I also started marriage counseling in April. It saved our marriage. The traumatic months that we had lived through now seem like a nightmare that took forever to awaken from. The reason we managed to stay together through it all seems to be the fact that buried under the stress and agony, behind all the walls we had built between us, we genuinely loved each other. In our case, we were able to build from that base. Now, we are back to being a very good team.

We are luckier than most parents of children with physical challenges because Jon has a built-in peer group. The reason Jon did so well on his second evaluation (and is now within normal range on all developmental levels except gross and fine motor) is that we sat back and watched what Andrew did each day, and whatever Andrew did, we made it possible for Jon to have that same experience. This meant we've had to change some rules occasionally. It was OK to climb on the end table, because Jon did it by himself. But, it was only OK a few times. We stop and make the time for Jon to have as many normal experiences as possible.

One of my favorite things to do with my boys is to take them to a grocery store. We look at everything, we feel stuff, and we smell things; the produce department is the best. It may take us two hours to get ten items, but we all have fun. It's a normal experience that teaches, and it's easy to incorporate into our day.

Jon currently has therapy seven hours each week. He is physically at about a ten-month level. In December (1988) his physical therapist started teaching Jon how to walk using a special walker; it's really hard work for him. He hates it, but he's coming along. He may always need some kind of support to help him walk. I don't really care. The important thing to me is that Jon has an inner drive to keep up with his brother. He is by nature a fighter. Life is going to be hard for him at times, but I know within my heart that he will be able to adapt to any given situation. His presence in our lives has made adapters of us all!

Our physical therapist told me recently that the first few months she worked with Jon, she thought he might never walk. What struck me about her comment was this thought: if I hadn't changed doctors, found a good physical therapist and battled to get appropriate services for my son, he very well might have been wheelchair bound and speechless.

Our doctor, whatever his motives, made a horrible situation horrendous by his refusal to say the words we needed to hear in order to get on with accepting our son and our new life situation. No one but a medical doctor can legally give a family a diagnosis of cerebral palsy, nor is it anyone else's job to do so. Everyone around us, including the members of our local support group, knew what was wrong with Jon. Denying us the diagnosis for so long simply prolonged our agony, and left us in a state of limbo for far too great a time. It would have been much kinder and much better for Jon if, with compassion and directness, we had been told of Jon's condition as soon as it was suspected. I can't help but wonder where Jon might be now if we had explored the possibilities of therapy and early intervention at three or even six months.

I trusted my doctor. I believed that he was doing the best for Jon and for us. The realization of what really happened in our situation has shattered my confidence in the medical profession. I know that most M.D.'s are not like ours, but the bitterness at what he did to our lives remains. I have become a wary consumer of medical services. Never again will I take what a doctor says at face value; I believe in second, and even third opinions. I will never again fall for the same "band-aid" treatment that we received from our doctor.

Some Thoughts for Professionals to Consider:

First, *be honest with parents.* Tell us the truth; tell us the possibilities even if you are not sure. Not knowing is agony and simply prolongs the time it will take us to pick up the pieces and move on with our lives. If you don't know, or can't take the time to research a problem for us, please send us to someone who can. Or provide us with enough information that we can do the research ourselves.

Listen when we speak. We quickly become proficient, if not masterful, at dealing with the special needs of our children. We can be resourceful, inventive and valuable allies on the team which serves our child's needs. We may fall apart occasionally, but with time and knowledge, most of us will be alright, and even *happy* with our lives.

Steer us toward a support group. Nothing helps more than finding someone else who has stood in our shoes, particularly if they have gone on to lead accepting, productive and happy lives.

Just today, as I've been writing, Jon discovered for the first time that he could pull himself up onto his feet and reach the light switch. He's been in his room playing with it all afternoon. Off and on, off and on, off and on — *all by himself.*

CHAPTER 5: SARA

"Daddy, Phone's Busy"

Bud Mariska

Bud Mariska works as an independent consultant and sales representative, and is the father of Jamie, Jessica, Sara, and Hope.

In most of our lives, at some point or another, we face a major traumatic event. This event can change how we look at ourselves and how we deal with situations in our lives. It may be the loss of a loved one through death or divorce, a career change, a serious accident or illness, or anything that can have a profound effect on one's outlook on life. Such an occurrence is known by psychologists as a "significant emotional event." March 30, 1983, was the date of my significant emotional event. It was the day that my daughter, Sara, was born with Down syndrome. Before this date, having a child with disabilities was something that happened to somebody else.

As well as having this genetic disorder, Sara also had heart and eye complications. Her mother, Jan, and I knew little about this abnormality when the doctor gave us the initial diagnosis, 24 hours after her birth. We began immediately to try to learn more about her condition. Due to Jan's previous occupation (seventh and eighth grade teacher), she had a good understanding of what it takes for children to learn, and this skill proved to be invaluable for Sara. Through referrals and reading, she discovered some new techniques, generally known as "early intervention," and we started to carry out these procedures to give Sara the best possible start in life. The early intervention techniques were an intensive set of procedures that enhance and build upon the natural learning phases that children go through as they grow. One explanation describing a rationale for early intervention sees a child with Down syndrome as traveling at 40 miles per hour, while a normal child runs at 55. That is why it is so important that Sara be kept "up to speed." If the proper input was not there, she might fall even further behind as she grew.

Sara's pediatrician did not have much experience dealing with Down syndrome and explained his feelings about his experience level. One of his first comments after his initial diagnosis was to give us the option of changing doctors. It is, as I understand, common for people to feel uncomfortable with the doctors that give the initial diagnoses of severe problems. I suppose some people have a tendency to either blame the doctor, or, when returning for future appointments, to feel unpleasant memories triggered by the environment. I believe he clearly felt uncomfortable dealing with Sara, not because of her disability, but because of his lack of specialization in dealing with Sara's specific conditions. He is a very good physician, with broad general experience and had done a great job with Sara's two older sisters. Therefore, we felt that it was better to stay with someone we already trusted. Another thought that occurred to me was, if we had to deal with Sara's problems the rest of our lives, *he* shouldn't be able to escape that easily. As it turned out, it was a rewarding learning experience for everyone.

In the first few days, I was actually encouraged by the opinion of some professionals who told us Sara would have a shortened life span, probably only into her twenties. This seemed to put a limit on how long we had to care for her. As I look back on that initial emotion, I cannot believe how I could have felt those things. Maybe I was just looking for an end to something that seemed impossible for myself and my family to face. A short time after, I realized how selfish a reaction it was . . . sort of an easy way out. As time went on, we learned these opinions were based on very old data. The reality is that people with Sara's condition generally experience close to normal life spans, given that related physical problems are correctable.

I value Sara every bit as much as my other three daughters. Sara's courage is unique; she faces ridicule, rejection, conflicts, and challenges in her everyday life, more than any "normal" person does. Her reaction is to remove herself from those individuals and situations that cause her discomfort. She's a smart kid.

Soon after birth, like any child, she started to develop her special personality. Sara, at an early age, became very sensitive to our feelings, more than most "normal" children do. She always tries to help if someone is feeling unhappy. More than once, I have arrived home after a stressful day at work and just wanted to sit on the couch for a few minutes to collect my thoughts. She always comes over to greet me and, finding me in this state, gives me hugs and tells me that she loves me, all the while patting me on the shoulder. If that doesn't break the ice, she starts to do funny tricks until I smile. With that task completed, she goes on to her next "happiness assignment."

We have been through some very traumatic experiences with Sara. She was 21 months old when she had open-heart surgery at Primary Children's Hospital in Salt

Lake City, Utah. It was an extremely difficult, highly emotional experience for both Jan and me. The most intense memory I have of that time is when we met the surgeon at the door of the operating room before the surgery. When we attempted to hand Sara over to him, she somehow knew that something was happening. She hung on to Jan's blouse so hard that I had to peel her little hands off, finger by finger. I will never forget the look in her eyes; they seemed to say, "Help me Daddy!" I will carry that moment with me for the rest of my life. I returned home after a couple of days to be with our other two daughters, while Jan stayed in Salt Lake City with Sara. It was a week to the day after the surgery when my two daughters and I met Jan and Sara at the airport. Jan was holding Sara as they left the plane and when we came into view, Sara reached out to hug us all. She was so happy to be back with the whole family again.

Sara really started to grow and function better after the surgery. She helped turn that difficult experience into something wonderful, as only Sara could. The only really negative effect that it had was to give her a deep distrust of anyone in a white uniform, especially if that person has a stethoscope around his or her neck. Even if there is a program on TV with medical personnel wearing white uniforms, she will immediately come and find me and say, "Doctor on TV, can't like him." I guess I have an enduring reaction as well, mine being a fear of an envelope containing a bill from the hospital.

Now that Sara is over six years old she is really coming into her own. She has just completed her first school year of being mainstreamed in a morning kindergarten class, with an afternoon special education class. She insists on getting on and off the bus by herself and if you forget and try to help her, she reminds you that "Sara's a big girl." She puts the important things in life first and doesn't worry about the things that bother most of us.

Sara's way of looking at life is, as one would expect, a little different from other people's. When she is around my older two daughters and they start getting into a fight (unfortunately, this is not a rare event), she comes looking for me to break it up. She usually says, "Can't like Jamie and Jessie fighting; come on Daddy." Then she takes my hand and we go break up the fight. She always likes to keep me informed on the actions and whereabouts of our other three daughters, Hope being the youngest by two years. The word "special" is used to describe kids with disabilities. Sometimes it strikes me as overused, but here it *does* apply very well.

Sara, unfortunately, is an early riser and will wake up everybody in the house, always happy to see them. I look forward to these mornings to see what insights she may have. She has a special way of seeing things that sometimes the rest of us just miss. Just the other day, as I was stepping out of the shower, I heard a knock at the bathroom door and, of course, knew it was Sara with some morning news. I told her to wait a minute while I got dressed, but she just kept knocking at the door. Hurriedly, I dressed and opened the door. Then I heard my alarm clock in the bedroom buzzing with a steady beep-beep-beep. I had forgotten to turn it all the way off. I looked down and Sara was holding her hand out to take mine. She led me into the bedroom and pointing at the alarm clock said, "Daddy, phone's busy."

Sara is learning a lot as she grows, but most of the learning is done by the people around her. In our quest for our dreams, we often lose track of the things that are the most important. I think Sara has a rare ability to focus on the things that are most important in life. I am looking forward to my continuing education from my daughter and, with some luck, hope to someday gain her level of understanding.

"It's OK, Because She's Sara..."
Excerpts from a mom's personal journal

Jan Spiegle

April 8, 1983

My father brought me this book some time ago, a relic of his mother's past found in a garage trunk. A book for keeping memories, left empty that I might receive it someday. It was too special for a diary, too much a part of me to leave empty. So it sat for months, on a shelf by my bed. I'd pick it up occasionally, wondering if ever there would be time in my life to fill it. A two-year-old and a four-year-old make it impossible to think sometimes, let alone write your thoughts down. And a new baby was due soon. Would the book be wasted again?

Sara Jane Mariska was born a few days late on March 30, 1983. She was to be the "finish" to our family, the third and last baby for us. I anticipated her arrival as I had those of her sisters, with loving impatience. But with two children for previous experience, I had no anxiety. After all, I knew how to make formula, change diapers, treat the croup, potty train. This child would be such a joy. All the love, and none of the fear that I might "do something wrong."

She came into the world and I shouted, "What is it? Count her fingers, count her toes," I demanded. "She's all there, she's just fine," my doctor reassured me as he lay Sara on my now empty belly. She squirmed and let out a lusty cry. She was here and she was perfect and I couldn't hold her near enough or stroke her lovely little body enough with my shaking hands.

We went to our room. Sara had her first "meal." All the waiting friends and relatives were phoned. I fell into a blissful sleep; Sara snuggled in the warming bassinet so near I had only to reach my hand out to touch her.

When I awakened, she was gone. Taken to be weighed and bathed and fed again. I showered and walked to the nursery to retrieve my baby girl. As I entered, the nurse stood over her bassinet, examining Sara with one hand as she held the phone and spoke to our pediatrician with the other. I caught only snatches of the conversation as I gazed enraptured at Sara. Later that day, those snatches of conversation would haunt me and eventually become a living nightmare:

"No, her tongue looks OK. Her eyes are very swollen, so it's hard to tell. Yes, the crease is on only one palm. No, her heart sounds good and strong. Yes, she's a big girl — 8 pounds, 3 ounces."

The nurse hung up, saying that Sara could come to my room if I wished. Walking down the hall, I noticed the corner of a green paper sticking out from under the clear bassinet. In my room, I read the delivery room nurse's examination sheet. I smiled at the Apgar score — a nine — I had always had big, vigorous babies. Then I noticed some notations on the section reserved for comments: "Slightly floppy. Simian crease on left palm. Slant eyes? Fatty deposit on back of neck. D.S. baby?"

Hurrying back to the nursery with the paper, I asked the first nurse I saw what all those comments meant. Was something wrong with my Sara? Three nurses came over immediately to reassure me, trying to stop my panic. "Just a routine report," they said, "Don't worry."

Uncertainly, I made my way back to my room. Holding Sara close I began to examine her. Her eyes did seem to slant, didn't they? One by one, I examined her fingers and toes. They were perfectly formed. There just couldn't be anything wrong with *my* baby.

I slept until midnight, but after being awakened by the nurses to feed Sara, I found myself unable to sleep. The comments on the green paper played on my mind. Wandering in the hall, I found myself a quiet refuge in a lounge the nurses used to relax and give reports to the changing shifts. It was empty at this time of night; one wall was lined with a medical library. Not wanting to, but unable to stop myself, I reached for a text titled *Birth Abnormalities*. The text carried two chapters on chromosomal abnormalities, one devoted entirely to Down syndrome.

And that's what Sara was — a baby born with an extra 21st chromosome, a tiny bit of matter that would alter our lives forever. Unable to believe this could be true, unable to quit reading, I read and reread the chapter until morning crept into the lounge and a nurse came to find me for breakfast. I knew then, of course, that Sara had Down syndrome. Inside myself, I wept, denying in my mind that it could possibly be so, yet knowing without a doubt that it was true. I didn't need the sad or averted gazes of the nurses to tell me so. I didn't need the kindness in the doctor's voice as he spoke the words; I knew. The hardest part was not in my knowing. It was in knowing that I had to tell my husband, my parents, and my friends. The words came with so much difficulty, they stuck in my throat; they choked me as I spoke them. There will *never* be a more difficult thing, not ever.

Now, two and a half weeks later (it seems like two and a half years) we have been contacted by innumerable people offering help, innumerable friends offering support, and genetics people offering plausible (but never positive) reasons why this happened. They try very hard to be helpful, but in the end, nothing helps.

April 18, 1983
I am so lonely. My parents were here this weekend; now they are gone. Bud's back to work. The burden seems incredibly heavy as everyone leaves and I am left with my thoughts. Three children are demanding all the time. Every minute of my time must focus on their needs. Sara does not rouse herself to eat; I must set an alarm clock to remind myself to feed her, lest she not get enough nutrition. Her sucking reflex is incredibly weak; takes nearly two hours to feed her four ounces. One feeding runs into another; the days pass in a blur. I need to cry; only I must do it in the shower so as not to upset the children.

April 25, 1983
Bad night last night. Sara was fussy and each time I laid my head on the pillow she began to cry again. By 2:00 a.m., I was crying, too. It hits me at odd times, not so frequently as before, usually when I'm tired. Sobs that come from a depth within me that I didn't know existed; it's gut wrenching. All the hurts I have known before in my life are nothing in comparison.

Sara seems to bloom each day. She wakes to smile at Jamie, who loves her with the uncomplicated, undemanding, unconditional love of a four-year-old. She always said while I was carrying Sara that "our baby will be very special." How right she was.

May 9, 1983
Mother's Day was hard to get through. I wanted to shake everyone and scream. Don't they realize what I am going through? My life is a semblance of normalcy, interspersed with periods of absolute, total anguish.

One hot July night in 1982 I awoke with a desire. Who put the desire there? What quirk of fate awoke me at that particular moment? Awoke me to love my husband, beget a child, and produce a baby that conceived one month later or earlier surely would have been normal. Why us? Why now? *Why me?*

Sara was diagnosed at her two-month checkup as having a congenital heart defect — it may be something she will be able to live with, but it probably will require major surgery. My brother said, "It just seems when you get into these things, it's one thing after another."

Sara smiles and coos, recognizes her family; it's hard to believe that anything is wrong with her. People ask how she's doing and when I answer, very honestly, that she's fine, they look at me either suspiciously or sorrowfully. They all seem to feel that I am somehow different. And I guess I am changed.

October 4, 1983
The pain has eased immeasurably. Sara is doing very well. Her infant stimulation program, begun when she was 4 days old, is helping. She's almost sitting independently. I love her as I have never loved before.

Time does ease all pain . . . eases, but doesn't erase. My parents are hard to face. The pain in their eyes is a reflection of my own and I feel responsible for this burden they too must learn to bear.

For the first time in months, I believe there is hope. Hope that Sara (like any other child) will reach her full potential. In my heart, there is a certainty, a resolve. I will see that she is the best person she can be. No one really knows her capabilities better than I. She *will* be what she *can* be. I will see to it.

June 26, 1984
Eight months have gone by. This journal has been with another mom who has a child with Down syndrome for that long. She tells me it gave her strength, eased her isolation. She didn't want to let it go.

Sara's 15 months old now, belly-crawling, into everything. Her laughter permeates our days, allows no time for the sorrow of past months. These pages seem at times so melodramatic as I read them now. Yet those feelings are still with me. Again and again they resurface, surprising me with their intensity, filling me with bitterness, resentment, anger, denial and finally an overpowering grief. (I envision myself tearing at my hair and wailing like a member of some primitive tribe.) I mourn intensely for the child I did not have, overcome with guilt all the while, because to mourn that child is somehow to deny Sara. As I write this (lying on a blanket in a park) she crawls around me, over me, pushes her face in front of mine, demanding that I play with her. She shuts this book and grins at me impishly. How can I possibly feel these contradictory feelings? If I let her, she will make a path for me out of my grief.

I lie here surrounded by children playing and mothers chatting happily. I cannot look at an infant without my heart breaking; cannot see a pregnant woman without wondering if she will share my story. In my most selfish of thoughts, I hope she will. Then I would perhaps not be so alone.

I read this again and think what a resentful person I have become. To wish what has happened to me upon anyone is unthinkable. Will I ever work past this sorrow? Will there be a day when Sara is not the first thing I think of every morning and the last thing I think of before I go to sleep?

August 2, 1984
Just realized I haven't cried in a long time. People told me when Sara was born that she would bring great joy, that she was a special gift, that our family would be better because of her. I wanted to scream, they said it so often. I wanted her to be theirs so that they would know how empty all those words really sounded. They offended me in their effort to comfort me. I thought they would never understand, and in very many ways they never will. They would be astonished to know how true their words really were. Sara has brought to us joys we would have never known without her. Her arms around my neck, the smile that says "hello" to me each time I look in her eyes, the utter joy she experiences when she learns something new; these things are ours, hers and mine. She *is* a blessing, a mixed blessing to be sure, but a blessing nonetheless.

August 14, 1984
In the last year I have gotten to know many families of children with disabilities. *All* of them have this unique sense about them. They were ordinary people who faced extraordinary problems. They did so with tears and anger at first, with fists raised to the heavens asking "Why me?" But they have come through it in triumph. They have grown in courage, self-worth, sensitivity, understanding and sharing. Without Sara, I would not have known them, would not have their friendship, a friendship that I cannot now imagine being without. The depth of sorrow that we have known and shared has somehow made us each a part of the other. In my soul, I will treasure these people forever.

God may not be able to undo the circumstances that brought us together, but He has compensated us tenfold because He has given us each other. He has given us children, however imperfect they may be in the eyes of the world, that bless our families with gifts others will never know.

How good it feels to say these words and really mean them. Like a marathon runner who has "hit the wall" and persevered, I can go on. I have endured and I have triumphed. It feels very good to know I can finish the race. Perhaps I will even win.

October 16, 1987

I was doing better than anyone else, they said. I was a marvel, a super-mom personified. The role thrust upon me, I took it on willingly because the alternative was "to *not* do OK," to fall apart. Too many people were depending on me not falling apart.

In the beginning, each time I looked at Sara, I felt my heart break as if tiny pieces of me were dying every day. I worried what would become of her when no one was around to care for her any more. I worried that my husband would kill himself trying to meet the financial burden of her care. I worried that we would grow so far apart I would never be able to see the man I married behind all the pain in his eyes. I worried what her sisters would go through simply because they were her sisters. I worried that if I fell apart, they would, too.

I felt at the matrix of a giant puzzle, the key piece without which none of the others would stay together. This child would need me for a long time; she would need me in ways that most children never need. I wanted desperately to be equal to the task of raising her, not just raising her, but doing it well. Perhaps doing it better than anyone had done before. If I could do that, maybe I could compensate for what I had lost: the "normal" child she will never be in the eyes of the world.

I wanted, above all else, to be a good mother to her. I wanted to give her a chance to be what it was she was capable of being. I wanted to change the world so that it would give her that chance, too. Now I realize that I wanted too much. Oh, she still needs a good mom, and the chance to be what she can be. But in the end, she needs exactly what every other child needs, to be nurtured, to be loved, to be given every chance to learn and grow; no more, and no less. And I have found that the world is changed *one person at a time.*

I am not "super-mom." The role was a way of compensating, but there is no compensation for what has been taken from my child and from myself. There is no way to make her whole in the eyes of the world (though, in my eyes, she is *more* whole than most people). It has taken me a long time to realize that no matter what I do, Sara will always be Sara. And really, truly, that's okay. Because being Sara is not such a bad thing to be. She will have some things in her life that other children need, and never have. She had two grandpas who loved her unconditionally; two men who valued personal achievement above all else found out through her that there are other ways to value people. She has a father who delights in her very existence. She has a grandmother whose caring is matched only by her will to help Sara learn. By simply being, she has changed and touched lives that would have been very different without her. She has a power that few of us have, because in her unknowing innocence she has taught many people about the basics of trust, beauty, and love. She has taught us all how to be survivors. And, now that we realize we *can* survive, perhaps she can teach us how to live.

I will probably never stop asking why all this happened to me. I don't think I did anything to deserve all the pain I have felt. But who among us deserves it? On whose shoulders would I place this responsibility, if not on my own? Who would have survived it better than I? Who could have loved her the way I do, save me? When it comes right down to it, who better than me? If I have been changed, been made stronger, more resilient, who will have more benefit than I? Sara will never be the child I dreamed of and planned for. But, that's okay. It's okay because, instead, she's Sara . . .

The Birthday Invitation

Jan Spiegle-Mariska

Four years ago I chose to mainstream Sara. It was one of the hardest choices I have ever made. Having lived within the sheltered and supportive environment of early intervention programs and "special" preschools, I had reached what the professionals would call "acceptance." However, considering the change to a "real world" environment frightened me. It was one thing to watch Sara within secure surroundings, her every need attended to closely by people who not only were trained to deal with her specific needs, but who had come to truly love my daughter. It was quite another to anticipate placing her with "regular" teachers and "normal" kids.

Educationally, I knew it was the right thing to do. Intellectually, I was extremely pleased that she was ready for such a step. Emotionally, I was scared to death. What if the children made fun of her inadequacies? What if the other parents objected to her presence? What if she wet her pants (a rare, but still possible occurrence)? How would they handle her sometimes noncompliant behavior? What if the teachers found the situation unworkable? In short, what if the transition failed?

Knowing it was important to take the risk, I did place her. The first few weeks were difficult for me; I had a smile tattooed to my face and great fear in my heart. I couldn't bear to be in the classroom for very long. I fell back into the trap of making comparisons between Sara's development and that of her new peers, all of whom were chronologically younger than Sara. Rather than focusing on her strengths, which I had done for many years, I saw only that she was woefully behind in some areas. It simply hurt too much to be there.

Sara, on the other hand, was doing beautifully. She delighted in being with the (developmentally) older children in "Susan's school." She was tired of teachers and aides monitoring her every move, and relished the freedom of the less restrictive setting. Aided by supportive staff in both the sending and receiving schools, she was getting along quite well, although she did wet her pants one day as she played at the "water trough." Some children did give her a wide berth, bewildered by her speech, or her different appearance. Others were intrigued by her differences. She spoke often and enthusiastically of playing with Zach and Maia, Sarah Lynn and Jillian. Eventually (much later than Sara), I began to see that the change had been exactly right for her. I was then able to smile genuinely and feel more at ease within the classroom.

The sweetest day, however, came that spring. Picking Sara up from her class, I found in her locker a birthday party invitation. She had, of course, been to parties before, for her sisters and a couple of neighborhood friends. This was different. Her sisters had no choice but to include her. The neighbors had been good friends of ours before Sara's birth, and had worked hard to fit our special child into the neighborhood. But this was an invitation that Sara had earned on her own. It came from Zach, a little boy I knew only in passing. It came from a mom I really didn't know at all. I had nothing to do with it.

I had not cried in a long, long time, but as I stood reading the colorful dinosaur birthday card inviting my daughter to a "real world" birthday party, tears flowed. Feeling elated and very silly, I retreated to the car, Sara demanding all the way to know why I was crying, and me at a total loss for words. How could I explain that this simple invitation meant more to me than one engraved in gold? How could I explain that it meant the risks were well worth taking? How could she know that, for me, the card symbolized hope in its purest form? Hope that acceptance, not just from me or people close to us, but from regular people in the "real world," was not just a dream, but an attainable goal.

So, to Zach and his mom, my thanks. To the teachers who made the transition possible, my gratitude. And to Sara (who never once considered that she might fail) my love and deepest respect. You have taught me a significant lesson about the dignity of risk.

As I did the day I found the invitation, I feel a bit silly recounting such a seemingly insignificant event. I wonder if I will ever overcome my great motherly instinct to shield Sara from the big world outside the door of our home; I suspect not. Yet, I do know that I have learned that risking failure with my daughter also empowers her with great dignity. It is the same dignity we grant any child as we raise them to be more and more independent of us.

As we let go of "normal" children, allowing them slowly to be more responsible for themselves, they grow and mature and make many mistakes. From those mistakes, they hopefully learn how to be better decision makers. Those are lessons that Sara must learn too, if she is to function successfully in society someday. They are lessons best taught by her peers in as normal an environment as possible. All children must make their own mistakes in order to learn and so, motherly instincts in check, I intend to empower my daughter at each new transition she faces; I expect there will be failures along the way. What is different now is that I am not so afraid to let her take the risks, fail or succeed, and learn to go on.

Sister of the Heart

Jamie Mariska

Jamie is Jan and Bud's oldest daughter, and Sara's sister.

NO MATTER WHAT THEY ARE

Sara is a falling star
from heaven.
Sent from God to our hearts
So it doesn't matter
because we're all the
same inside.
So be good to all
no matter what they are.

WHY

If I could fly I would fly.
I'd fly to God and ask:
Why didn't you make people the same?

Why? Why? Why?

He says: "World would be boring if all were the same,
So everyone is the person they are to be."
Just like Sara: the same.

SARA

Ducks swim,
Flowers bloom,
Horses jump,
Kittys purr,
Puppies bark,
We all have different senses and sounds,
So Sara is neat, but different.

POLITE SARA

We give her juice
She says "thanks"
She gives us her plate
We say "thanks"
She says "welcome"
No matter what it is
She is always polite.

ROSES AND SARA

Roses are red,
Violets are blue,
Sara is special,
But, then, so are you.

Skyriding

Jan Spiegle-Mariska

Soaring higher and higher toward
The neighbors' trees
Skyriding on a scooter that
Two weeks ago
She was afraid to sit on.
When did she conquer it?
Getting off, she pushes, watches,
Does it again.
Chagrined,
I realize what I thought was
"REPETITIVE STIMULATION"
Was actually problem solving,
Experimentation.

To share
She runs inside
Persuading
Cajoling her little sister to
"WATCH ME OUTSIDE"
Soaring, both sides of the scooter
Full
With giggles and screeches and
Windblown hair.
Teaches pumping and "be carefuls"
Likes the big sister role
Denied in so many ways
How good it must now feel.

Spring greens and grows
Unsteady at first
Like her
Fits and starts
Cold and warm
Undecided
Then, progress.
Plateau.
Inevitable, they say.
I think not.

CHAPTER 6: SEAN

Isn't Testosterone Wonderful?

Fred McGlynn

Fred is an associate professor of philosophy at The University of Montana and the father of three sons.

Our second child has nocturnal epilepsy, possibly resulting from a protracted labor and traumatic birth. Our oldest boy was adopted at the age of 20 months, so our second child was my wife's first birth experience. She was in labor for more than 36 hours, completing the delivery only with the aid of Pitocin (a drug used to enhance the strength of uterine contractions, thus speeding delivery). I mention this only because the issue of his being our firstborn loomed large in our subsequent dealings with various doctors.

By the end of our son's first week of life we were aware that his health was not what it should be. He had lost significant birth weight and suffered from projectile vomiting. By the time he was a month old he had gained so little weight that the skin was shriveling on his back. A battery of tests was unable to establish any precise reason for his difficulties. One doctor thought that he might be suffering from cystic fibrosis, but was unsure. He suggested that we would probably not know whether our son did or did not have this dreaded and fatal disease for several more years. Our son's projectile vomiting was attributed to an intolerance to breast milk, so he was put on a goat's milk substitute. The substitute worked, and he quickly began to gain weight. This first, life-threatening trauma seemed to be over. Our troubles, however, were just beginning.

By the time our son was two months old, he began to suffer very unusual sleep disturbances. Within an hour or so of his falling asleep he would begin to whimper loudly as though he were suffering extreme fright. It was difficult to wake him from sleep, but when we did manage to wake him, he would seem fine. After returning to sleep, however, the pattern of extreme whimpering would begin all over again, lasting intermittently throughout the night. My wife and I would take turns getting up to try to comfort him, but to no avail. When we woke him up, he was fine; he did not cry nor did he seem frightened in any way.

We had heard of colic and at first assumed that this might be his problem, although if it were colic, we could not understand why he would not continue to fuss once he was awake. My wife took him to our pediatrician several times, giving detailed accounts of the symptoms which we had observed. The doctor checked him thoroughly and found nothing amiss. He suggested that she not worry, that this would pass.

It did not pass. Rather his sleep difficulties increased in both frequency and intensity, now accompanied by physical spasms, extreme jerking of arms, legs and head. His crying was very loud; it seemed to me more like the crying of a small, terribly frightened animal than any normal crying of a child, even a child suffering from a nightmare.

As the months went by, I eventually became inured to his crying, managing to sleep through these episodes, but his mother was unable to do this. Since these bouts of crying and thrashing lasted throughout the night, my wife was barely able to sleep at all. She began to record each episode in a journal, noting the duration and frequency of the symptoms. Armed with this detailed information, she once more sought medical help. Our pediatrician suggested that our son see a neurologist and we followed through on the suggestion.

The neurologist administered both a waking and sleeping electroencephalogram (EEG) and motor tests. None of these tests, however, indicated any neurological abnormality. Both the neurologist and the pediatrician suggested to my wife that perhaps, as a "new" mother, she was overreacting to what might be just slightly more than "normal" crying in our child. They both insisted that there was nothing wrong with our son. One even suggested that she close both the doors to our child's room and to our bedroom so that she would not hear him cry and thus be able to sleep.

My wife became increasingly frustrated with her inability to communicate the seriousness of our problem to the doctors. Lacking any restful sleep for months on end, she became exhausted both physically and emotionally. She began to observe occasional episodes of nystagmus (an involuntary, rapid movement of the eyeball, usually from side to side) and blank staring in our son during the day. Neither I nor my mother, who was living with us at the time, noticed these symptoms, nor were the doctors able to observe them when she took our son in for checkups. Despite her almost total exhaustion, she continued to carefully record the date, time and symptoms of every episode she observed. About a month after she first noticed the nystagmus and staring episodes, I also began to observe these occurrences.

Since my wife was becoming increasingly frustrated at the doctors' unwillingness to take her reports seriously, she suggested that I take our child to the pediatrician for his next checkup. I did. After he reported that our child seemed to be in good health, we began to talk about the sleep disturbances. Given the lack of test confirmation of any neurological disturbance, the doctor suggested that perhaps my wife was an overly anxious first-time mother. It became clear to me that he was dismissing her reports as the product of the overwrought imagination of an hysterical, novice mother.

I told him that my wife was not hysterical, that I had seen all of the symptoms which she had reported to him, that she had very carefully observed and recorded the details of each episode, that she had a graduate degree in language pathology and had been trained in careful scientific observation techniques, and that she came from a family in which both parents were practicing child psychologists who were experts in brain damage and learning disabilities. In sum, I insisted that her background, training and character suggested a patient and careful observer, not an hysterical first-time mother. I then repeated many of her observations and mimed the sharp animal cries which our son emitted during his nighttime disturbances. I noted that his body spasms were often so severe that, even though he then was only about two years old, I sometimes had a difficult time restraining his movements when I picked him up. I insisted that, while I had observed him far less frequently than my wife had, I was convinced that his behavior could in no way be described as "normal."

I am a forceful speaker with a deep bass voice; my wife is somewhat shy and has a soft, feminine voice. I would hate to think that something as irrelevant as the tonal placement of the voice carries authority in the medical community, but I do know that after my visit to the doctor and our little "chat" about my wife, he began to take her reports more seriously. She heard no more suggestions that she was overreacting to our son's difficulties.

After the pediatrician began to take her more seriously, he suggested that we go to a research hospital in a distant city for more sophisticated tests. He particularly wanted our son to have a CAT scan which, at the time, was not available where we live. The trip was arranged and our son's files were forwarded to the "expert" with whom we were to meet. We were told to anticipate a two- or three-day stay for tests. We took our son to the "expert" who, to our surprise, seemed to know nothing about our son's case. He administered the same waking and sleeping EEGs and motor tests which had already been done in our community. Finding the same lack of any abnormal results on these tests, he quickly concluded that our son suffered from a "behavior problem" and was simply seeking attention, which we were clearly generously providing. I informed him that I thought it was fallacious to assume that simply because the tests had shown no abnormality that therefore there could not be any. I said that I thought it unlikely that a behavior problem would have developed at six weeks of age, and that, besides, our son could not be "behaving" to draw attention since he was asleep when the incidents occurred. In addition, our son had no memory of these bouts when he was awakened. The "expert" was not moved by my arguments and quickly dismissed us.

It was clear to me, when I reflected back on this incident some months later, that our inability to get a hearing from this doctor was not the result of his dismissing either my wife or me as hysterical first-time parents but was, rather, the result of another impediment which parents with problems like ours seem to frequently encounter — what I call "the medical technology blindness syndrome." Rather than undertaking the very difficult task of investigating the cause or causes of symptoms which do not manifest effects discernible by present medical technology, the doctor simply retreats to the comfort of the presumed exhaustive accuracy of present diagnostic technology. Thus, if his or her tests don't show there is anything organically wrong, then there can't *be* anything organically wrong. The remaining facile explanation is that any abnormality in behavior must be psychological, not organic; that is, my son must have a "behavior problem."

At the time of this incident, however, I simply returned home in furious frustration, feeling that there was nothing more we could do. My wife, fortunately, was not as resigned to our impasse as I was. She began to spend her evenings in the library doing research on sleep disorders. After several months, she came home one evening with a Xerox copy of an article that contained an almost word for word description of our son's symptoms. This article suggested that our son suffered from nocturnal epilepsy. Our local neurologist had never heard of such a condition and did not seem to appreciate my wife's independent research efforts to enlighten the local medical community. She had better luck with our pediatrician, who by now had become increasingly impressed with my wife's tenacious observation techniques.

After one more futile effort to gain help at another major research hospital (they diagnosed "night terrors" and prescribed treatment with Valium, the effects of which lasted only a few days), we finally received an accurate diagnosis and instituted a regimen of drug treatment which brought my son's condition under control. This came about because my wife wrote to the author of the article which she had discovered and he confirmed our suspicions that we were dealing with a seizure disorder.

Some years later, when a new pediatric neurologist moved to town, we again encountered a double resistance to my son's problem. That is, once again my wife found that when she took my son to this doctor, he seemed not to take her concerns seriously. She became uncomfortable in the face of what she perceived to be his attitude toward her. Once again, I was called upon to take my son to his appointments. It was not long before this doctor, too, suggested that my son's problems might be behavioral in origin. Ironically, this neurologist had done his internship under the "expert" to whom we had previously taken my son and who had given the same "explanation" of my son's condition.

This time, however, my very firm rejection of the absurdity of this hypothesis (including a scathing account of our reception by his former mentor) overcame his tendency to retreat to the medical technology syndrome. He was willing to admit that the previous diagnosis obtained by my wife, and the subsequent success of the drug treatment of our son's condition, did indeed suggest that the problem was neurological in nature, even if no tests confirmed this fact. This doctor continues to be our son's neurologist and we have established an effective working relationship with him.

The ultimate irony of our long odyssey to discover what was wrong with our son through the aid of the medical community is that it was my wife's diligent research, not the many doctors who dismissed her as "overwrought," which provided the key to our finding a diagnosis and gaining an understanding of his problem.

My wife does not have the testosterone which produces chest hair, large muscles, and a deep authoritative voice which "gets listened to" in the male medical community. But without her patient observation, tenacious research and an unwillingness to accept that she was merely an hysterical "first-time mother," our son might not have had the chance to experience the general success in life which he currently enjoys.

Dispensing More Than Drugs

Kathy McGlynn, parent, with Byron Dodd, R.Ph.

Kathy McGlynn and Byron Dodd are a parent/pharmacist team who have worked together to manage the seizure disorder of Kathy's son, Sean. Kathy and Byron collaborated on two manuscripts for Changes, the second of which, "Pharmacists Helping Families: A Unique and Untapped Resource," can be found in Chapter 11, The Health Care Professionals. *Together, the manuscripts offer a comprehensive and exemplary picture of effective family/ medical professional partnerships.*

I first met pharmacist Byron Dodd when I ducked into Smith's Drug Store to obtain a prescription for my ailing mother-in-law. He asked me several questions about her, explaining that he liked to keep individual records on patients so that he would be aware of any allergies they had or any previous drug reactions they had experienced. That way he could notify physicians should a prescription come in that had an offending ingredient and hopefully he could obtain a safer substitute. I liked the personal touch and the active interest in patient welfare that our brief encounter revealed. I hadn't expected anything more than a perfunctory sale.

Many months later, my son Sean was born with a number of medical problems that required multiple medical tests, endless doctor's appointments, and many and various drugs. The first prescription was for Mycostatin, an anti-thrush product, which my husband obtained at Smith's. When I went for a refill there was a middle-aged woman ahead of me, whom Byron came over to greet. When he said, "Hello, Mrs.__________, how are you today?" she burst into tears saying, "I'm so worried about my mother." I distanced myself from this personal exchange and watched as Byron talked with her for several minutes. I was very moved by his kindness toward her and the discretion he showed — this was not my image of the pharmacist/ businessman.

By the time we needed a second refill of the Mycostatin, I was exhausted, stressed, and angry. My son, by then diagnosed as a "failure to thrive" infant, continued to have repeated vomiting and diarrhea and cried almost continually day and night — and he wasn't responding to the Mycostatin. Why, I wondered, was

I buying more of it?

I went into the store and saw Byron talking with a nattily dressed man carrying an attache case. Various customers were also present. He interrupted his conversation to take my order and soon handed the refill to me. "That will be $7.50," he said, whereupon I shrieked, "But I don't *have* $7.50!" I saw the man with the attache case and the nearby customers begin an immediate physical retreat, but not Byron. He responded, "That's okay, you can charge it." This offer rendered me speechless. Why should he let me charge it? He didn't know me. I might skip town without paying. Why should he take this unknown risk? He must care more about helping my child than making a dollar. How unexpected — how wonderful! I finally managed an "Okay" and left, never dreaming what doors had been opened to me.

Within a few weeks the questions of immunodeficiency had subsided and the metabolic problems were under control, but a seizure diagnosis loomed next. (What? Did my son have brain damage?) I froze as I turned in Sean's first prescription for phenobarbital, praying that the pharmacist wouldn't say anything revealing in the presence of other customers. Byron volunteered the comment, "We will be glad to work with you and to answer any questions you may have." I figured he was simply responding to the tension that must have been evident in my face. Nice . . . maybe he *was* really interested. At the very least, he was discreet.

Following multiple refills of the phenobarbital, Sean's behavior took an unexpected dive. Dismay and fear prompted me to seek yet another medical opinion to explain his violent sleep patterns and erratic reactions to ordinary situations. From this physician, I obtained a confirming diagnosis of "neurological problem", and a prescription for Dilantin. This drug comes in two strengths; we were given the stronger one. I didn't have time to get to Smith's that day, so I went to a nearby chain store. This experience was most aggravating. After I waited a full twenty minutes, the druggist informed me that they didn't stock the stronger form and then walked away; he did not offer to obtain it. My dismay changed to panic. If this, a major chain store, didn't stock it the others probably didn't either. What if no local store stocked it? Fortunately, Smith's did, and I clutched the precious bottle, breathing a sigh of relief, and left with exhilarating confidence.

The consulting physician couldn't believe it when it became evident that Dilantin was not going to work. "Are you sure you got the right strength from the pharmacy?" he asked. We had the right Dilantin; he gave us another prescription, this time for Mysoline. I began to feel suspicious and *guilty*. My son seemed to be getting half of his calories from the drugs he was taking! It felt as if he was being used as an experiment. We seemed to be flitting from one drug to the next, adding others, and changing doses and strengths so often. Uncomfortable as those thoughts were for me, we didn't seem to have much choice. I started to keep much more detailed and accurate records and to talk more openly at Smith's. At this point, Byron believed that Sean's response to the medications which had been tried pointed to an unusual or rare form of epilepsy. However, the attending physicians were slower to accept such a conclusion.

With no relief from Sean's sleep-activated screaming/crying/growling outbursts (averaging 25-35 a night), and repeated illnesses, I was going crazy from worry and lack of sleep. Would the Mysoline bomb too? Byron assured me that it was not unusual for it to take a while to find the right drug and the right amount of it to control a seizure problem. Further, we might need more than one drug to establish seizure control before we were through. "I must have fifty different anticonvulsants on these shelves; we're not limited to just a few that can be tried." This conversation was tremendously reassuring: it offered hope that my son's exhausting and frightening symptoms could be controlled and that, as a result, our lives might someday return to a semblance of normalcy. *That hope meant everything.*

Gradually, it became evident to the doctors that a single drug was insufficient. We had to find a winning combination of drugs — and soon. By now, I had entered a downward spiral of terrifying despair. Later, at our local support group for parents of children with special needs I remember saying:

> "I'm scared. I'm afraid I'm going to kill my child — drop him on the sidewalk or something. I'm so tired I barely have the strength to hold him anymore. I got less than two hours sleep again last night. I can't think; I can't react. I just spent half an hour reading the front page of the newspaper, but I don't remember any of it. Yesterday, I almost set myself on fire while fixing breakfast. I just stared at the red burner with my cuff only an inch away, when I should have instinctively jumped back.
>
> Each day is worse than the one before. I am going to die of exhaustion within the next few weeks unless we can get his constant sleep-screaming stopped. It's very much like being in the home where Valerie Percy's murder took place, except that this happens three or four times an hour, six or more hours each night.* Why can't the doctors see how desperate I am and get the problem under control? *Our entire household is in an uproar."*

---

*Valerie Percy was a U.S. senator's daughter who died violently, the victim of a multiple stabbing by an unknown assailant. She was attacked while asleep in her room at the family home. We lived only a few miles from the Percy residence at the time.

Somehow Byron recognized that I needed more to go on than I'd been getting, and he correctly guessed that reading would help me cope. Upon giving me the Mysoline, he also handed me a piece of paper he called a "package insert." "I want you to read this," he said, "I think you'll find it helpful." The insert gave a brief description of the drug, how it was composed, how it was to be administered, how to figure dosage levels, contraindications, etc. It also stated that blood levels should be checked periodically. This was news to me. It also turned out to be news to my pediatrician (not the prescribing doctor), who immediately responded by ordering blood tests at regular intervals. Close call, I thought. What if I hadn't seen the package insert?

Without too many increases the Mysoline began to have some effect, but the seizure control was not perfect. At this point, neurologist #4 wanted to switch Sean to Klonopin by phasing him off the Mysoline as we added in the new drug. During the rocky period that followed, I kept studying my own records and graphs, which by now were becoming quite detailed. I became convinced that if we used both drugs in the right amounts we could probably achieve total control. The doctors agreed to pursue the idea. The neurologist said I could experiment by using up to one level of Mysoline and up to another level of Klonopin. Finding the right combination was up to me. Why, I wondered, was he leaving it up to me? *I didn't know what I was doing.*

If ever I needed Byron it was now. When I talked to him I said: "I think there is a winning combination here. The pediatrician is leaving it up to the neurologist and the neurologist is leaving it up to me. Now *I'm* leaving it up to you." My heart was pounding and my stomach churning; what if he said "no"? I knew we could not solve this problem without the Rx factor, and that was known only to him.

Without hesitating, Byron took the sheet with the minimum and maximum dose levels and devised a four-stage plan. I was to use a specific level of each drug for a period of two weeks; if that failed I would move on to the next, higher-dose stage for another two weeks and so on through the remaining two stages. I was too numb to be very hopeful, but at least I had something to try.

My heart sank as the details of each stage were recorded, each phase evidencing abysmal failure — until we hit the last one, and voila! It didn't seem possible that after three miserable years and umpteen false starts, we had actually found the answer. How could such a seemingly small increase make such a difference in seizure control?

Our success immediately unleashed a barrage of endless questions. For months on end, I asked, read, and asked more. Byron was almost always at the store and almost always able to talk. He gave me copies of drug information sheets, drew diagrams to explain the drugs' chemical flow in the blood, discussed conversations he had had with Sean's physicians, helped me formulate questions I needed to ask the doctors (most important), and gave me a better grasp of the overall picture than any physician had. It was wonderful to know I could get so many answers so readily and that Byron continued to be interested in following Sean's progress.

This interest involved much above and beyond the call of duty. For example, no one else told me that one of the drugs we once used required the patient to take extra amounts of Vitamin D. No one else, including the prescribing doctor, offered to check on the unstated, long-term side effects of Klonopin, something I had been very concerned about since we were exceeding the recommended doseage listed on the package insert. Byron volunteered to call the company and find out for me when my inquiries to the company spokesman failed to yield any answers. He got it all, and ten pounds were subsequently lifted from each of my shoulders. Additional benefits came to me personally. I got rid of the guilt I had been carrying, and developed a more realistic attitude toward health care consumerism.

Thus, Sean's symptoms were controlled by the time he was three, the year my son went through sixty-nine prescriptions and refills. It took an additional three years to sift through all the events and information and begin healing from the trauma we had experienced. Sharing information and funneling questions through Byron enabled me to finally feel on top of my son's overall situation. His willingness to listen, advise me, and sympathize helped maintain my sanity. I never dreamed how crucial and supportive a pharmacist's expertise could be. No one referred me to Smith Drug; I simply stumbled into the right place at a critical time.

Dear Mom and Dad

Joel McGlynn

Joel is currently a Private First Class in the Marine Corps, and Sean's brother. He wrote this letter when he was 13.

Dear Mom and Dad,

Sean is getting hard to live with. I mean he has to take those pills and he has a very short temper to go with it. Sometimes he misplaces his wallet with all of his money in it and he blames it on other people and yells at other people. The day he lost his wallet Dad wanted everyone to look for it, and we could not do anything until we found it. Sean had made all of our friends go home until we found the wallet. He was yelling at us to look for it and all he did was sit down and watch television! *He* misplaces stuff and cannot remember where he put it and expects other people to look for it.

The thing I like about him is when he is nice to a lot of people. He will do good things for them if you ask him very polite and nice. Like one day I had to do the garbage, he wanted to help me with it. But sometimes he will stall when you ask him to do something he has to do that needs to be done fast. He says he will get it done, but he never does it in time and sometimes you have to use force to get him to do it and then he yells at you for it and you get in trouble.

Some days he forgets to take his pills and gets mad and hyper and starts to yell at people like it was their fault. He is smart, but he looks kind of dumb because he gets up in the morning and never combs his hair. But once you get to know him really well he is a good person, but he still may be a little strange. He is O.K . . .

Joel

CHAPTER 7: LISA

Conversation on Butler Creek Road

Lisa DeLand, Virginia DeLand and Jan Spiegle

What follows is the transcript of a conversation that I had in 1989 with Lisa DeLand and her mother, Virginia. Lisa is a young adult with developmental disabilities. Since Lisa was a very small child, Virginia has been aggressively designing, obtaining, and implementing educational programs and life skill programs which custom fit her daughter's needs. As a result of that work, she has had a dramatic and positive impact on the lives of many parents and children whose needs are similar to those of her own family's. Virginia now works as an advocate and parent support person for a regional advocacy network. Lisa works presently for a local Pizza Hut restaurant.

I think of Virginia as a mentor and a colleague, but most often simply as a very good friend who understands my life situation. Her work on behalf of her daughter has paved the way in western Montana for all of us who follow; many of the services we "newer" parents take for granted (most notably respite services) began as one of the "unrealistic parental expectations" which Virginia speaks of in this conversation. She has taught me much about my own power as a parent advocate. But she has also taught me, by example, how to persevere.

In the spring of 1989, I approached Virginia and Lisa to ask if I might interview them for *Changes*. Virginia agreed and Lisa was enthusiastic. As I approached the driveway into their heavily wooded lot on a spring afternoon, in a clearing stood a ten-foot replica of a dinosaur skeleton. (This "project" is explained in detail in our conversation.) The dinosaur greets visitors to the DeLand home, a symbol of a family which has realized many "less than realistic" goals. To many in mainstream society, those goals must have seemed unattainable and nearly as out of place as a dinosaur made of cast-off bones culled from fields left unplowed. Yet there it stands.

The issues talked about that spring day ranged from sterilization to family pets.

At first, I intended to segment each topic to help the transition from one subject to another. But, as I transcribed and edited the conversation, it became apparent to me that retaining the flavor of an informal conversation was important to the tenor of this manuscript. It lends the reader the position of a mouse in the corner and allows a form of honest eavesdropping. To change that tone, I felt, would be to take from the reader the spontaneity, humor and sometimes very tangible melancholy that were a part of this experience for Lisa, Virginia and me. So, instead, I have inserted editorial comments and a few logistical notes to clarify transitions.

Jan: Lisa, when did you graduate from high school?

Lisa: Let's see. When did I graduate from school, Mom? A month ago?

Virginia: No, June of '88.

Jan: So it's been almost a year now. What job were you working at when you graduated?

Lisa: Um, Dale's Dairy.

Jan: What did you do there?

Lisa: Well, I did cleaning shelves, doing milk.

Jan: You cleaned shelves in their store? And what did you do with the milk?

Lisa: I had to do the big milk tanks.

Jan: What did you do with those?

Lisa: Had to wash them out with soap and dry them off.

Jan: Make sure they were clean for the next time? Are they big?

Lisa: Yeah, but they don't have the dairy anymore.

Jan: What happened to the dairy, Lisa?

Lisa: Arsonist.

Jan: Arsonist?

Lisa: Did it. Did the barn and store and everything else.

Jan: It all burned?

Lisa: Yep. I think he did a lot of damage to everybody in this whole world.

Jan: What kind of damage did he do to you, Lisa? When the dairy burned down?

Lisa: I was angry.

Jan: I bet you were angry. I would be.

Lisa: I hope they throw the book at him before I do.

Jan: Did you have another job right away after the dairy burned down?

Lisa: No. I had to stay home for four months! Until December first? Right, mom?

Virginia: No, Lisa, you stayed home for almost n*ine* months.

Jan: That's a long time to be at home. Did you like being at home?

Lisa: No. I was just tuckered out. I stayed home. I didn't do anything. I just stayed home and went to bed and...

Jan: Was it boring?

Lisa: Yeah.

Jan: You just didn't like it?

Lisa: No, but I started a new job.

Jan: You got a new job?

Lisa: Pizza Hut!

Jan: What are you doing there?

Lisa: I do pasta. I do measuring. I do cleaning. And I didn't have to make pizzas today because somebody else did that.

Jan: What do you do with the pasta?

Lisa: Pasta. We use it for noodles and spaghetti I think. I get them ready to go for when the people order them and I put them in the fridge.

Jan: The same with pizza? Do you usually make pizzas?

Lisa: Yup. All kinds. Pepperoni and I can't think of the others.

Jan: Do you like doing the pizzas? What's your favorite part of your job?

Lisa: Making those pizzas.

Jan: What's the hardest part of your job, Lisa?

Lisa: Making the stuff. It's so messy.

Virginia: The tomato sauce?

Lisa: Yeah. Pizza sauce is the worst thing I've ever done.

Jan: Do you work with somebody, Lisa?

Lisa: I have three job coaches. Three women.

Jan: Is there one with you all the time at work or do you work on your own?

Lisa: Well, she helps me part of the time.

Jan: Are there other people working there at the same time?

Lisa: A few work in the morning; a few work at night and half work during the day.

Jan: Do you like the people you work with?

Lisa: Sort of. Some of them, I do. Some of them, I don't.

Jan: Tell me about the ones you like.

Lisa: I like girls better than men cause the men treat me wrong than the women do.

Jan: How so? What do the men do that you don't like?

Lisa: They just like to be grouches. In the mornings they are real grouches.

Jan: I think I know what you mean! So, you find the women easier to work with?

Lisa: Yeah, they're easier.

Jan: Do you have fun at work, too?

Lisa: Yeah, I like it.

Jan: So it's not like being home all day long?

Lisa: No, it keeps me busy.

Jan: How many hours each day do you work?

Lisa: Until it gets done!

Jan: That's a good way to put it! Just like everyone else. How many days a week do you work?

Lisa: Monday through Friday.

Jan: Do you get paid well?

Lisa: Absolutely!

Jan: All right! What do you do with your money?

Lisa: I started saving it. Half for the fair and half for something else.

Virginia: What about your animals?

Lisa: Yes. My animals.

Jan: You use it to take care of your animals? Tell me about them.

Lisa: Four goats, two dogs, a pony and a horse.

Jan: Wow!

Virginia: And a rat.

Lisa: No, that's not my rat. It's Loren's. (Loren is Lisa's younger sister.)

Virginia: We have four goats right now. Elizabeth P. Goat, Venus, Maybelle, and Mrs. G. Carrot.

Lisa: Three are pregnant.

Jan: Whoa. You are going to have an exploding goat population around here!

Lisa: Do you want one?

Jan: Oh, no! I don't need a goat. We need a bigger house and then we would need a goat.

Lisa: She's gonna have twins, I think. Yep, we may have twins this summer, Mama!

Jan: Do you take care of all those animals, Lisa?

Lisa: Yep. I have to do the dogs cause Mom has to do the taxes. (The interview took place in early April.)

Jan: What do you do for them?

Lisa: Water them. Feed them. Hay them. Grain them. But I don't have any grain right now, so . . .

Jan: So, it's just hay now? Do you enjoy working with them?

Lisa: It's hard work. You gotta shave them for the darn fair.

Jan: Do you show them at the fair?

Lisa: Yep.

Jan: Have you won some ribbons?

Lisa: How many ribbons have I won, Mom? Maybe thirty-eight or thirty-nine?

Jan: Just for your goats?

Virginia: For the dinosaur fossil and lots of other projects, too.

Jan: That's right! I remember reading a newspaper article about the dinosaur.

Virginia: She's won a lot of ribbons for that and for the various 4-H projects. She did a project one year called "Safe at Home." We spent the whole summer going over things she could and could not do at home . . . what was safe for her. Activities she could do to keep herself busy. We put them in categories like "things that are fun," "things that are jobs." No stove. She couldn't turn on the stove, but she could run the microwave. All those things you need to know about being home alone. She won a lot of ribbons for that.

Jan: Was this all for 4-H?

Virginia: Yes. It's all for 4-H. That has been wonderful.

Lisa: I will not be able to go with my friend. I have to work at fair time and it's gonna be a disaster!

Virginia: You won't be able to go in the mornings anyway. Two years, Lisa won the

Herdsman Award. It's an award that the Kiwanis Club has been giving out for 40 years. They give it to the individuals who do the best job all fair week of keeping their pen clean, and they come by twice a day, randomly, different judges to interview the kids. The competition is bloody! They are down there scooping up every piece of poop . . .

Lisa: Mom!

Virginia: . . . practically before it hits the ground. And Lisa, one year Lisa got a perfect score! And she was the only person . . .

Lisa: Everyone was very surprised.

Virginia: . . . in the history of the award to get a perfect score. And no one has done it since.

Jan: If you've kept those things, I'd love to look at them.

Virginia: Ok. Why don't we go and show you Lisa's trophies?

(From the dining room table, the conversation moved to Lisa's downstairs bedroom, where I was able to see a treasure trove of ribbons, trophies, and medals which document Lisa's accomplishments in her leisure-time activities.)

Virginia: Well, as a friend of ours said, this is probably the only house in town that you can come to and see a dinosaur in the front yard and a tent in the living room!

(Lisa's younger sister, Loren, had been practicing her camping skills in the DeLands' living room. There was a large orange tent affixed to the open-beamed ceiling and draped over fully a fourth of the living room area!)

Lisa: But my room is probably a mess!

Jan: That's OK. I've got four daughters, you know . . . Oh, Lisa your room is really pretty! That's a beautiful trophy for, let's see, best dairy goat. And this one?

Virginia: Best dam and daughter. There's one for best milk-producing goat. And here's her Herdsman awards.

Jan: I see bowling trophies, too. Do you like to bowl, Lisa?

Lisa: Oh, sort of. I haven't done it lately.

Jan: I like your room, Lisa. Thanks for letting me see it. It is obvious from everything here that you like all kinds of animals.

Virginia: What a pit!

Jan: Compared to my daughters' rooms . . . Well, at least in here you can see the floor to walk on!

(The conversation resumed back at the dining room table.)

Virginia: And here are the other 4-H projects.

Jan: This one is great — about learning consumer skills.

Virginia: This one was about recycling papers. And here's the one about selling her goat's milk and spending some of her money; cutting out pictures of the things she wanted . . .

Jan: . . . and comparing prices.

Virginia: She cuts out all of the pictures. She finds the magazines. We take photos as she does the work on the projects.

Jan: These are *all* ribbon winners!

Virginia: She got a purple ribbon (denoting outstanding achievement) on this "family adventure: cooking together."

Jan: This you did as a family? Planning dinners and shopping and preparing meals.

Virginia: Yes, you had to do four "adventures" and that was one that we chose. Then you have to create a scrapbook/notebook about it (with a big sigh as she surveyed the pile of memorabilia). It's really been a lot of work.

Jan: These projects are all wonderful, Virginia! It sounds as if all your long hours and enthusiasm have empowered Lisa to be a capable young woman.

Virginia: The projects have had real practical worth — tailored to her needs. This year she will be doing a self-determined project. She is going to pull all the pictures off all these posters and we'll do a huge scrapbook of all her years in 4-H. (There is a long pause.) This is her last year. We're going to have to find something else to fill in the gap this will leave.

Lisa: But, Mom, I don't want to miss the fair.

Virginia: You won't miss the fair, Lisa.

Lisa: Maybe I could be in another 4-H group?

Jan: Do they have an "older" level 4-H?

Virginia: Nope. Twenty-one is it.

Jan: Is that how far Public Law 94-142 follows kids through the system, too? (Implemented in 1975, Public Law 94-142 is the law which guarantees a free appropriate public education to children who have disabling conditions.)

Virginia: No. It follows them until they graduate. That's why I thought . . . You know, Lisa was eighteen in 1987. That's how we got that second year of high school. (More on this later.) It is "permissive" in Montana. ("Permissive" is a term used to denote services which are recommended, but not required by law.)

Jan: Lisa, tell me about when you were working at Dale's and the dairy burned down. You had to be at home. What happened with your family then?

Lisa: Well, we were angry and depressed, really angry the whole time. I was frightened to see my life get ruined like that!

Jan: For nine whole months you were without a job? Did that make people crazy at home?

Lisa: It made my mom bonkers! (Virginia nods vigorously.) I guess just because I didn't understand why this guy did this. Just hard for me to understand why he did it.

Jan: It's hard for anyone to understand why he would do it.

Lisa: I had two ladies (job coaches) helping me because of the stress. And they didn't rebuild the barn, but they rebuilt the store.

Jan: But there wasn't a job for you after they rebuilt?

Lisa: No. I . . . there just wasn't.

Jan: How did you feel when you got your new job?

Lisa: I felt happy. I'm still sticking with this job for a long time.

Jan: Sure. Because you know what it feels like to be without one now.

Lisa: Yeah.

Jan: I wonder if the man who did that realizes how hard it was on you?

Lisa: I don't think so. I don't know what the people are gonna do with him.

Jan: What did happen to the man who set the fire?

Lisa: They arrested him.

Jan: So he's in jail?

Lisa: No. He got out. But they haven't decided what they are going to do with him.

Jan: He hasn't gone through a trial?

Lisa: No, he hasn't.

Jan: Does that make you angry, too?

Lisa: Yes!

Jan: Makes you feel like, for now, nothing's happening to him?

Lisa: No, nothing. Hope the cops put him in jail for what he did. Put him in there and leave him in there. Betty Jo and her husband (the owners of the dairy) were just so sad. They lost three 4-H pigs and a horse in the fire. But they didn't lose any cows.

Jan: So they had the ability to produce milk, but no place for their cows to be?

Lisa: Yeah. They had to take them somewhere else.

Jan: Are they running the dairy now?

Lisa: No. No money. They just rebuilt the store.

Jan: This really changed a lot of people's lives.

Lisa: Yup.

Jan: Lisa, your mom told me that the other day at work you lost a knife.

Lisa: Yeah, but they found the knife this morning.

Jan: Good. Did it make you feel badly when you lost it?

Lisa: Yes. I was scared to lose my job. I was depressed. Just because everyone knows how I've been since this tragedy (the fire at the dairy) came. I was just scared and lonely as ever. I tried and tried and now...

Jan: You felt like you had failed? Because you lost the knife?

Lisa: Um-hm.

Jan: Did it worry you a lot?

Lisa: Yes. I had nightmares.

Jan: You had nightmares about losing the knife?

Lisa: I was so sad. My mom came in my room. She looked at me and she said, "You sad about that knife?" I said, "Yes, I'm serious!"

Jan: So things like that really bother you — like when you don't do something right at work?

Lisa: Well, they found it in the garbage. And they are doing fine now.

Jan: Was anyone at work really angry with you?

Lisa: No.

Jan: That's good. So they didn't think the knife was all that important, huh?

Lisa: No.

Jan: Good. Tell me what you like to do for fun, Lisa.

Lisa: Me? I like to listen to music and I don't know what my career will be, but being in the band business would be fun . . .

Jan: What would you do?

Lisa: Don't know.

Jan: Would you like to live some place other than your house here with your mom and dad and sister?

Lisa: I want to move to a house where I don't get calls by anybody . . . (Lisa stops to grin at her mom) . . . but I'll let my mom call me once in a while.

Jan: That would be nice. You feel like you'd like a place that's more private for you?

Lisa: Yeah.

Jan: A place that's just yours?

Lisa: That's right. So many of the kids got their own jobs and I already have my own job. But I can't do anything right now until the fair begins. Gotta get up real early.

Jan: For the fair? I'll bet you do. Do you think that after the fair is over and next fall comes around you and your mom will try to find a place for you to live?

Lisa: Yeah. I'm gonna keep a few animals. Some belong to Loren. Some belong to me. I'm gonna take the baby and the mama and leave Venus and Elizabeth. Maybe. I don't know which ones.

Jan: So wherever you go you'd like to take some of the animals? They would be good company?

Lisa: Yeah.

Jan: Would you like to live alone or with some other people?

Lisa: I'd like to live by myself and try it out cause . . .

Virginia: (surprised) You would? With no one else around?

Jan: Why do you think you'd like to live alone?

Lisa: Cause it's more easier so I don't have so many people calling me at night. (Lisa had been the recipient of an obscene phone call and clearly did not want it to happen again.)

Jan: People call you at night?

Lisa: Well, just friends, you know. They call me at night.

Jan: So you have lots of friends?

Lisa: Well, not very many.

Jan: Do you have good friends? Friends that you really like?

Lisa: Um. I have a friend that lives in town. But me and her aren't friends very much anymore.

Jan: What happened?

Lisa: She was just depressed of me because I was out with my friends in the band and she hated them.

Jan: Oh, she was upset because you went out with some other people?

Lisa: Yeah.

Jan: Sometimes friends feel that way.

Lisa: Are they just jealous of me? Is that the point?

Jan: That could be. They could be jealous. Where did you meet these friends? From school?

Lisa: No. From a band concert. When I graduated in 1988.

Jan: What do you like to do with your friends?

Lisa: Well, I don't usually call them because they're so busy. I love doing things the right way!

Jan: And the right way is not to bother people when they're busy . . .

Lisa: Right!

Jan: Well, Lisa, show me the things *you* wanted me to see here.

(We go back to the scrapbook items that Lisa and her mom had assembled for my visit.)

Jan: Oh, look, here's the wonderful article from our local newspaper about the fossil you built! You won an "outstanding achievement" award for this. You made a "bovine-saurus"?

Lisa: Yup. My granddad had a heart attack. A bad one. No one couldn't save him. He started the dinosaur stuff.

Virginia: The whole thing started when Lisa was eight years old and someone sent Lisa this "dinosaur hunting" packet of materials in the mail. So my father and mother took Lisa on a dinosaur hunting expedition. They went up to a state park. And you know, of course, that all dinosaur hunters eat lots of Kentucky Fried Chicken? Well, they found lots and lots of bones. My father came back and said

"Well, we didn't actually spot a dinosaur. We almost saw one but he was going over the hill as we got there." When they got back, Lisa decided that we should *build* a dinosaur just like they do in the museums. So, we all spent the summer building a dinosaur. (Laughing) We had to have an emergency expedition over to a friend's ranch because we ran out of bones.

Jan: Your family is amazing! Lisa, I'm sorry about your grandfather. My father just died of a heart attack too. You must have wonderful memories of him on that dinosaur hunting expedition. Did he die a long time ago or was that just a little while ago?

Lisa: It was a month ago. We had a funeral for him . . .

Virginia: It was 1987, Lisa.

Lisa: Yeah. 1987.

Virginia: The year Lisa went through the graduation ceremony at her first high school. Then she went one more year to another local high school.

Jan: How did that situation come about?

Virginia: I went to a conference and discovered that you lose all your rights once you are out of school and Public Law 94-142 isn't there . . .

Jan: . . . doesn't protect you anymore.

Virginia: No. And at that time supported employment was just an idea. I came back from the conference and for the second time rejected the Child Study Team's recommended placement in our local sheltered workshop.

Lisa: I don't like the workshop. The workshop's been so dangerous because that cowboy's been around for four months and I can't stand him. (More about the cowboy later.)

Virginia: Anyhow, I rejected the placement and then the high school staff worked out this arrangement. One of the teachers at another local high school was doing supported employment all on her own. She had no backing from the school, nothing. She went to two nearby towns to look at how they were doing it, came back and just started. Went out, found the jobs for the kids and pretty soon she had them out working.

Jan: Sounds like her personal initiative made a difference for lots of folk?

Virginia: Yes. And she actually got into some trouble with the administration because she pushed for more integration, more job placements and a few other things like that. She was awfully good, so we switched Lisa to her supported employment program. The following spring, right before graduation, they evaluated her again and, of course, she was by then no longer a candidate for the sheltered workshop.

Jan: Because by that time the supported employment program was up and running and they had trained her?

Virginia: She had a job! She had the training. She'd been on the job since October of that school year . . . so for eight months, I guess.

Jan: What would have been your options, Virginia, for Lisa's employment had she graduated that first year and there had not been a supported employment project in the works?

Virginia: Whew. I don't know. (A very long pause.) I just came back from that conference with my mind made up that she wasn't going to ever leave high school until she had a job. I really don't know. Some of the things that I do . . . there aren't any logical reasons why I do them. If you look at what's out there, what exists . . . you can't just be satisfied with it . . . We started a trust fund when Lisa turned fourteen and started high school. At that time, of course, all of the legal advice, and it was accurate, was to disinherit (children with disabilities).

Jan: In order to remain eligible for state and federal help.

Virginia: So we just started plunking some money each month into a reputable stock. I did that on the assumption that somehow, eventually, there was going to be a way to use that money for Lisa's benefit without it having to take away other services . . . that something would happen, that parents would band together, that laws would get changed . . . something would come together that honestly met the needs of our kids. I came back from that conference with exactly that belief and knowledge. I didn't know *how* we were going to do it or how it would all work out. I just knew that was where I was headed.

Jan: That's where it had to go for you and Lisa.

Virginia: Yeah, and it didn't have a whole lot of basis in reality. (Laughing) I think I've fulfilled that definition of "unrealistic parent."

Jan: And, yet, all those goals, to date, have been realized because there now *is* a way to make a trust fund work and now there is supported employment.

Virginia: If the governor signs the bill. The bill for the self-sufficiency trust is now on his desk.

Jan: So sometimes those "unrealistic expectations" have gotten us far more for our kids than anyone would have thought possible.

Virginia: Yes, but just *deciding* that you want this or that to be in future for your child doesn't relieve you of the responsibility for knowing the system and knowing the rules. We kept all of this stuff out of Lisa's name. We just went ahead and did it.

Lisa: (looking very bored) I had to have surgery two times and ten or twelve people came to visit me in the hospital.

Jan: So you *do* have lots of friends.

Lisa: Yes. I have twenty-nine of them.

Jan: Lisa, how did you come to decide to have the sterilization done?

Lisa: I don't know.

Jan: Did you talk about it for a long time with your mom?

Lisa: Yeh, but for a while I didn't think if it was right for me to have the surgery. It's just that I don't like having kids. (with great emotion) I don't need to be the same as everyone else. It's just that for me it was the right thing to do. Then I got real sick all over again (after the surgery Lisa had an infection) and I felt hopeless.

Jan: From being sick again?

Lisa: Um-hum.

Virginia: We're not keen on surgery!

Jan: My daughter's not keen on it either and with darn good reason. She knows all about it too. Do you feel OK about not having kids, Lisa?

Lisa: Yup.

Jan: You feel like that was right for you?

Lisa: Yes, it was. Some of my friends, a few have had kids. Sometimes its just a mess. I was just afraid it would be complicated for me to handle this situation. I can't tell any of my friends about this cause this is *my* personal life, not theirs.

Jan: I think you're wise to understand how complicated having kids can be. I guess it must have been a hard decision for you to make.

Lisa: Yes. It was. I didn't want to have kids cause I'm scared that other people might hurt me, desert me. Right, Mama? Remember when that cowboy came along?

Virginia: Well, I'm not sure that I'm following, but I think your reasoning is probably sound.

Lisa: Cowboy and I don't agree with each other. This guy and I haven't been friends. Some other girl got raped. She was a friend of mine.

Virginia: I don't think that was rape. I think he made advances, "came on" to her.

Lisa: Yeah. He "came on" to her...then he came to me.

Jan: What did you do when he did that, Lisa?

Lisa: I got very depressed at him. See, he's been having troubles with his life, but *I* can't help him with anything. His family abused him and he wanted me to help him. I thought to myself, "This is ridiculous." I don't know what to say. It's hard for me to deal with something like this.

Jan: Sometimes you just have to say "No", huh?

Lisa: That's right.

Jan: Virginia, you were telling me about how far P.L. 94-142 follows our kids through the system.

Virginia: Usually for severely affected children and young adults they will let them go on to twenty-one. The problem is that there is no post-secondary program that adapts well to our needs. Vo-tech centers and universities need to jump on this one. Heck, even the sheltered workshops are "permissive" and not required to serve anyone.

Lisa: I *don't* like the workshop!

Virginia: We *know* that.

Lisa: After my last year at 4-H, I'd like to do something that *I* like to do...that's more personal to me.

Virginia: We need to find some recreational programs for her, but we've got 4-H until it ends, and then...it has to be something *she* finds as absorbing as all this.

Lisa: Like the band business!

Virginia: Well, I've never heard about the band business until today; I haven't given it any thought. I can't quite see you as a groupie! (Laughing) How do you think you'd fit into that?

Lisa: Maybe I could help them go around.

Virginia: (teasingly) You know what I think? I think you like those guys with the open shirts and the long hair!

Lisa: (clearly embarrassed) Mom! The band business would be better for me than those goats and the fair!

Virginia: (clearly surprised) Are you getting tired of goats?

Lisa: No, I'm just done. It's just hard for me to handle all of them.

Virginia: You want to get rid of the goats? All you have to do is say the word to your dad.

Jan: Sounds like maybe your mom and dad are ready to jump right on that one!

Lisa: I might sell all of them and the horse.

Jan: Maybe you've just grown up and grown out of them and want to move on to other things?

Virginia: Well, it may come to that, but as passionate as she has been about animals . . .

Lisa: I'm not gonna breed my goats next fall either!

Virginia: OK. That's fine.

Jan: Did the supported employment program look for jobs . . . perhaps as a veterinary assistant or . . .

Virginia: Yeah. One of the problems with the job coach, of course, is that she's got eleven clients. She is supposed to do all the matching and training. This job coach meets Lisa at 8 a.m. at the job, works with her til 11 a.m., goes with another girl whose job is at a day care center, then she goes back to the office, does all of her staffings, all of the Individualized Habilitation Plan (IHP) paper work and logistics, then at 4 p.m. she works with a crew that cleans City Hall, and then she's got a person that she checks in on regularly at 9:30 p.m. This lady is also supposed to be out developing jobs for these people and others?

Jan: I understand. Understaffed and overworked is the norm; the same old story.

Virginia: What has happened often is that *I* have developed jobs, most of which didn't work out for Lisa, but many of the areas I explored ended up in job placements for other kids. There was one at a local ice cream parlor; it didn't work for Lisa, but it worked out for someone else.

Jan: You've been "beating the bushes" then, finding what you can.

Virginia: Yes. I have learned to "call in all my markers" and use all the contacts I have. Like the person up the road who is a physician at a local medical clinic. I had the job coach call him; he said to go ahead and use his name. He even went to their personnel department personally to see what he could do. He recognized that there were, as he put it, "a million jobs that could be done in the clinic by young adults like Lisa." But, even with his help, nothing's ever come of that one. For every time you "score" there are ten more closed doors. We need to figure out how to get in those doors. Once we do that, all things are possible.

One Bite at a Time

Virginia DeLand

Virginia is the parent of two daughters, Lisa and Loren. She works as an advocate for families in the state of Montana and as a parent consultant for Parent's Lets Unite for Kids (PLUK), a parent-run advocacy network.

As the parent of a young adult with developmental disabilities, I was asked to write about some of the dilemmas I have faced and feelings I have had as our daughter approaches adulthood. I've spent most of one summer resisting the exploration of my feelings about our current situation; it's too much like taking my tongue and probing a sore tooth. I'm just trying to get through it.

The problems are harder now; Lisa is less malleable. In the past two or three years, issues that could no longer be postponed have been forced upon me. Hopes about the level of independence she might achieve have had to be reconciled with the actual skills she has been able to acquire; and the future, dependent on so many variables over which I have no control, is hard to contemplate. It sometimes seems like a piece of tough meat growing larger and more indigestible the longer I chew it. The only way I have been able to deal with the trying predicaments of Lisa's adult life is to break them into smaller pieces that I take one bite at a time.

The First Bite

Supplemental Security Income, or S.S.I., is a subsistence program for people with disabilities, with approval based in some measure on income level. Once accepted for S.S.I. in Montana the person with disabilities is automatically accepted for Medicaid and eligible for food stamps. In addition, group homes receive an extra stipend for each person with developmental disabilities on S.S.I who resides in the facility. Job training programs such as the Targeted Jobs Tax Credit Program and vocational rehabilitation monies are also income-related. Thus, being on Supplemental Security Income is key to any residential program, day work program or job training placement for the person with disabilities.

I was never keen on the S.S.I. process and spent a number of years trying out various savings and investment plans in an effort to avoid applying on Lisa's behalf. In 1982, when Lisa was fourteen, I was *turned down* (which has to be a first) by an insurance company salesman when I applied for an annuity policy for Lisa. We calculated that to assume total financial responsibility for Lisa's care for her lifetime would require we invest *$1,427.73 a month* for the next sixteen years. Since this simply wasn't possible and I could find no other alternative to applying for S.S.I., when Lisa turned eighteen, and our income was no longer a consideration for approval, we applied. I have concluded that no one (except the very wealthy) has a choice about it.

The process was every bit as awful as I imagined it would be. We were required to apply in person. The purpose of the interview at the S.S.I. office was to establish that Lisa was so severely disabled that she was incapable of ever supporting herself. This interview took place *in Lisa's presence.* I had spent days organizing her records, dating back to the original diagnosis, in an effort to prove my daughter's total incompetence. What a role reversal for me!

The woman who conducted the interview almost salivated over those records, commenting in her report to the state that I had "voluminous records that measured five to six inches in height." The state office quickly deemed Lisa eligible based on her disability. They then took over a full year to determine her "economic eligibility," whatever that means. Thirteen months and eleven days from the day she applied, Lisa received her first check.

Now that we are in the system, as Lisa's "representative payee," I am required to keep complete records on how her money is spent. I am responsible for informing the Social Security office of any changes in Lisa's income, resources, or living situation that might affect her Social Security status. Lisa's eligibility is redetermined by Social Security periodically and all financial records they wish to see must be produced on demand. They have the right to come into her home without notice. (I have never heard of this happening, but they do have that authority.) The value (above $20.00) of any gift that is made to Lisa, such as Christmas or birthday presents, must be reported so that it can be counted as unearned income, and her Social Security payments can be reduced according to their formula.

I seem to be adjusting slowly to this business. I now find presenting her Medicaid card at the front desk of every doctor and dentist we visit only mildly degrading. Because it is so vital to her well being, I have gone from frantically trying to avoid S.S.I. to being afraid of losing it. Every time I see an envelope with the S.S.I.

return address or get a call from them, my palms get sweaty because, with S.S.I., even when it's settled, it's not settled. It is as if Lisa is a prisoner of war and will be a captive of the system for life.

The Biggest Bite

Independence was my dream for Lisa: she would be able to live unaided and hold her fate in her own hands because that *is* real security.

I never wanted to become her guardian, but that is what has occurred. If it were feasible, I would gladly petition the court to reverse its decision. The guardianship is a defeat of the highest magnitude and I covet my old dream.

I started early enough; I contacted our lawyer when Lisa was seventeen and fully intended to have completed the process before she came of age (18). She was nineteen before I could drag myself through the process. Avoiding the necessary steps became an art form; I dreaded the hearing.

It was, in fact, the morning of the hearing before I decided it was time to stop evading. At that point, it occurred to me that if there was ever a time to "dress for success," this was it. My husband wore his "power suit," the only tie he had which was narrower than his lapels, and polished his cowboy boots. I chose my black silk and pearls. If I had owned a Rolex watch, I would have worn it.

Looking the epitome of middle class respectability, we met our lawyer at the courthouse and waited to be called into the judge's chamber. The lawyer, my husband, myself and Lisa filed into a messy conference room off the court, identified ourselves and were duly sworn. The judge asked Lisa if she understood the proceedings and agreed to them. She looked at me. I told her she understood; she told the judge "Yes, sir," and we were out of there. I had spent a year and a half twisting in the wind trying to summon the strength to face the death of my last, best dream for Lisa. Yet, in a matter of minutes, it was done. I had been able to face the loss and *the system had made it easy.*

I was weak with relief. But as I accustomed myself to the notion that this ugly business was, at last, in the past, and my feelings of deliverance abated somewhat, the thought began to permeate that *nothing this momentous should be so facile.* While I did not want or expect to be put through the Spanish Inquisition, I definitely wanted to see care exercised. We spent longer waiting to see the judge than the procedure took. Lisa's fate was decided in less than five minutes. We could have been well-dressed criminals for all the judge knew. Our lawyer tried to reassure us that it had all been investigated before the hearing. But, I wondered with bewilderment, can a judge strip a human being of her rights and place her in the care of two people he has never met in so cavalier a fashion? You bet! With feelings verging on panic, I have thought about the fact that the next time a judge assigns a guardian for my daughter, it won't be me.

The Third Bite

In Montana, a sterilization procedure can only be performed with the "informed consent" of the individual. When Lisa was fourteen, I could see with distressing clarity that the responsibilities and pleasures of motherhood were well beyond her capabilities. However, it was anything but apparent to Lisa. She stubbornly resisted all efforts to persuade her of its necessity. And, even though I could have pushed her into it, I wouldn't. It took a nervous five and one-half years with counseling on the subject before she would agree. It was a decision that Lisa made with hesitation and an aching heart. For no matter the cost to me, this was truly Lisa's bereavement. The depth of the loss, even when the outcome is desirable, cannot be denied.

In my mind's eye I will always see a vision of Lisa, whole and wonderful, soaring to extraordinary heights. I can envision the life she might have had and know it will never be. The children she will never bear symbolize to a degree *all* the losses. I know I have not only lost the child that I dreamed of before Lisa was born, but also the grandchild who might have followed.

The Toughest Bite

It is part of a parent's job to protect and nurture his/her children. When one's child has a disability the job is done with such a sweet, tender intensity that one can almost reach out and touch it. I thought those feelings would be there for the whole of my life and half of Lisa's. But it's not so. I love her; I would kill for her, but the days of physically caring for her are nearing an end, and I am not sorry.

Lisa and I are engaged in the difficult dance of parting which all parents and adolescents perform. The growing apart has made things difficult for us. The warm companionship we enjoyed when she was younger is no longer comfortable for either of us. The seamless friendship is, of necessity, being torn apart by our divergent needs; hers for self-determination and mine for release. Our relationship is marked by mutual touchiness these days. It sometimes makes us long for a return to our old closeness. At other times, we are impatient to get on with it. Enough of the old fun remains to remind us both of our love (and also how much we really like each other). I operate on the assumption that when she firmly establishes her adulthood and we discover the proper mix of distance and independence, we will be free to resume our old friendship. Until then, Lisa desperately needs to try her wings. But *how*?

I find it hard to picture Lisa in a group home where they go everywhere in a group of eight and dress oddly. Transitional living doesn't really fit her and independent living is beyond her capabilities. I can visualize her owning her own home with a couple of acres and her animals. She would have a living coach (much like the job coach she has now) augmented by current technology to facilitate this arrangement. But, that is all it is right now — a vision.

I have been driven by many emotions as Lisa grew up: disbelief, depression, the need to make something positive grow out of all the negatives, a compulsion to understand my emotions, and anger — especially anger. But I am afraid to look at my feelings now; afraid that I will discover that the emotions that have propelled me in the past will be gone and something worse will have taken their place: weariness. I fear a lassitude so absolute that it will enfeeble me and I will never be able to go forward again. If I stop working on a solution for the sort of "customized" independence I envision for Lisa, will it ever happen? Even if I keep working and it *does* happen, will it be soon enough? Can I last as long as it will take?

I have loved, raised and now continue to live with a young woman who struggles to become an adult under her mother's eye. I hope she can do the job under such adverse conditions. There are so many scary risks to be taken and the possibilities for disaster are so many. As Dorothy Parker said:

> Three be the things I shall have til I die:
> Laughter and hope and a sock in the eye.

Summing Up

Sometimes when I stop to assess just how all of this has changed me, it looks pretty good. I am stronger, tougher, more resilient and capable of change than I would have thought possible. I have developed skills and discovered talents of which I wasn't aware. I will always feel Lisa was cheated, but I also know I would never have pushed myself so hard if it hadn't been for her needs. Because of her, I have been forced to face what I thought was unfaceable. I have discovered the pure joy of loving another human being unconditionally. I would never have believed in 1970, as a devastated parent in the doctor's office, that there would be a day when I could say, with honesty, that I had been blessed, but it's true. Today, however, it is a blessing tempered by reservations. How ironic it would be if the result of all that hard work to secure Lisa a decent future was simply my own personal growth.

In providing Lisa with a childhood dense with opportunities in order that she might realize her potential, I also created the expectation *in her* that realizing that potential would be possible. It would be more than I could bear if I broke Lisa's wonderful, innocent heart. So, one bite at a time (with lengthy rest periods in between), we move on.

CHAPTER 8: AUSTIN

The Decision for Out-Of-Home Placement

Delanie Baker

Delanie is the parent of two children, Austin and Sharon. Austin has autism. Delanie is now an educator and, as an associate member of the Montana Committee for Children with Severe Emotional Disorders, she is an advocate for persons with emotional, behavioral, and/or mental disorders and their families.

In 1983, I was the head of a low-income, single-parent household consisting of myself (a thirty-two year old licensed practical nurse), Austin, a beautiful ten-year-old, and (also beautiful) seven-year-old Sharon. At this time, though we knew there were serious behavioral and personality problems with my son, we had no "label." Evaluations by numerous professionals had led to much speculation but very little concrete knowledge. Inadequate (and sometimes late) child support payments, along with health insurance, were all we got as support from the children's out-of-state father. And, although we qualified in all financial respects, due to the lack of a diagnostic label for Austin it was impossible to obtain the treasured lifeline of Supplemental Security Income (S.S.I.) from the Social Security Administration. With it, we might have been able to maintain a minimally well-rounded, healthy, positive existence. But as things were, we pretty much aimed at just surviving the best we could. I had ceased to be committed to any kind of personal growth for myself, focusing only on keeping my checkbook in the black and my children (especially Austin) cared for adequately.

If I could have found abundant, affordable child care settings and/or providers trained to care for Austin's increasingly outlandish behavior, I could have worked more hours and been more flexible with my work schedule. That was not to be. A large share of my income went to the care of Austin and Sharon because I often had to use two separate day-care settings. And, of course, Austin's care cost more. It wasn't worth it in terms of money or physical stress on me to work more.

Our home was rather stormy — I could say missing "adequate tranquility." I became increasingly exhausted and brutally overextended just dealing with day-to-day matters. Austin created a continuous stir and upset. Mealtimes, bedtimes, public outings, and "get-ready-in-the-morning" times were nightmares. By the time he was ten, I knew we would require big-time help (and soon) to continue as a family unit. With great sadness and guilt, I began admitting that despite my best efforts, things were going downhill.

Austin could best be described as existing in his own world, in and out of reality within minutes. Sometimes this manifested itself as an emotional "spaciness," the sense that he was not really present or not hearing what was going on around him. Occasionally, he could display quite run-of-the-mill behavior and conversation. But sometimes his "own world" was a grossly uncomfortable place for him (and consequently, those around him) due to the presence of highly tormenting, self-described "bad thoughts." Whatever caused him distress usually expressed itself in difficult-to-deal-with actions, including destruction of household property and aggressive behavior. "Voices" seemed to torment him and he often spoke aloud to them, saying, "Get out of my head!," "Leave me alone!," or "I'm not going to do that."

He frequently obsessed aloud about happenings in outer space with imaginary space creatures and super-beings like Spiderman, Superman "with a white neck," and the Hulk. His most prevalent unanswerable, mysterious concepts and questions centered on the nature of "good" and "bad," along with other baffling conversation topics like hell, heaven, God, devils, angels, and the number of atoms in the kitchen table. His fixation on these topics became a constant source of frustration, and I eventually refused to allow much of this talk in my home; it had the effect of frustrating, astounding, and agitating most everyone who listened, though there were a few people who journeyed with him and enjoyed his imaginary world adventures. Though I limited, and at times refused to allow, such verbal harangues, I always did so with mixed feelings; any of these conversations served to stimulate speech development, vocabulary, and human interaction, goals that were all important for Austin.

His emotional response range was limited, though his anger remained readily available for expression. His low tolerance for frustration, whether real or imagined, whether of the present or from the past, manifested itself in socially unacceptable or emotionally unhealthy manners. Any perceived frustration, his "bad thoughts," changes in routine or setting, and God knows what else, could unpredictably send him into repeated, loud, hysterical rantings, complete with body contortions at times. These episodes varied in degree and duration. At any given moment, he could be found hammering holes in a table or pulling a curtain down, with gritted teeth, angrily resolving to "nuke" our home town, and/or hitting and shouting at his sister because she was "the enemy" and he "just felt like hurting someone." The capricious nature of his behavior left Sharon and me waiting for the "other shoe to fall," ever vigilant and ever stressed.

Interactions with other children were strained, to say the least. Because Austin was so lacking in social skills, his sister became his main "buddy." I rejoiced at the times they could play together in a normal fashion. Most kids liked Austin, but lost interest in him quickly (with the exception of a few who found him rather weird and fascinating). Some boys took on a protective attitude toward him which I heartily welcomed. I worried and stewed that there were insufficient opportunities for social interaction. I wanted him to be as similar as possible to other children and *to have friends.* This worry was one of my worst and most frequent. I remember thinking that it might be worth the peace of mind to actually pay for a friend for Austin.

While I had taken a parenting course, I lacked an "industrial strength," professionally monitored, home-based behavior management program to offer me expert advice and support. I learned early on that corporal punishment would backfire (he would feel compelled to hit back at someone). I frequently used "time out" as a means of controlling his behavior. I enforced a "cooling off" period or "get your act together" time by requiring him to be alone in his room (which often led to his "trashing" that area) or I placed him out in the car if we were at a store or another outing. Perhaps eight to ten times a week his unleashed aggression required physical restraint until he got himself under control. Often I would try to forestall such occurrences by talking to Austin about the hazards and consequences of these episodes *before* going out. This seemed (sometimes) to remind him that he was responsible for his own behavior. Once in a while it proved fruitful. Ah, the countless times we exited from public outings or family get-togethers because of his inability to "pull himself together," that is, to quit screaming and cease bizarre behavior.

There were times I'd lose my cool and just scream at him, shaming and scolding. Often I would later cry over my lack of control and my thwarted efforts to make things better. By this time in our lives, I no longer believed a loving God existed; maybe there was a God, but I felt I didn't possess the time or energy to maintain a relationship with an apparently rejecting omnipotence. My spiritual state was barren. Mostly, I'd feel raw and burned out, sometimes lonely and isolated. Rarely did I feel confident that I was doing enough or the proper things for Austin, for my daughter, or for myself.

There were also negative repercussions, at times, from Austin's periods of relative quiet, lost-in-his-own-world behavior. I remember him at five years old, just wandering out onto a softball field totally oblivious to the exciting, competitive game he was disrupting. At that time I was newly divorced and had attended the game to make some new friends, having just moved to a new town. I wanted and desperately needed a support network, and saw this as a chance to begin building one. Instead, some of the people glanced at me with skepticism and disbelief as I hastily retrieved an oblivious Austin from the field. What in the world was wrong with this kid? What in the world was wrong with me? What kind of parent was I? Hadn't I managed to teach him anything in five years? The unspoken questions in their eyes translated in my guilt-ridden mind as an indictment of my parenting. Predictably, I reacted with embarrassment and anger toward Austin. It seemed most of the kids at the picnic and game were above-average, highly stimulated, and had managed to be born to intellectual parents. The sad fact became glaringly apparent—denial disappearing—that Austin had serious dysfunctions, but in that town, at that time (and for years to come), we could not get firm answers to what had caused the problem, what label to give it, or what to do about it.

The reaction of the people at the softball game was by no means the worst or most dramatic of the incidents we have lived through with Austin. In fact, it pales in comparison to the kindergarten teacher whose first question to me about Austin was, "Do you ever hug your son?"

Hoping for more of every kind of assistance, we moved again when Austin was six and a half. I believe I explored every avenue for help for us when we arrived in Montana, but it seemed there wasn't a whole lot more offered than what had been available in the previous settings. We plodded along with a meager income, food stamps, and some low-cost recreation; what else were we to do? The one service agency in town which might have been able to help us dealt with children only up to the age of five. And, again, our lack of diagnosis (despite evaluations by numerous new professionals) allowed us to "slip through the cracks" of service delivery.

Support from the kid's father was unthinkable. He rarely called, wrote, or visited our children. He made many grandiose promises when we did talk to him, but delivered little. Summer and Christmas visits were discussed, but rarely happened. Thus, my children were left with unfulfilled promises and I with an (always) unanswered need for time off. All in all, my ex-husband refused any real involvement with handling Austin, Sharon, or the problems arising from Austin's behavior. This had been the pattern throughout our six-year marriage. Austin's early years were full of turmoil and family dysfunction. The fact that I had remained too long in that life situation caused me even more guilt and led me to take on the "noble martyr" complex which kept Austin in our home longer than he should have been. Guilt is a strong motivator. Austin's father's continuing unpredictability and self-centeredness generated resentment and frustration in me which raised my already dangerously high stress level.

Fortunately, I did have my parents, my sister, and some friends who offered support in many different ways. Though I chose to handle most of the problems on my own, their support at crucial times allowed me to survive the crises and maintain our family unit.

Austin's eating habits had always been of concern to me, also. He was very slow to accept solid food as an infant; he didn't seem to recognize physical hunger in the same manner as the rest of us. His stature was slight and he was small for his age. And over the last few years, he had developed the habit of being particularly disruptive at mealtimes.

By the time he was ten, I would have to ask him to leave the table at mealtimes on a regular basis due to his unsettling, disorderly behavior. He repeatedly halted the digestive process for the rest of the family, or for dinner guests when I was courageous enough to invite them. His mealtime disruptions triggered a virtual shut-down of crucial family communication during the dinner hour. He spent one rather unusual weekend during this time in his life deciding to consume hardly any food. His reasoning on this matter was that to eat food would kill him. Where this notion came from, I'll never know. I rejoiced when this self-destructive thought left his mind by Sunday evening. This incident was out of the ordinary even for Austin, and it induced in me new, fresh fears about what was going on in this kid's head, and *what was yet to come.*

Austin had extreme difficulty shutting off his thought process and entering the world of sleep; once asleep he'd have such disturbing nightmares that the whole household suffered lack of sleep. These times were some of my worst. It was very hard to detach emotionally and not react with exasperation after dealing with him all day. I felt at night when the kids were bedded down, I certainly deserved to have some solitude and a break from parenting. Think again, Delanie! If I were cut out to be an abusive parent, it certainly would have happened at these times. Mornings when we had to get a sleepy, "lost-in-space" Austin off on the school bus (with him dawdling over dressing himself and battling over breakfast) made such thoughts dart through my head on many a bright new day.

I couldn't convince a physician (out of six I had asked starting when Austin was five) to prescribe even a mild sedative to use before bedtime. I listened, again and again, as these physicians and other professionals told me how injurious drugs are for children and that "there were various other ways to induce sleep." As a nurse, I knew those things. I also knew they didn't work for my son. But because I was guilt-ridden about Austin's condition, lacking self-confidence, and insecure about *everything* I was doing for my son, I never challenged them. Doctors might have more readily prescribed something if they had lived with Austin.

But, more than sleeping aids, we critically needed a diagnosis — some label which indicated to the world that we needed more help than we were getting. I remember wishing Austin had Down syndrome; then I'd know what I was dealing with, grieve sorely, and *get the help we needed.*

It is interesting to note, in retrospect, that the summer before Austin entered the public school system, and fully five years before we had a label, I had employed a special education teacher to tutor him. Having spent one year in private kindergarten, he was still not ready in any aspect for school in the fall, but I had high hopes that tutoring would help. This teacher was the first person to mention the word "autism" to me in reference to Austin. She performed a tremendous service for us by alerting the school district that Austin would be needing special education services. Because of her foresight, Austin only had to spend six grueling weeks in a regular education classroom proving that he wasn't able to function in that setting.

Austin (and in turn Sharon and I) had some great luck that year. Austin was placed in an excellent self-contained special education program for educationally and behaviorally challenged elementary-aged school children. The expertly trained and experienced teacher set up wonderful behavior programs, stimulating play activities, and creative learning opportunities. These teaching strategies often required a one-to-one teacher/student ratio with Austin and included nearly constant prompts, reinforcers, and consequences. They were just what Austin needed.

I credit this teacher for her tireless efforts with my son, but mainly for facilitating Austin's ability to read, write, do simple math and follow directions. Since then, I have learned that not all teachers pour their energy so generously into difficult, challenging children like Austin. Many children like him end up institutionalized or in group homes by this age. I do wish I hadn't been so exhausted at the time; I could have followed through more consistently with her suggestions for cooperative behavior management. This teacher also turned out to be a neighbor of ours and throughout our acquaintance has maintained an understanding, supportive, tolerant, loving attitude towards me and my children. She often listened patiently to my evening phone calls concerning my worries and woes about Austin. That positive attitude was, and continues to be, precious to me and has been a renewing force in my life.

Of course, the six hours a day spent in school for 180 days a year alleviated considerable expense in terms of money for childcare and provided some relief from the intensive parenting I had been doing. But there were still 185 days (7680 hours) when I was alone with the problem. What we really needed was predictable, hands-on services when the children weren't in school: things like respite care money and providers, a family trainer, a financial boost, a family counselor, a case manager, clothes and bikes for the kids, and a scheduled weekend once a month (or every two months) when I could be without parenting responsibilities.

When Austin was nearly eleven years old, I cast my lot with yet another professional. Austin was evaluated by a local pediatric psychologist. With my fist clenched on his desk I said, "Something is wrong with this child, and we are going to find out what it is." Something had clicked inside me; this time I knew that my family's survival depended on getting an answer. I was assertive enough to let this professional know, before he evaluated Austin, what was going on in our family. And he had the courage and compassion to do for us what no other professional had done thus far. He labeled my son as having a "childhood onset pervasive developmental disorder" (autism falls under this rather broad categorical umbrella) with mild mental retardation. I suspect he never would have made such a "rash" diagnosis had he not understood how badly we were in need of services. (It was four months later, when Austin was a patient in an out-of-state children's hospital for diagnostic, referral, and medical evaluations, that autism was decided upon as the official label.)

Finally getting a label meant many things to my family. First, it validated my gut level feelings that something was wrong with my son. Second, it allowed me to realize that I was not to blame, and that I didn't have to carry this burden alone. A label also meant short-term survival. We were immediately admitted on the rolls of S.S.I. We were now qualified to receive respite monies, and with it came a treasured list of trained respite workers.

There are no words to say how very much I wish these answers and this assistance would have come early enough to keep Austin in my home. During those respite breaks, I was able to have blocks of time when I could think rationally about our future. I knew that Sharon needed at least some of the time and attention returned to her that Austin had innocently demanded and received for so many years. In my less sensible moments, escape fantasies played on my mind — I'd just leave the children and drive far, far away in my car. This was, I guess, an option, but my sense of responsibility prohibited such an escape. One of my best friends shared with me recently that, at that time, I appeared to be "barely keeping my head above water, swimming to beat the band to find anything to help." She couldn't believe that in our sophisticated, wealthy society something couldn't be done to help our household.

Significantly, the decision for out-of-home placement came shortly after the school's two-week Christmas break the year that Austin was ten. I was able to see with serious alarm during that time that controlling Austin's behavior was just too much for me. I was simply too weak for those two weeks. And I realized that I didn't just desire control over his behavior, I wanted him to get well, get better, get something!

Propelled by that desperation, something "clicked" again inside me. I knew I needed an extended break, perhaps a month of Austin residing out of our home for me to be the kind of person (and mother) I had long ago set standards to become. The respite time was precious, and it helped me to make some decisions about the direction my family was headed. It helped in that way, but in many other ways, it simply came too late.

Through the local county human/social services agency, we were blessed with finding a family that would take Austin for a month, and longer if it was deemed necessary. It took three months of waiting for a family, being interviewed by various professionals, and filling out forms, but it was worth it. The month that we spent without Austin in our home allowed many positive changes to occur in our lives. Sharon had blossomed socially (for the first time, she felt comfortable bringing friends home) and I felt a nearly tangible sense of relief and freedom. I could actually have a complete thought sequence. I was able to *choose* the two or three times a week I spent time with Austin. I had the time necessary to recognize and confront the grief that I felt about my son's disability. And because this family rolled up their sleeves and delivered care for Austin, we avoided a residential/institutional care placement for him.

There were rumors floating around at that time about a new, wonderful, "supportive-in-all-ways" program that was in development and particularly suited to our needs. It is titled Specialized Foster Family Care, and is now Austin's lifeline to realizing his potential in the least restrictive environment. It prevented him from residential care placement and also from doing the "foster home drift." It became apparent in implementing this program for Austin that other households required expensive, extensive support services to maintain him effectively and ethically on minimal drug dosages. But, both in the long and the short run, it has proven that it is more cost-effective and better to maintain Austin outside of residential/institutional care.

Except for a five-month break in foster care placement (during which time Austin lived, again, with us) he has been out of our home for six years. The first foster family had "our boy" for two and one-half years. The current foster home has been administering care for three years to "our boy." I call him "our boy" because I remain, as always, his mom.

I have always co-parented Austin with his foster families, sharing concerns, strategies, and his (always) overwhelming care requirements. We have come to realize that the job of parenting Austin is too large for any one person to handle. (One social service professional has said to me that she believes it takes three to four involved families to maintain a child like Austin out of a group home or an institution.) Overall, the system that we have developed is working well for all of us.

Austin was three and one-half when I began to search for help and answers. I was motivated initially by his language delay and his development of a "self-constructed" language. Most professionals (child psychologists, one psychiatrist, and numerous physicians) who evaluated Austin and consulted with me over the years postulated that Austin would be getting better. I heard an array of comments such as:

"I know autism and he doesn't fit the mold."

"He's just going through a phase."

"These things just have a way of working themselves out."

"After a divorce kids can get quite freaky."

"Austin has a dysfunction, but doesn't fit into any boxes for labeling."

"Getting him into preschool will turn him right around."

"There's light at the end of the tunnel."

"You're doing everything possible, just hang in there, it'll be a while, but Austin will turn his behavior around."

"He's a real smart kid — that might be his problem."

"I hate to admit Austin [to the state hospital] for testing and more in-depth evaluation, because a stay there would permanently be on his record and might possibly hurt him in later years."

If these professionals didn't have an answer, I wish they would have referred us to someone who had a more in-depth understanding of childhood disorders, or at least, recommended that we seek another opinion. Some of the professionals I dealt with actively sought to convince me that "social programs" (like S.S.I.) were to be avoided. Hindsight is always 20/20, of course. But if I knew then what I know now, I would have taken a more assertive, determined, directed approach to do whatever was necessary to get much better help, much sooner for my struggling family.

I've paid some very expensive dues for my present peace of mind. Yet, motivated by whatever forces, I know I gave and continue to give my son many things: a sense of humor, better social skills than we have a right to expect, the ability to live in his present "least restrictive environment," and his capacity to survive in a classroom atmosphere and make educational achievements. He has retained his sense of family and mended his relationship with his sister (a rewarding development for me to watch!). My efforts on his behalf have kept him from a group home or institutional placement.

All these things leave me today feeling proud to have survived. I have a sense of well-being and self-confidence. Austin has given me a voice, a connection to the world, and a compassion has grown in me that serves me well in my nursing and teaching careers. Though the road I traveled has been fraught with detours and obstacles, I am who I am today because of having traveled that path. Yes, I would do it all over again.

Respite Care: A Most Necessary Choice

Tane and Tim Walmsley

Certified in elementary and special education, with an emphasis in early childhood special education, Tane is a classroom teacher for the CO-TEACH Kindergarten Readiness Program. Tim has a Bachelor of Arts in Elementary Education and Special Education. He works as an outreach specialist for VIDEOSHARE and the Montana Early Intervention Outreach Program. They have, as a couple, been respite care providers for many families whose children have special needs.

As respite care providers, we have had the opportunity to understand how all-consuming the parenting of a child with special needs can be. Having previous experience teaching preschool-age children with disabilities, we thought we had a good grasp of the struggles parents go through when caring for a child with disabilities. As we took on respite care duties, we in effect became "instant parents" with all the responsibilities that parenting encompasses. What we had not fully realized was that the amount of caring and energy we put forth a few hours a day in the classroom was vastly different from a parent's never-ending commitment to their child.

As we began working with Austin, an adolescent boy who has autism, we did not expect the complex and emotional world we encountered. The amount of time and energy needed to provide a nurturing and stable environment for Austin was overwhelming. Being versed in behavior management techniques, we thought there would be a minimal amount of time spent on behavioral interventions. Yet, as we cared for him for forty-eight hours every other weekend, it seemed that every minute of every hour was controlled by his presence in our lives. Even when he was in another room by himself, we felt our attention could never be totally focused on the task we were doing. Our time was filled with thoughts of his safety and well-being. In the back of our minds, we would keep a running tally of what might be happening outside our view.

We enjoyed a variety of activities together, but one incident immediately focused our fear and anxiety. It occurred in a situation that would normally be considered an enjoyable leisure activity. We knew Austin enjoyed playing games, so we thought this might be a starting point for our new relationship. Checkers and Battleship were his favorites. Losing a game was difficult for him and he would always emphasize who won and lost at the end of every game.

One evening Austin lost a checkers game and decided he no longer wanted to continue playing. He chose to color some pictures in the kitchen instead, an area he often used for his private leisure-time activities. As we sat in the living room, there was complete silence in the kitchen. When we went to check on the boy, we found him jabbing himself in the chest with a corkscrew, resulting in numerous small puncture wounds to his chest. When we asked him why he was doing this, he told us he wanted to get the "mad feeling" out of his chest. This scenario was shocking to us since we thought he was making progress and thought he had learned to better control his behavior. What should have been an enjoyable evening of playing games instead initiated a long-term process of understanding the inner feelings and emotional responses of this young man.

For the first time, we had a true understanding of what it would be like to parent a child with special needs. We wanted to know all of the answers so that life could be made more enjoyable and less traumatic for Austin, as well as less stressful for us. We became immediately involved with the emotional and physical nature of this child, trying to provide the most stable and fulfilling environment for him that we possibly could. We wanted, very simply, what every parent must want — to do what's best for their child.

In providing respite, not only did we give Austin's parent a break from the emotional and physical turmoil of being his parent, we gave something of ourselves to Austin. In return, we were given something back — an appreciation for life as we know it, as well as an appreciation for life from Austin's perspective and that of his family. We also became very aware that, although we only cared for this boy for a forty-eight hour period, we found ourselves physically and emotionally drained and in need of a break as each weekend came to a close.

This scenario and others we have experienced illustrate to us the great need for skilled respite care providers. Most importantly, it focused our attention on the fact that no matter how well-adjusted and sincere parents may be, they deserve and need a break from their child and time to themselves. Since the time that we served the respite needs of Austin's family, we have gone on to work with other families with special needs as well. We always hear parents say how relieved and rejuvenated they feel after taking some time for themselves. More often than not, they also say they should have done it sooner.

Now we know from first-hand experience how crucial it is that parents give some time to themselves so that they are better able to give the best of themselves when "on duty." Whether the respite time be for meetings with individuals who work with their children, unforeseen emergencies, a quiet dinner, a movie, or a weekend away, respite time needs to be a top priority.

Taking the first step in realizing a need for respite, and entrusting the care of their child to someone else's hands can be very hard on parents. But, we cannot envision a sane life for these parents without a "break in the action." Making the move to regularly scheduled respite care may be the most necessary change parents can make to ensure personal well being and family stability.

CHAPTER 9: MIRANDA

On Miranda

Anonymous

Wholeness,
in a body or a mind,
so judged by those of us
who believe
ourselves to be Whole,
is only that —
a judgment.

On some other level
who of us can say
with certainty
we would be judged as Whole?

Who of us could say
(to those speaking in a foreign tongue)
what our minds can comprehend,
what depth of feelings lie behind our eyes
and in our hearts?

She did not speak my language,
yet
I *know* she had one.
I was without the tools to understand.
But
I saw beauty bloom in her cheeks
I witnessed innocence alive in her eyes
I knew gentility in her touch

Entirely unspeakable by me
(The table's now completely turned)
Her bequest — the knowledge that
up on some other level,
by measures unlike our own,
she is now Whole.

CHAPTER 10: JOHN

An Eye in the Storm

Sally Freeman

Sally is an assistant professor of special education at The University of Montana and the mother of two sons.

> "I want a loving and caring life, a life where I get the job that I want and a family that I need . . . a life that has fun in it and happiness, love and friendship . . . a life that has only simple problems and not big ones."

These words were written by my fourteen-year-old son, John. His goals are not unique. Most people desire successful careers, loving families, caring friends and few problems. But John, like many children with emotional disabilities, has found that the attainment of success and happiness is not easy and often seems an impossible dream.

John began life with many advantages. He was a strong, healthy child who had a wonderful sense of humor and easily made friends. At an early age, John showed signs of athletic ability. When he was six and seven, John was the star of his little league baseball teams — running faster, throwing straighter, and hitting farther than his teammates. John loved all physical activities and often found school too confining for his boundless energy. He was bright and had an insatiable curiosity, preferring tree climbing to counting, tag to coloring, and the sandbox to the classroom.

John's life changed dramatically when he was eight years old. While playing with friends on New Year's Day, John was struck by a car and suffered a traumatic head injury. The doctor was unsure about the prognosis for recovery and gave John only a 40% chance of full recovery. John had sustained a serious head injury, and there was always the possibility of permanent brain damage and lingering behavioral or learning problems.

In the months following John's accident, I observed a number of behavior changes. From John's point of view, one of the most serious problems was the loss of most of his athletic ability. He joined another Little League baseball team but was now the child who always dropped the ball or struck out. He tried football but couldn't remember the sequence of movements in a play. Peers teased John about being slow and clumsy and often excluded him from their games.

More serious than the loss of athletic ability was John's difficulty with anger. His temper flared over trivial matters and he would respond without thinking or considering the consequences. If teased by a peer, for example, John would act on his first impulse which usually would be to hit the offending child. Afterward, John would feel badly. He really didn't want to hurt anyone, but some children became afraid of John. Others enjoyed teasing him so they could watch John lose his temper; few children wanted to play with him.

John realized that his temper and impulsivity were ruining friendships, but he couldn't control his behavior or make constructive changes, so he tried other methods of dealing with peers. When John was in the fifth grade, I caught him using his lunch money and allowance to pay children to play with him at recess and after school. He soon discovered that bribery didn't create lasting friendships. In time John adopted a defensive attitude toward his peers. He assumed that other children would be critical and not like him. Consequently, John was critical and unfriendly first.

John's relationships with his teachers were often no better than those with peers. At the elementary school level, teachers found John's out-of-seat, impulsive behaviors irritating, but manageable. Despite severe deficits in reading and written expression, John was motivated and worked hard to improve his skills and cooperate with teachers. When John entered middle school, his teachers expected more maturity and were not as accepting of his behavior. Some teachers refused to believe that there was a relationship between John's behavior and his head injury and blamed his behavior problems on willful misconduct. At times John was punished excessively for behavior he couldn't control. In the seventh grade, John was given at least 85 detentions and numerous in-school and out-of-school suspensions. John became increasingly frustrated and his motivation to learn decreased. He was less cooperative with school personnel and more defiant of authority. John concluded that he was a "bad kid with no future." One day we saw a rather scruffy looking man sitting on the street with a sign that said, "Will Work For Food." John pointed to the man and said, "That will be me in a few years." John's life was in turmoil.

I was having my own problems coping with John's disability. When he was in the hospital recuperating from his accident, I felt confident that I could handle any problem which might surface in the future. After all, I was a special educator with a doctorate in learning disabilities. *Boy, was I wrong.* All my years of learning and experience did not adequately prepare me to be the parent of a child with emotional disabilities or help me to cope with the daily — and sometimes overwhelming — barrage of behavior problems. I dreaded the ringing of the telephone or the door bell. I was sure that an irate neighbor or the school was calling — again — to complain about John. There were days when I didn't want to be John's parent.

One afternoon I picked up John at school. He had been given a three-day out-of-school suspension for something now forgotten. I looked over at him as he slumped against the passenger door with tears in his eyes. I suddenly realized that I had not seen John smile in a long time. But, then, what did he have to smile about? There were few places in his world that were rewarding. John viewed himself as a failure both academically and socially — a view that was frequently reinforced by those around him. And how long had it been since he had seen me smile? At that moment, I decided to give him a place where he could find approval, acceptance, a measure of peace, and a smile — a place that would be an eye in the storm that had become his life. He would have a place *not* to hide, but to gather strength for the challenges he faced each day; that place would be his home.

John will start high school soon. He knows that there are struggles ahead. He only has a fifth grade reading level and his impulsive behavior is still difficult for him to control. However, John was fortunate to have a supportive eighth grade teacher who provided another "eye in the storm" and who helped him regain trust in teachers and in school. He now looks forward to high school with more self-confidence and improved self-esteem. Most importantly, John can smile again.

In conclusion, I would like to share some suggestions for teaching and living with children who have emotional disabilities. These ideas come from three sources — from John, from my own experiences, and from experts in the field.

Listen: Children with emotional disabilities are frequently in trouble at home or in school. And frequently behavior problems result from something the child has done that is not appropriate. Thus, it is easy for adults to assume that the child is to blame for every problem incident. Sometimes, however, the problem is not the child's fault. Listen when the child says "I didn't do it." Investigate before drawing conclusions.

Remain Calm: The behaviors of children with emotional disabilities can make parents and teachers angry. Remaining calm is difficult. I have seen adults become so angry that they yell, swear and/or threaten the child. In effect, adults model the very behaviors that get children in trouble. Children with emotional disabilities need to learn appropriate methods of handling conflict. Adults need to model good conflict resolution. When problems arise: (1) remain calm, (2) state the behavior infraction, (3) state the consequence. Do not argue with the child, or yell, or swear or threaten.

Be Honest: Tell the children that their behaviors are annoying, disruptive, or can hurt feelings. Children with emotional problems need to learn how their behavior affects others. Always address just the behaviors (e.g. "We can't concentrate when you're talking"). Never criticize or belittle the child (e.g. "You're a real pain today").

Be Positive: Children with emotional disabilities receive a lot of negative feedback from their environment. They are constantly being told — in actions or words — that their behavior is "bad." Eventually, they come to see themselves as "bad" and stop trusting in people. To build self-esteem, (1) praise the child immediately for any and all appropriate behavior, (2) give rewards more frequently than punishments, and (3) never use physical or excessive punishment.

> "Some day, maybe, there will exist a well-informed, well-considered, yet fervent public conviction that the most deadly of all possible sins is the mutilation of a child's spirit."
>
> Erik Erikson

CHAPTER 11: THE HEALTH CARE PROVIDERS

To Know Them as People. . .

Ethan B. Russo, M.D.

Ethan is a pediatric neurologist practicing in a small Montana town and the father of two young children.

I have often been asked why I chose a field like pediatric neurology. There were several elements in my personal history which influenced that choice. My father is a veterinarian and his selfless work was a strong influence. Early educational exposures led me to an interest in the workings and intricacies of the mind. I had decided to pursue a career in neurology by my second year of college, but there was one key exposure that refined that interest and taught me the importance of developmental influences.

I had a job one summer as a counselor at a day camp run on the grounds of Lakeville Hospital, a residential and rehabilitation facility in Massachusetts for children and adults with developmental disabilities. Because I had just completed my first year of medical school, the hospital administration was kind enough to allow me to go on medical rounds with the doctors and nurses, as well as to observe the outpatient evaluations done by a pediatric neurologist who came down from Boston two days a week. This provided me with a rich background in seeing common and unusual clinical problems in people who were neurologically affected, and the opportunity to learn the medical ramifications. However, I was simultaneously working with the same people as a camp counselor, getting to know them as people, how their disabilities might affect their capacity to engage in camp activities, their attitudes, and their lives. I remember the feeling of waking up those summer mornings and looking forward to going to work, something that had never occurred with any job I had held before.

For many patients, their problems had been dealt with medically, but their underlying deficits remained. Because of those needs, the work of rehabilitation continued. I had the opportunity to see how the physician was part of a much larger management team including nursing staff, physical, occupational and speech therapists, and social service workers. Since many patients had terminal conditions, their medical complications were treated as they occurred. The ancillary services provided useful and therapeutic activity and attempted to increase patient comfort and allay feelings of uselessness and boredom that could lead to depression.

Although some fifteen years have passed, a few of the people with whom I worked still provoke poignant feelings: There was little Kim, a seven-year-old who had spastic quadriparesis, was wheelchair bound, and had profound mental retardation (secondary to infantile spasms, an extremely severe seizure disorder). Her seizures continued on a daily, and hourly basis, even with anticonvulsant medications. Despite these problems, Kim had an unusual "air" about her, a unique appeal that many successive staff members felt. Despite the medical certainty that behind her gaze lay a vacuous mind, her eyes bespoke understanding. I remember talking to her, working with her, attempting to establish some contact, while one of the senior physicians commented on the fruitlessness of my effort. After all, so many others had tried. When I returned two summers later for a six-week community medicine project, Kim was unchanged, but new people continued the attempt at communication.

The adolescent ward at Lakeville was home to a large number of youngsters with severe disabilities. Several had Duchenne muscular dystrophy. Some of them had even lived to be my age, which was unusual in those days. Bob had to spend each night in an iron lung, and had passed weeks at a time in such confinement, plagued by recurrent pneumonia. When I first met him, Bob seemed to have a confrontational and angry attitude. He appeared to have a caustic demeanor, and was highly critical of others. This was surely understandable considering the ravages of his disease which had rendered him essentially immobile; he required assistance for every human function. His family had disappeared years before, perhaps unable to deal with his needs. Despite these desperate circumstances, Bob had a different side which I eventually came to know. His guard would sometimes fall when he was around the head nurse (called "Mom" because it seemed she had been at Lakeville forever). She would stand closely by during those long weeks in the iron lung, reaffirming the resolve to continue the fight. She encouraged Bob to write his poetry, which was amazing stuff. Although no one would consider it polished, it had a stark realism that I have never found elsewhere.

Then there was Noel, a young man with severe choreoathetoid cerebral palsy. Noel's speech was sufficiently difficult to understand that many counselors limited their contact with him, or assumed that he must be quite retarded. (His I.Q. actually tested out at 115.) Noel was very "stand-offish" around me for reasons I did not initially fathom. Finally, someone let me know that Noel was angry with me for spending too much time with Judy (a youngster with Friedreich ataxia, a form of spinocerebellar degeneration). Noel considered Judy his girlfriend. Over the course of a few weeks, by spending time with him, I was able to get the hang of Noel's speech, and reassure him that my interest in Judy was purely professional. He had realized this all along; the attitude displayed toward me had been a ploy to see my reactions. It provided an example of his amazingly sharp mind. In these conversations, I came to appreciate his remarkable wit, which, by chance happened to inhabit a body that impaired his mobility and his ability to communicate. His social and verbal communication was limited to the people who were dedicated and caring enough to take the time to learn the patterns of Noel's unique speech. I was honored to pass his test. Later I was to hear that Noel attended college classes.

These experiences at Lakeville were my first in clinical neurology. Instead of a warehouse of hopeless and forgotten "cases," I saw Lakeville as an island of hope for the *people* I had gotten to know there. It has colored everything I have done in medicine since.

After medical school, I began internship and residency, the apprenticeship of medical training. Pediatric training was a study in contrasts. By day, I might be seeing basically healthy kids of middle class families in an outpatient clinic, while at night, I would deal with the life-threatening illnesses and traumas of Chicano children in the county hospital. There were the children with cancer, and many trying months in the neonatal intensive care units, where mortality often exceeded 50% at any given time. Along the way, there were very many physicians to serve as role models. Some were inspirational, while others posed a striking contrast to all I would want to be. For some, the job of neurology ended with diagnosis, since there might be no current treatment. This was a common attitude in classical neurology — after all, many well-known texts on neurology had elaborate facts and figures, and descriptions of disease symptoms, but *nothing* about treatment. There might be lip service tendered to physical therapy or supportive care, but nothing directed to the families left wondering how to manage a child with "so-and-so's" disease, which they probably had never heard of before the diagnosis.

Another physician's approach might be characterized as "cold, hard and clinical," where the discussion with the nodding parents included nothing but polysyllabic medicalese that parents had no way of understanding.

One additional philosophy I saw demonstrated was quite different — lighthearted, superficial and misleading. The neurologist in question (who actually was very knowledgeable) would examine children through play, and joke with them to establish rapport. Unfortunately, this playful approach did not end with the examination. Instead, during the family discussion, it led to frequent refrains of "Johnny has a little problem with this or that, but he's basically okay — he'll be fine." Often these parents left smiling, only to return later, angry and bewildered, because Johnny was *not* fine. I remember one such family in which a girl with Reye syndrome was labeled as "fine" one day, but succumbed to the disease the very next day.

Obviously, in life-threatening situations, or with life-long disabling conditions, there are no formulas for giving bad news. Each doctor cultivates his or her own approach. I had to learn how to be the one to tell parents that their child had a brain tumor, an incurable disease, or a permanently disabling condition. It has never gotten easier for me. It is sometimes necessary for a physician to maintain a certain "protective shell" in order to insure his or her own emotional stability and be able to continue to do the job. Otherwise, depression, "burnout" or a callous attitude can and do occur. As Shakespeare observes in *Antony and Cleopatra,* "the nature of bad news infects the teller."

These same issues continue for me in private practice, despite seven years experience. I hope I have learned to connect and empathize better with patients and their families, although there are always variations in how imparted information is received. I knew I was not connecting with one mother a few years ago when she asked me if I were a parent. I answered "Yes" sheepishly, and watched surprise register on her face.

I have dealt with referring doctors who may have soft-pedaled a child's problem and wondered why my discussions with the family had to include so much bad news. When that happens I tell myself, "It is my job to tell people what they need to know, not what they want to hear." I would refer any reader who disputes that sentiment to Mary Pielaet's manuscript, "Untold Diagnosis."

The task of the neurologist may be compounded when families are unsure why their child has been referred for evaluation. A doctor or agency may suspect a child has a certain problem, but not articulate the suspicions to the family. The doctors or agencies may prefer to get an "expert's opinion" before making a diagnosis. Although this conservatism has obvious motivation, the family's apprehension and shock may consequently be compounded.

In spite of hearing bad news, I have frequently had families tell me how relieved they felt that their child's condition finally had a name. Having a diagnosis allowed them to study, learn about it, and ultimately, to deal with it. One of the unique attributes that sets us apart as humans is this need to know, the need to master the mysteries and attempt to understand. Ignorance really has no place and no function. In fact, many disabling conditions have a genetic basis. In such cases, knowledge may be critical to family planning for this, and future generations.

Reactions to bad news can vary as much as the personalities of those who suffer its receipt. In addition to the reaction of relief at knowing the diagnosis, families commonly work through gradual stages of grief, much like those outlined by Elisabeth Kubler-Ross: denial, anger, bargaining, depression or chronic sorrow and, finally, acceptance. Discussion of difficult news with a family in a certain stage of the grieving process may not be well received. This may lead some families to resurrect the ancient tendency to "kill the messenger." Alternatively, the family may seem accepting and acquiescent, while privately rejecting the medical opinion. Some such families are lost to follow-up or seek care elsewhere.

Breakthroughs can occur, however, both in parental understanding and the doctor/family relationship. A good example would be the case of J.K. He was sent to me by a doctor in a distant town for evaluation of "failure to meet developmental milestones." His mother really had no complaints and was unsure why the referral had been made. She did not seem to acknowledge that it was unusual that her son did not speak by age three, or that he would periodically jerk his arms suddenly, and then appear distant and disoriented for ten to twenty seconds. I felt that J.K. showed "autistic-like" behavior and was suffering myoclonic seizures. We made little headway in the initial visit. Conversations with the boy's father by telephone revealed him to be equally resistant to my pronouncements. It was only after *two years* of repeat visits and discussion that this family recognized and accepted J.K.'s deficits and really began to deal with the situation constructively. It took that amount of time for this family to "hear what I was saying." Ultimately, in this case, the family considered a residential treatment facility.

We have seen, then, how the doctor may be guilty of exaggeration, minimization, rationalization or intellectualization, while parents may demonstrate various forms of acceptance, denial, reluctance or desperation. Often the family may be rendered financially and emotionally impoverished by the process of medical testing. And, after the diagnosis, there remains the issue of treatment. Often, this is merely symptomatic; a muscle relaxant may reduce spasticity, but does not cure it.

Any treatment may have side effects. All of these factors must be weighed, pro and con, and decisions made as to what is cost-effective, therapeutically effective *and* acceptable to the family. For obvious reasons, I am a big proponent of ancillary services, such as physical therapy. I feel they are instrumental in helping the patient to achieve maximum potential; they also provide families with the assurance that everything which can be done to help is being done.

It is also the duty of the physician to protect patients from and inform them about controversial, unproven or dangerous approaches to treatment. In cases where the practice of medicine has little to offer, alternative modes of treatment may be very attractive to families in that they offer continued hope. In such cases, I can only offer my opinion and hope that it does not sound too judgmental or dogmatic.

A growing movement in ancillary treatment is the concept of support groups. These arose from ideas originally espoused by Alcoholics Anonymous — that talking with similarly affected individuals is instrumental to the healing process. This is especially helpful to the adult patient. In the case of the affected child, their acceptance of the situation may seem easier or even natural. They often adapt and compensate, whereas the pain of the parents may continue for a prolonged period. In that instance, the family may be the ones to benefit from the support group system. Many groups have national clearinghouses and local branches with support meetings, informational brochures, speakers, etc.

When no support group exists, sometimes people can create their own in an interesting and sometimes serendipitous fashion. I have followed a patient of mine, L.W., who has amyotrophic lateral sclerosis (A.L.S.), for several years. She is a local artist who has continued to pursue her art well into the course of her illness. There was no local support group devoted to A.L.S., so she joined in the local chapter for multiple sclerosis (M.S.). Subsequently, another patient of mine, J.D., came to her attention. J.D. has a juvenile, genetically based motor neuron disease that is very slowly progressive. Pathologically, the two diseases are very closely related.

When I first met J.D., he was non-ambulatory and, though obviously very bright, he seemed prone to bouts of sullenness and depression. He, too, was interested in art. When J.D. began taking art lessons from L.W., I was obviously tickled! Both seemed to benefit greatly from the relationship — L.W. was pleased to be helpful to her young charge, cultivating his talent, and J.D. seemed to develop a new confidence and self-assurance that has definitely carried over into his daily attitudes.

It is just this type of happening that keeps me working in this field. This kind of personal triumph in the face of adversity demonstrates the strength of the human spirit. To know my patients as people has taught me much about that spirit; it is something from which we all can learn.

Decisions and Objectivity

Charles E. Bell, M.D., Bruce G. Hardy, M.D., Kathleen S. Rogers, M.D., and Scott Werner, M.D.

This article was co-authored by four pediatric physicians who practice in a small Montana town.

Physicians caring for infants and children with disabilities are frequently faced with situations that require making important decisions. The ultimate decision is in the hands of the parents, but the physician(s) involved can help make the process easier and, hopefully, better for all concerned. It is often difficult for parents to look in an objective fashion at the problems a child may present because they are, in fact, the child's parents and have great emotional bonds. This is understandable; in all truth, this is exactly how it should be.

The physician's most effective role is to provide an objective (though still caring) evaluation of the situation so that the problems and treatment options can be discussed in an atmosphere of clarity and mutual understanding. Some decisions are of an immediate nature, some can be put off for days or weeks, and some may not need to be made for years. Some decisions are "yes" or "no", while others involve many options. In medicine it is usually very difficult to say "always" and "never," and we must not forget how other biological factors may enter into the final equation. These factors may affect the final results.

When dealing in disabilities in children always remember that throughout infancy and childhood the individual is in a constant state of growth and change. This factor is frequently overlooked in research studies that compare methods of treatment. The natural history of what happens *without* medical intervention is also often overlooked.

The child with a disability is intimately involved with parents, siblings, extended family members, and care providers. How a medical decision will affect those relationships is important and needs to be taken into account as well. Tentative decisions that may not go into effect for months or years, must remain tentative. They need to be flexible and subject to change as the effects of prior decisions, growth, unanticipated accomplishments or setbacks, and new scientific information become available.

Changes in the lives of children with disabilities are brought about by and large by decisions others make for them (usually out of necessity). Physicians should welcome the opportunity to facilitate the decision-making process with the ultimate goal being the welfare of the child and his or her family.

As pediatricians who take care of general pediatric problems in a smaller sized town, we are often left with the duty of having to inform parents that their child has a serious or chronic problem. In its own way, it is as difficult to deliver such information as it is to be the parent who has to receive it. The "objective" manner with which the information is often given and later dealt with is perceived at times as being indifferent or uncaring. This truly is not the case; most of us become very involved with our patients. But that objectivity and seemingly unemotional attitude is sometimes necessary in dealing with problems that evoke a tremendous amount of emotion and stress for everyone involved.

We often are perceived as "the bad guys" because of the type of unpleasant news or the amount of disruption we have to deliver to our patients' (and their families') lives. Management of these chronic problems is also difficult when, as the physician, we have to tell a parent that we *do* need to deal with the behavioral problems, or we need to do *one* more blood test, or we need to do one *more* invasive procedure. As parents, we all want to protect our children and decrease the amount of trauma they have to endure; that is a very important parental role. As physicians we have to be sure that we don't leave something undone that may make a difference, simply because it is one more intrusion. Striking the balance between what is *necessary* and what is *optional* is the key.

As parents, it is most difficult to be objective about our children, particularly when the child is disabled in some way. As physicians, we try to view children in an objective fashion simply because it makes us more effective in dealing with the problem. It also gives the parents a set of data from which to make what can be very formidable decisions. The two roles complement each other and often merge as each of us, as physicians, becomes more involved with our patients. Still, it is left to the physician to make some of the critical decisions that are often the most immediate and demanding, particularly during times when the problem is new or seems to have reached a crisis state.

No one physician, as no one parent, knows all the answers or does everything correctly. We do our work to the best of our ability and our training. We think that when dealing with a chronically ill child, the most important thing to develop and maintain is open, ongoing communication between parent, child and physician. Establishing strong rapport is essential. The loss of it creates additional problems, while the improvement of it almost always helps find solutions that work for everyone.

So, as in any relationship, talking to one another and listening to one another are the pivotal requirements. They are essential elements if the physician's objectivity and the parents' knowledge of their child and family are to come together in a trusting, effective partnership.

Through the Door

Scott Werner, M.D.

Scott is a pediatric physician with a special interest in the needs of children with disabilities and their families. His work includes not just a pediatric medical practice, but evaluative, support, and advocacy work under the auspices of a regional child and family service agency.

Nearly every morning at about breakfast time, I walk from the newborn nursery down the hall of the maternity ward to visit the mothers of the newborns I have just examined. What a light step I walk with when I carry good news! What a pleasant way to start the day; to walk into a new mother's room and say, "I have no bad news. There is nothing missing, nothing extra and everything is functioning properly."

On a morning when I must deliver sad news, there is hesitation in every step, in every breath, in every thought and, I think, even in my metabolism itself. The task that is mine, to walk through the door into a new mother's room and give the news that a baby has been born with a permanent defect, is a task that I would do almost anything to be able to wish away. Birth means that now the invisible can be seen, and the promises and hopes are becoming just a memory. The baby that was dreamed of, the toddler, the school child and the teen, doesn't exist anymore. The family's future that was envisioned and hoped for is not to be. My news will replace all of that with shock, helplessness, isolation, emptiness, sadness, and finally, grief. I hope there are family and friends who can be supportive in the right ways and at the right times. At least let there be communication between spouses of strength and love — at least — please.

It doesn't get any easier having done this before. The pain is new each time. Of course, each mother, each family and each support system deals with it differently and in their own way. But, they all want to know "Why?" They want to know what the future will hold. They expect accurate information, although the shock of discovery may not allow them, at first, to comprehend or remember much of what I say.

How can I word my news and my answers to make this traumatic life moment less wrenching? How can I be there enough for this family? How can I help them react? How can I react to their reactions? What can I do that will not only make the news understood, but also start the healing process toward an optimal adjustment. Help me to avoid a word, a phrase, a reaction that will always be looked back upon and remembered with pain or bitterness.

Meanwhile, with each walk down the hall, I confront my own attitudes, emotions, life philosophy and the hollow pit in my gut knowing that I must walk through that door to tell and teach and help and cry.

Pharmacists Helping Families: A Unique and Untapped Resource

Byron Dodd, R.Ph., with Kathy McGlynn, consumer/parent

During the summer of 1991, many authors who wrote for Changes *were guest speakers at a class offered by The University of Montana's School of Professional Education entitled, "Families and Disability: Diverse Strategies for Growth." The following manuscript originated with a presentation that Byron Dodd, a community pharmacist, delivered to that class.*

Families who deal with the complexity of a disability typically have extensive contact with numerous and assorted medical professionals. Pharmacists can be a unique and invaluable resource to such families. Many people still view pharmacists as simply glorified clerks, but we are medical professionals. We have a different perspective and emphasis from that held by physicians or anyone else in the health care field. Usually, people are very surprised when they learn how much information we have to share and what services we can offer.

Qualifications

Pharmacy is a five- to six-year program of study, depending on the specialization chosen. The initial courses, including anatomy and physiology, are similar to the ones required of medical students. During the study of the causes of disease (etiology), physicians are trained to look at the course of a disease and its treatment, while pharmacists are taught the preparation, qualities, and uses of drugs (pharmacology) as they apply to specific diseases. Doctors get one to two quarters of training in pharmacology, compared to the five or six quarters pharmacists receive; it is this emphasis which gives pharmacists their unique perspective and makes them most useful as allied health professionals. Their skill and expertise make them an especially valuable resource for families who deal with acute and chronic health problems.

Developing Partnerships with Families and Physicians

To be effective, community pharmacists (the professionals who work in drug stores as opposed to those who work in hospitals, nursing homes, or research labs) must enjoy interacting with people and be genuinely interested in the individual patient and the clinical situation at hand. Their availability and concern can encourage people to open up more readily than one might expect. Some people are afraid to talk to a physician, but may talk to a pharmacist, especially if a problem persists or answers aren't forthcoming from the doctor. When that situation occurs, a pharmacist might suggest a second opinion from another physician or specialist. He or she may also consult on a professional/medical level with the doctor and suggest (not prescribe) a different course of treatment or alternative medications which the doctor may not be familiar with. (Physicians ordinarily stick with a limited number of medications which have proven effective with their patients.) A pharmacist may also suggest different dosage levels or alternative diagnoses which the doctor might consider.

Pharmacists consult with and make referrals to physicians in a variety of situations. Often, a consumer's comments to the pharmacist — "This stuff doesn't work," or "Those pills always make me dizzy" — will prompt physician/pharmacist consultations. In other words, a consumer's comments may well provide the missing clue to a more accurate diagnosis and/or a better treatment plan. It is particularly helpful when these comments come from a regular customer, because then the pharmacist has some basis from which to make pertinent observations. For example, when one such gentleman came into my store saying, "I just can't get rid of this cough! What do you recommend in cough syrup?" I noted that he exhibited several signs of heart trouble. Because he was a familiar customer, I was in a very good position to encourage him to see a doctor right away. My judgment would have been much more tenuous had I never seen him before. It was my long-term familiarity with the man that allowed me to note the changes in appearance and symptomatology which prompted my referral. And it was his familiarity with and trust in me which prompted his quick trip to the physician. It saved his life.

In order for consumers to be accepting of this type of assistance or level of care, there has to be an element of rapport with, and trust in, the pharmacist. For most people those things develop only over time. The key to the development of such confidence is often the ongoing communication and genuine concern evidenced by the pharmacist in his or her contacts with people. Many people come to the pharmacist with a prescription immediately after seeing their doctor, where an unsettling (or even frightening) diagnosis may have just been made. At such times, stress levels are very high. The pharmacist's sensitivity at these crucial times sets the pattern for subsequent contacts (see Chapter 6, Sean, "Dispensing More Than Drugs"). Other patients may be very uncomfortable turning in a prescription which they suspect broadcasts their personal condition (or that of a family member) to the pharmacist. Reassurances that information given in a prescription is confidential unless a patient releases it, are timely and important at this juncture.

In a typical community pharmacy, encounters with patients lack the kind of immediate privacy available in a physician's office, making it difficult for people who are more timid to discuss matters that may be pertinent or helpful to the pharmacist. Discretion at such times is key to gaining a consumer's trust.

Conversely, the open-store atmosphere may be less intimidating to some people than a physician's office. For those people, communication can be greatly enhanced when the pharmacist simply exhibits an open, caring, and helpful manner. As repeated and positive contacts occur and patient records accumulate, pharmacists begin to have at their disposal the information they need to best assess a patient's situation.

Additionally, getting to know the patient and family situation over a period of time helps the pharmacist to develop a holistic perspective on patient treatment. In fact, the personal or family history and immediate life situation are often as important as medication in determining the course of action to follow. In the case of the gentleman with the heart condition, a cough syrup would have been of no help, and it probably would have delayed or prevented life-saving treatment.

Keeping Home Records

In addition to keeping accurate and updated records, making assessments (not diagnoses) and referrals, the pharmacist can often help consumers to obtain better health care by teaching them how to keep appropriate and useful records at home. Without specific tangible information (such as when swelling occurs, under what circumstances a coughing spell hits, what events seem to trigger seizures), it is very difficult for any professional to determine the nature and severity of problems which arise. Keeping a simple calendar log, noting the incident or symptom, the circumstances under which it occurred, its duration, and any other pertinent data, may be all that is needed to help a physician make an accurate diagnosis. Other data which pharmacists and patients can track together include adverse reactions to prescription or over-the-counter medications. While such information sometimes bypasses a pharmacy's record-keeping system (because it gets reported only to the doctor), a pharmacist's awareness and maintenance of such information is vital to patient well-being.

Generic Drugs

Problems are sometimes encountered when lower-cost generic substitutions are made for name brand drugs. A generic tablet may not, for example, dissolve in the body as readily or completely as its brand name equivalent, resulting in a reduced (and possibly insufficient) amount of medication circulating in the blood. Generic drugs are cheaper for a reason. Manufacturers of generic drugs often do not have the level of quality control or follow the same standards of content used by name brand manufacturers. Additionally, they are not required by the Food and Drug Administration to meet the same standards as are the latter producers. Much of the time a safer way to cut prescription costs is to buy *half* a generic prescription if there are any doubts or concerns, so that the patient, pharmacist, and physician can evaluate its effectiveness over a short trial period. No one likes or should have to spend money for something that doesn't work or which might produce other unacceptable side effects or symptoms. The same is true for any new (untried) medication.

Package Inserts

A package insert is an informative printed summary concerning a given pharmaceutical product. It includes a list of all possible complications and side effects. It is a patient's prerogative to receive the package insert with the product, and patients often feel reassured and more in control when they are well informed about the medications prescribed.

However, it is a rare person who doesn't worry about the side effects a drug may cause, particularly if he or she has obtained and read the package insert. It should be emphasized that physicians prescribe medications because they are needed. A patient should *never* quit taking the drug because of information in the package insert. (Sometimes doctors may even choose certain drugs over others in order to obtain a particular side effect which may be beneficial to a patient's overall condition.) If the package insert raises concerns in a person's mind about whether or not he or she (or a family member) should be taking a certain medication, both the pharmacist and the physician should be consulted.

Consumer Assertiveness

The field and practice of medicine is constantly evolving and pharmacy is no exception. New drugs are coming out every week and patients' reactions to them are as individual as the patients themselves. The importance of communication cannot be overemphasized. Consumers need to ask questions about the drugs that are prescribed, particularly if they have any problems with a product or don't "feel right" about it. It is often difficult for pharmacists to identify which consumers need to talk; that's why it is important that the patient take the initiative. In general, people who get in trouble with their medication are likely to be in need of better communication with both their pharmacist and physician. Consumers need to remember that help and information are available for the asking.

The Pharmacist as Ally and Advocate

If a patient or family experiences problems with prescription medication, the pharmacist can be their most valuable ally. They can serve as an effective go-between for doctor/patient communication. They have access to the most current information and expertise available directly from pharmaceutical companies (information typically not available to consumers), and they are constantly updating and expanding their knowledge. (A minimum of fifteen hours of continuing education per year is required to maintain pharmacy licensure.)

The amount of research and consultation pharmacists do for their patients varies widely according to need. The needs of families who have a member(s) with a disability are, almost without exception, bigger and more complex than the norm. Such families need to seek out a pharmacist with whom they can build an effective working partnership. It may be necessary to look for a second or even a third pharmacist before being satisfied with the services they receive. Some chain stores require their pharmacists to fill a certain number of prescriptions per hour, which limits the amount of time they can spend on individual concerns. Others, including mail-order prescription companies, simply cannot give individualized care, let alone the consultation that goes with it. The point is for a patient or family to find someone with whom they can work and in whom they can trust.

The story I assisted Kathy McGlynn to write, *"Dispensing More Than Drugs,"* Chapter 6, graphically illustrates the kind of technical and personal assistance pharmacists can offer. While it represents one of the tougher situations I've ever encountered, it is by no means an isolated case. A summary of the lessons that Kathy and I learned through our experience, and our suggestions for consumers and professionals are detailed in the section which follows.

Implications for Consumers

- The community pharmacist is in the unique position of being able to provide personal support because he or she has a good chance of getting acquainted with the family situation and, in general, is usually accessible. Cultivate a good, long-term working relationship with your pharmacist; you never know when his or her help will be indispensable. Remember that family histories and situations are often as important as medication in terms of the course of action to take.

- Involve your pharmacist as consistently as you can in your family's care. The more they know about your medical situation, the better they are able to serve you.

- If you have any questions about the drug(s) being used, check with the pharmacist first. Then you are in a much better position to ask the doctor pertinent questions. It never hurts to check on the amount of a drug that has been prescribed and to familiarize yourself with possible adverse reactions and known side effects. The package inserts summarize this information. *Ask for the package insert* but remember that it lists all *possible* side effects, most of which never occur in most patients. The idea is to be an informed (not panicked) consumer.

- If a prescribed drug doesn't do what it's supposed to, find out from your pharmacist if there are others that can be tried or added; then ask the doctor about those specific ones.

- Don't wait until you are desperate before seeking relief from troublesome symptoms. Ask your pharmacist first for information about medications which may be appropriate. (Are they applicable to the particular symptoms or disease state in question? Are there patient variables to consider, such as a possible allergic reaction?)

- When feeling overwhelmed, ask the pharmacist to pursue your drug questions for you. Let him or her do the telephoning and follow-up. Often pharmaceutical companies will give the pharmacist information that they will not release to the general public. In addition, pharmacists can be of great help in completing insurance forms or following through should a prescription claim be questioned or denied.

- While not always the case, you are more likely to get personalized care from a community pharmacist than one in a large chain store. If dissatisfied with service from one source, by all means try someone else.

- Keep accurate and current notes and records. If you are unsure what to record, seek advice from your pharmacist as to what specifics are important.

- *Ask questions until you are satisfied. It* is very important that you know what you're doing and why you're doing it. Your welfare (or that of your family member) ultimately is in your hands.

Implications for Health Care Professionals

- Give patients credit for knowing what they are talking about. It's their problem/illness/disability or their family member's. They live with the troublesome symptoms on a daily basis. They are experts in their own right; recognize and validate that expertise.

- Don't let symptoms that trouble patients (or their family members) persist without offering some kind of help, even though at first there may not seem to be anything particularly wrong. Unresolved situations may catapult patients or families into needless frustration and even despair, states of mind that certainly don't help them cope any better with the health problem in question.

- Pay attention to casual remarks. (Read between the lines.) When the patient/family refers to something which is bothersome, try to pursue specifics and implications, not just for the patient, but for the family as a whole. (For example, in Kathy McGlynn's situation, "Dispensing More than Drugs," Sean's night-screaming disrupted *everyone's* sleep, putting the whole family in a constant state of fatigue and stress.)

- Body language may tell you more about levels of stress and fatigue in your patients (and/or their families) than their words. Parents are often very protective of their children with disabilities, making them less inclined to verbalize problems to medical practitioners who are not yet judged to be "safe." The aware and sensitive health professional will take note of the hidden signals.
- Volunteer help that may not be explicitly asked for; make more than one overture. Patients who have dealt with less-than-sensitive medical professionals in the past may be wary of you out of fear that you too will have nothing to offer (or might give them the brush-off). Patients and/or family members who are preoccupied or exhausted may not always hear what you are saying the first time. Let them know that you are there for them, and *keep letting them know.*
- Don't underestimate the value of rapport. Effective health care partnerships cannot take place without it. Make a conscious effort to show patients and their families that you care. They will feel much more free to level with you, enabling you to serve them more effectively. The bottom line is: "People don't care what you know until they know that you care" (Dr. Dan Saddler).

CHAPTER 12: THE TEACHERS

Kids and Labels

Jim Denny

Jim is the principal of an integrated elementary school.

As the principal of a school which integrates regular education classes with special education classes and children with disabilities into mainstream classroom settings, I have learned about labels: O.I., E.D., E.H., M.R., M.M.R., V.I., S.I., E.M.R., D.D., L.D., T.M.R., S.E.D., O.H.I., and others.

My school has three classes of special small people who are labeled by the letter descriptors which attempt to identify their specific disabling conditions. Sometimes the labels themselves *become* disabling conditions. Some of these small children have caused me to learn about IEPs, CSTs, Least Restrictive Environments, P.L. 94-142, and why their teachers want to take lots of field trips.

There is K., a child with Down syndrome, who laughed in kindergarten even though she had a hole in her throat and a brace attached to her skull. Nearly every day now, she walks hand in hand with "my friend, Mr. Johnson." What a pair to see — little K. and tall, white-bearded Mr. Johnson, visiting their way from the lunchroom to the playground.

Then there is A. His daily reward for doing his work and being "compliant" is to visit me in my office at lunchtime. We visit together well, if I remember to wait at least 30 seconds for him to form replies. What a far cry these visits are from our first encounter: an eight-year-old boy in a rage trying to kick me and straining to overturn my desk!

E. memorizes spelling words using a computer. She plays a few simple tunes on the piano, and has a well-developed sense of humor, yet has part of her brain missing.

W. wears heavy braces on both legs. He walks with crutches and falls often, but never cries or complains.

B. came to school recently after graduating from special education classes seven years ago. He came to see his former teachers. B. was wearing his U.S. Navy uniform, standing straight and tall, and proudly displaying the laundry and dry cleaning unit insignia on his arm.

These students and others have taught me to look beyond the labels to the human being. **E**motionally **D**isturbed could as easily mean **E**n**d**earing or **E**n**d**uring! **L**earning **D**isabled could mean **l**oving and **d**ear. **D**evelopmentally **D**elayed could signify a **d**arling **d**aughter and on and on . . .

There is always a lump in my throat when parents and I are waving goodbye to a big bus loaded with kids going to the Special Olympics. The parents go home to an empty house; I go inside to empty classrooms. I am reminded again how the school is graced by the presence of these children, and how very barren the halls are without them.

Every school should be so lucky!

From a Classroom Teacher's Perspective

Susan Harper-Whalen

Susan is a specialist in the field of early childhood education with extensive experience in integrating children with special needs.

"Transition" is a very important term to a preschool teacher. Often the preschool serves as a child's initial step from home to the school setting. Parents and children count on that step to be a gentle, caring move into the world of school. It is their introduction to teachers, circle time, learning centers, parent\teacher conferences, and a new peer group.

It is always tempting for me to stop right there. I've often thought that if families (parents and children) leave the preschool feeling good about themselves in the school environment my greatest goal has been achieved. However, as I watch these children moving on to academically rigorous kindergarten classrooms that focus more and more on seat work and readiness for math and reading, I realize that preparation for this next step must also include teaching skills that allow children to adjust and cope with many different environments and challenges.

Usually, I see families through two tremendous changes in one short school year — from home to preschool and from preschool to kindergarten. These transitions are challenging for all families, but perhaps most of all for children with disabilities and their families. My conviction that these experiences *can* and *should* be positive for all involved in the mainstreaming experience — parents, children and teachers alike — has helped me grow and change alongside the children. As I reflect on the past ten years, I can see some of my growth in the way I have come to view mainstreaming.

My initial experiences with mainstreaming as a kindergarten teacher left me with grave feelings of inadequacy. While I welcomed all children into my classroom each day, I was left wishing I knew more. I also found myself wishing for more help, fewer students, and more time. I wondered how I could meet the needs of *any* child in a classroom of twenty-five, let alone those of a child with special needs.

My faith in children helped me move away from a tremendous fear that I was "doing it all wrong." As I calmed down, I began to note that the children with special needs enjoyed simply *being* in the classroom. The children, aided by appropriate materials and directions, took over, and I began to see all the children working and growing together. Each child participated at his or her own level and I began to recognize and enjoy their uniqueness as human beings. I could probably call this my stage of "isolated bliss." James Hymnes, past president of the National Association for the Education of Young Children, expressed my sentiments when he addressed the purpose of a preschool program by saying, ". . . the goal of their schooling is to help them live their four-year-old lives with richness and vigor — not to housebreak them for becoming five or six." I was not in the business of training pre-first graders. We were living for today!

I began to see that what was important to the "special" children in my classroom was simply the fact that they were *there* — that each day they were exposed to how "normal" children act and learn. That exposure, I came to realize, is the key to helping children with disabilities reach their full potential. As facilitator, I could be sure that opportunities existed for specific skills to be acquired, but the basic social skills that allow a child to mainstream successfully were being taught *by the children to each other*. Daily interaction allowed the educationally challenged children to understand what school was all about; peer models quite naturally were able to teach a nonverbal child that if they wanted to play, it was necessary to communicate. Whether that was accomplished by sign or speech, I saw children with very little language skill acquire a means to communicate when the incentive was peer acceptance. Rewarded with friendship and the good feeling of belonging, the mainstreamed children I have taught have gained immeasurable social skills because *they wanted to*. What better motivator?

In turn, I saw the typical children in my classroom become more accommodating, more accepting of personal differences and more sensitive to the fact that everyone has strengths and needs. They soon learned, to my great joy, that the smallest accomplishment for a child with a disability is worthy of celebration. They were delighted to watch a child who initially could not match colors accomplish that task; they took great pride in knowing that they had helped that child to learn. They also took huge pleasure in having that same child teach *them* how to express the colors in sign language.

Continued experiences these past four years have guided me into a new stage — one that attempts to create a better fit between my classroom and the rest of the world. My work with the CO-TEACH Preschool Program (a program which integrates all children in a model preschool environment) has added a dimension to my ability to meet the needs of all children. In 1985, the staff at CO-TEACH began to use my classroom as a site for the children in their program to "practice" mainstreaming. The children, accompanied by an aide, would join my group for various activities once or twice a week. The program had a dual purpose. First, we were allowing the children an opportunity to venture slowly into the "real world" setting of my regular classroom. Second, the staff from CO-TEACH was learning valuable information about what skills needed to be acquired for their children to successfully mainstream into a less restrictive setting.

I was learning too. The most valuable lesson was the willingness of the families of children with disabilities to communicate with me about their needs, fears, and joys. Their openness has added to my ability to understand *all* families, and to meet the needs of those whose lives have been changed by their special child. I am still concerned about the child "here and now." I still strive to make each day positive for today! However, I also now have my eye on the future and the imminent transition these children will make into the public schools.

Within this growth process, I have developed some convictions and ideas. They are my own list of insights into what makes mainstreaming not only successful, but delightful. I'm certain the list will continue to evolve as I continue to equate teaching all children with helping them "live their lives with richness and vigor."

Early childhood educators and special educators can and should work together. Our goals are the common ones of teaching children the skills they will need to survive in the classroom environment. We complement and strengthen each other. Special educators can offer their expertise in areas where regular classroom teachers are not trained. Regular classroom teachers can offer the special needs child what special educators cannot — the chance to learn and grow and risk in a normal classroom environment. Special educators and support service personnel may need to focus on isolated aspects of the child's development, but regular classroom teachers can always look at the whole child. The two can effectively work together to provide the child with the best opportunities. That is, by definition, the "most appropriate placement," in the "least restrictive environment."

My effectiveness as a teacher improved when I opened my classroom to incorporate the past, present, and future needs of the children. Mainstreaming meant opening my classroom to the observations and input of a multitude of specialists, including special educators, therapists, families and teachers from the environment that would be receiving the children I was mainstreaming. Human nature and the traditional "egg crate" structure of schools which house teachers in isolated classrooms can make accepting this situation much more difficult than it seems. So much of what goes on in our classrooms relates to us personally; we develop a strong sense of ownership in our teaching styles, routines and goals. Unfortunately, those attitudes can lead to a lack of continuity and skill deficits for the children who are moving within this system.

As I've learned to accept the talents and uniqueness of my colleagues, I've gained a better understanding of where my students have been and where they need to go. Simple changes in my routine have made transitions more successful for all children. For example, last year we had "chair days" when we practiced carrying chairs to sit in at circle time. I usually plan circle time as a floor activity; however, an alert parent noted that success in the mainstream kindergarten environment for her child would involve carrying chairs to the circle. It was a small change for me to make once a week, yet it enabled that child to have one more competency skill as she entered kindergarten this fall. Who is to say how many of the other children also benefited from learning that skill as they left my classroom for the big, new world of kindergarten?

Even earlier in my career, when I was teaching kindergarten, I remember working hard to create an activity-based program in math and reading readiness that demonstrated exciting gains in concept formation. However, I soon learned that workbook skills were also important to the first grade teachers. As a result, I began offering occasional workbook pages at the writing center in my classroom, to teach skills and terminology like finding the appropriate page number or circling "the one that is the same."

In addition to incorporating aspects of receiving programs in my classroom, I've learned to welcome the *people* involved, too. It's not uncommon for many professionals to be working with a child with disabilities in some capacity, and my classroom has proven to be to be an ideal place for them to observe the child in a "natural" setting. When the O.T. uses my classroom as a setting for therapy, he sees the environment in which the child must function. I, in turn, can observe the tasks and skills the child is working to master. If the speech therapist observes the child in my classroom, she sees the child use communication skills in a "real world" setting and can help me find ways to reinforce those skills. This willingness to be part of a team approach is essential in meeting my goal of serving the *whole* child.

Communicating with families has allowed me to continue learning and believing in the mainstreaming process. I have always been an advocate of the premise that strong home school ties are a critical component of quality educational programs. This tie has become even more important to me when working with children with disabilities and their families. First, these parents are the experts who have lived with their children, worked with specialists and watched their children grow and develop from birth. Their insights into the strengths, habits, likes and dislikes of their child can help ensure school success from the start. Second, these parents *need us to listen* if we hope to move closer to understanding and meeting the needs of all the children in our classrooms. During their child's first few years of life they may have experienced life-threatening surgeries, contradictory diagnoses, continual testing and evaluation, and role confusion between that of parent and therapist. All the while, they probably have been case managers, and provided transportation to two or three programs and specialists daily. Perhaps my primary realization here is that I really *can't* say, "I know how you feel."

My listening and questioning, and the willingness of parents to share their insights and concerns with me has helped me come closer to understanding. I look back and thank the parent of a child with Down syndrome for telling me how difficult mainstreaming can be for parents. My focus was on the exciting progress her child had made to reach this point. She shared in that excitement more than anyone, yet also felt painful reminders of her daughter's differences each time she entered my classroom of "normal" children.

This same parent helped me understand the importance of early mainstreaming and the fear of failure that parents may have for their child. We talked of the joy and learning that took place when her child worked with same-age peers in our classroom. Even with this success, the parent worried that a failed mainstreaming experience in kindergarten would mean an end to this opportunity for her child.

Sure, I've struggled with mainstreaming at times, wishing for more help, fewer children or a special education degree. But, I've never struggled alone. My efforts have been matched and exceeded by the most important partners in this process — parents.

Relax enough to enjoy the child. I've felt overwhelmed at times when my focus has centered on skill acquisition at the expense of appreciating the whole child. Relaxation seems so much easier when I allow myself to "kick back" a bit, enjoy the children and appreciate them as individuals. It's okay to let children know that we're glad to be with them, not just because they stood nicely in line or sorted the blue and red blocks, but because we *like* them. This acceptance of all individuals provides a necessary model for all the children in a mainstream classroom.

An emphasis on social skill acquisition has made my classroom a better experience for everyone. Mainstreaming has encouraged me to look more closely at the skills that help children work together in a social setting. Cooperation, acceptance of differences, a willingness to help and be helped, taking turns and sharing are not skills that *just happen* when we put 15 or 20 children in a classroom. Social integration of children with disabilities does not just happen either. I've learned to teach skills like asking "Can I play?" and role playing what taking turns "looks like" in order to facilitate better (and more natural) interaction between children with disabilities and their peers.

Modeling the "acceptance of differences" can also have a pronounced impact. I've moved away from projects designed to produce 20 identical pictures and now heartily praise and appreciate the uniqueness of ideas, processes and products I see. As a result, I've heard children marvel, "Oh, look! Everybody made a picture that is different."

This brings me to my most deeply held conviction:

There is room for all children within the four walls of my classroom. Indeed, some aspects of mainstreaming are difficult for all of us — parents, teachers, and specialists alike. But over and over, I see mainstreaming work to the benefit of all of us. My teaching skills have grown as I work toward individualized instruction for all children. The children sitting at our writing center are all working toward the same goal as one holds the marker and makes large strokes, another makes deliberate strokes and names letters as he goes and another asks how to spell the rainbow she has colored. They work at a meaningful level and each one feels success.

Of course, I'm not the only learner in this process. Our children are learning to live together in a world where we help and accept help. Children with challenges have taught others sign language, how to put our coats on using the "up-side-down" trick, politeness in the use of phrases like "thank you" and "excuse me," letters of the alphabet, and kindness by holding hands or comforting a crying child. At the same time, their peers have helped push wheelchairs, zipped coats, found the right place for a puzzle piece and clapped with joy as new skills were mastered.

Finally, perhaps the mainstream classroom has served to bring teachers, parents and specialists together. It has helped us realize that we are indeed a *team*. Our roles and methods may differ, but our goal is the same: we're all here for the children.

Feelings in a Manila Folder

Sharon Richardson, M.A., CCC-Sp.

Sharon is a speech clinician who works as an itinerant teacher in a rural school district.

I feel a charge to improve a child's speech/language skills has been given to me by my training as a speech pathologist, by my own personal standards for success with a child, and by parents' trust in me and expectations of me. The demands of fulfilling that charge have so many variables that they defy computation. At times the overwhelming needs presented to me to be fixed in the course of the school year in two or three twenty-minute sessions a week become a fearsome duty. I want to cry out against it as a ludicrous task.

I recently had to come to terms with a failure to effect change in a child. I thought my goal was appropriate and worked toward that goal for years — to no avail, all the while not knowing that the parents really did not put much hope in speech therapy. But it seemed totally obvious to me that the goal was proper — after all, the child could not communicate. She was unintelligible to most people nearly all the time. It so happened that she was a student in the schools that I served for four years. For one of those years I chose to be assigned to a specific school just to follow through with this child and my therapy plan.

More than once I have awakened in the middle of the night with this child on my mind and felt nightmarish panic at the prospect of not succeeding. I had sought opinions from other clinicians and tried other approaches, while still keeping my main goal of improving intelligibility. It finally became clear to me that this child had neither the physiological nor the neurological "hardware" necessary to meet my goal. It was a painful realization — I had pursued a faulty course far longer than I should have. I have recently changed her goals to cognitive and pragmatic development, and have quit beating the dead horse of intelligibility. Even when other clinicians hear me tell my story and assure me that my decision is correct, changing this goal still feels wrong because this child needs intelligibility nearly as much as she needs food and water.

All of us are unique, and our special children are even more so. Among most of us, our similarities are easier to count than our differences. But among our "special" children the differences can be overwhelming. A strengths-and-needs profile one might conjure up to compare them would appear chaotic. These children can be as different as the brain is complicated. Some disorders are so rare that they may never have been seen by a clinician in the school setting. So when it comes to teaching these children, even the professional can often only make educated guesses as to what potential a child may have.

We can measure some of our children's skill areas, but we do have invisible variables to deal with. The "rate" of learning of a particular task is perhaps one of the most frustrating. We have to combine that unknown "rate" with waiting for some immeasurable maturation point at which the child will be "ready." Add to that the other unseen effects of a variety of traumas, either physical or emotional. We can then only guess what the child's potential is through behavior as demonstrated over time by learning, or the lack thereof. As many of the unknown variables gradually unfold, we realize the only certainty is in hindsight.

With many misgivings, I speak of my frustrations as a clinician trying to work with and teach a child with multiple disabilities. The parents have had so many more incomprehensible facets of their child's limitations to come to terms with that the one I'm concerned with seems minor. The parents have at times, in fact, accepted their child's limitations *before* I have. It feels strange as a professional to be consoled by the parents of the child. I have learned that professionals must come to "acceptance" on their own terms, much as parents do.

So I tell you of one speech therapist and one child. She will move on next year to another clinician who has read the file, met the child with me, and with whom I have shared my feelings and fears. She is in good hands.

Sometimes I think it would be easier to put these feelings in a manila folder in a file drawer for future reference, if necessary. Instead, I keep her in my heart and thank her for what she has taught me.

From a Sibling and Physical Therapist's Perspective

Elizabeth A. Couch, R.P.T.

Liz is an itinerant physical therapist for a rural special education cooperative, and the sister of a young man with disabilities.

Finding a way to begin this manuscript has been a most difficult task, since my involvement with individuals who have disabilities has been essential to my way of life from a very early age. Someone once said, "Life can only be understood backward, but it must be lived forward." So I will start at the end of someone's life and work towards what I have learned in the first half of mine.

My grandparents had a son with profound disabilities — my Uncle Billy. My grandmother, who was herself an invalid for the last eight years of her life, cared for Billy at home with the help of her family. Her daily prayer was that she could die in peace if she knew that Billy would be taken care of. Her family reassured her repeatedly, and after her passing, Billy remained with my grandfather, who was a cardiac invalid himself. Despite the complications and extra work, he managed to meet Billy's needs for an additional nine years. After my grandfather's death, none of Billy's siblings' families was able to absorb him into their structure. He was institutionalized and later placed in a state group home in Alaska where he resides today at age fifty-seven.

Billy stayed with my family for a while after my grandfather's death, but by this time, my brother David (who also has disabling conditions) was requiring much in the way of financial and time/care expenditure. My mother simply could not handle the demands of both individuals. She has suffered tremendous guilt over the decision to place her brother in an institution. She has frequently said that placing Billy was the hardest thing that she has ever done, and that she could never go through anything like that again.

These experiences made lasting impressions on me as a small child. David required daily physical therapy after six months of age; this process took up half of my day as a preschooler. I never remember resenting the long ride into Anchorage, nor the time that I spent by myself in the waiting room while my brother was being treated. It was during those times that I realized how lucky I was to be "normal." I can remember watching in horror as children came and went: those without limbs, those with monstrous heads that needed artificial supports, those who could only propel themselves by rolling, and one little boy in particular who hollered, "Hi ya!" as he "walked" by me pulling his paralyzed body down the hall using his chin. It was then that I knew that my brother was different, he was "one of them." How unfair, this thing called life.

As my brother grew older, I saw the ridicule and teasing that he experienced and the unfairness overwhelmed me at times. During my early teens, I came to the realization that you can spend your life dwelling on how unfair life is or you can choose to accept it. Life is not fair and once you realize that, you strive to make life better for those who have gotten more than their share of unfairness.

We, as a family, never pitied David. As anyone associated with a person who has disabilities knows, it is harder to watch them "do for themselves," but it is in their best interest. There were many things that David would never be able to do, but we focused on what he *could* do and taught him to do his best. Many tasks that physicians said David was incapable of accomplishing such as walking, reading, toileting and reasoning, he in fact has mastered. My mother changed fourteen years of diapers for him, but so much greater was the rejoicing when he was trained! David spent sixteen years in special education classes. He now has the capabilities of a five- or six-year-old child and still resides with my parents.

We could be bitter about David's condition. It was caused by a physician who let him remain in the birth canal for twenty-two hours with decreased oxygen. With modern technology, David would have been "normal." This was not the case, however, and after thirty-one years, countless hours of therapy by professionals and my mother, many surgeries, multitudes of tests, and much work by caring teachers and friends, David can walk and enjoy life. Throughout the struggle, our family grew closer together. We learned the value of life and helping others, but above all we knew what David needed from us was to do all we could to help him reach his potential.

I can't say that I as a parent would have done anything differently, but I do feel now that David needs his independence. I feel that gradually introducing him into group home activities and life are in his best interest at this time. David has friends that reside in group homes and the transition would be gradual, and I believe exciting for him. Unfortunately, my mother cannot bring herself to this conclusion at this time, so I must trust and respect her judgment.

David has taught me so much. I knew while still in high school that I wanted to help people like him. While other students struggled with career decisions, I knew I wanted to be a physical therapist. Those thoughts and that focus drove me through college and graduate school — believe me, that was the only way I could justify getting through chemistry and physics!

I performed my graduate work at Children's Hospital of Los Angeles, where the cold hard facts finally hit me. There were going to be many people that I treated that I couldn't "fix," many with whom I could not accomplish what I wanted. No amount of education, dedication or experience can change the potential that an individual has. Those realizations brought me closer to understanding what my grandmother and my mother must have gone through, and I resolved to follow their examples. There are some things in life which we have no control over, but we must do the best we can with what we have. Our potential as parents, siblings, professionals and friends is our greatest asset. If we never give up, if we continue to set goals, if we use whatever resources and strengths are available, if we do all these things out of love and compassion (not pity), we can accomplish great things. More often, the things that we accomplish will not be so great, but that we have accomplished a small task and can start on another is a reward. We never know what an individual's potential may be. We must work within the constraints of their capabilities using what they have to offer in any way we can. By doing this, we are also challenging *ourselves* to be all that we can be.

As my grandmother's last prayers become my mother's, and my mother's thoughts become mine, the cycle will continue. What will happen to David in the future? I have faith that things will work out for the best. As a family, as a mother, as a father, as a sister or brother, we do what we humanly can, no more and no less. How much more have I experienced in my life because of my brother? How much more have I given of myself? Living life forward instead of backward is a disability in and of itself — one that we all share.

CHAPTER 13: NIC

From Provider to Consumer: An Involuntary Transition

Richard van den Pol

Rick is currently the director of the Division of Educational Research and Service and a professor at The University of Montana. He has worked in the area of service delivery to persons with special needs for twenty years.

In 1975, I enrolled in a graduate psychology program to specialize in the study of Applied Behavior Analysis. The discipline was then quite new, based in large part on a seminal article written only seven years previously by Don Baer, Todd Risley, and Montrose Wolf. By definition, applied behavior analysis relied upon scientific measurement of the effects of innovative treatments for socially significant human problems. Germinal research had suggested new directions in services for students in classrooms, for very young children and their parents, and for the elderly.

A key intervention tool was Positive Reinforcement: catching people behaving desirably and strengthening that performance with praise and other pleasant consequences. A key evaluation tool was direct behavioral observation: judging effects according to changes in an individual's actions. Required texts included B. F. Skinner's writings about behavioral assessment, as well as Dale Carnegie's 1936 text *How to Win Friends and Influence People* .

During graduate school we were taught that human service program evaluation can take many forms. Data analysis and other empirical methods allow us to conclude confidently whether or not a treatment "caused" an outcome. Less clear, and far more challenging for social scientists to test, is the extent to which a treatment outcome is "successful."

For example, it is a straightforward task to demonstrate that systematic teacher and parent praise for arithmetic achievement reliably increases students' productivity. However, we also must assess the effects of this treatment on other performances. Is there an effect on spelling or peer relations? How much productivity is desirable? Most of us would agree that encouraging a child to attempt and complete an arithmetic assignment is desirable. The value of this accomplishment generally is perceived as greater if the student was previously unsuccessful — and greater yet if the child now is able to do more work with great accuracy. But most of us also would agree that if the student were to work strictly on arithmetic, fail other subjects, and cease playing with friends, then there is a problem. *Maybe we can have too much of a good thing.*

For many of us, this caveat was disturbing. We had been ready to go out and "change the world." Now we were told that we had to be concerned with doing too much; we had to worry about spill-over and side effects. We were warned about changes that occurred outside of clinical and educational settings. These so-called side effects were problematic: if we couldn't directly observe and measure these changes scientifically, how on earth could we determine their success and desirability?

Fortunately, some of these dilemmas were addressed during the tenth anniversary of the advent of the field of applied behavior analysis. In 1978, Montrose Wolf published an article entitled *Social Validity: or How Applied Behavior Analysis is Finding its Heart.* This article, along with a similar one published in 1977 by Alan Kazdin, suggested mechanisms to measure the overall success and desirability of a treatment. Central to this model were two features: obtaining the opinions of experts and collecting evaluations by consumers of the service. It is noteworthy that a decade later we collectively are beginning to recognize that often *experts and consumers may be one and the same individual*. I think that my personal awareness of the role of "consumer as expert" occurred about six years ago when my single father, living in a distant state, was diagnosed with Parkinson's disease.

As an expert, I "knew" that there were residential treatment options that would afford him safety and security, as well as opportunities to socialize with peers. As his own expert, my father knew that his time was limited. While I visited nursing homes, he joined his church's single adult volleyball league. I warned him that his total disability was inevitable and that he needed to prepare for it; he warned me to remember my manners.

Some time later, I received an emergency phone call from a neighbor. Apparently my father had overdosed on his medication, was delusional, and had been admitted to the hospital. Before leaving for the airport, I put on a tie and slacks. During the airplane and rental car journey, I wondered at the cruelty of life. How could a man who spoke seven languages be stricken with a disease that would leave him mute? My father had been a diplomat for the government of the Netherlands.

His career spanned thirty years, involving public relations, advocacy for disadvantaged Dutch nationals, international commerce, and intelligence gathering. He once had been cited for bravery and upon retirement had been awarded the "Order of Orange — Nassau" by Queen Beatrice, which in Holland is equivalent to being knighted.

When I arrived at the hospital, I found my father tied into bed in a strait jacket. No one intercepted me as I entered his room. Perhaps my tie and slacks gave the appearance of a physician. Nic didn't recognize me, nor did he seem aware that anyone was present at all. I walked to the nurses' station and entered. Again, no one seemed concerned, or for that matter aware of my presence. Without permission, but also without having been denied, I removed his chart and read it, while copying relevant passages in longhand.

He had been admitted by an ambulance crew following our neighbor's call to 911. On admission he had been dehydrated and delusional; a heart attack was suspected. A neurologist later confirmed Parkinson's disease. During the course of his admission he had been resistant to treatment, complained of "voices" and people who were not really there, been administered a powerful anti-psychotic tranquilizer, been placed in restraints, escaped from restraints by removing his gown, and been recaptured — naked — in the hospital lobby. (I later learned that hallucinations and delusions are common both to advanced Parkinson's disease and to overmedication with drugs used to treat Parkinson's.)

During the course of my surreptitious review and copying of his chart, several nurses and nurse supervisors offered to "help" me. I dismissed them with what I hoped was a physicianlike manner. Eventually, a hospital administrator arrived with security guards at his heels. As the minutes of so many client-focused meetings say, "Extensive discussion followed." Somehow the entourage moved away from the nurses' station and ended up in my father's room. Perhaps I now looked like his son, and not like a physician. Or maybe my "tantrum" reminded him who I was, for he greeted me by name, and spoke to me in Dutch.

"See," said the cardiologist, "he can't even make sense."

Not once that day did the cardiologist speak to my father. Not once did he use his name. And not once was there any concern that my father was receiving "too much of a good thing."

Eventually, the blood levels of his drugs were stabilized and Nic insisted on returning to his home. A live-in aide was hired. Through direct observation, I knew that the quality of care provided was mediocre. My unannounced visits routinely discovered what I knew were shortcomings. But every attempt to arrange more appropriate care was rejected. In the final analysis, it was necessary to follow the prescription of a different expert.

CHAPTER 14: MARINA AND KATYA

And the Winner of the Rainbow Lottery is. . .

Kate Carlyle

My daughter Marina, who celebrated her fourth birthday last month and now tells everyone she is "four-and-a-half-going-on-five," is a miracle of health, intelligence, and physical ability. I know she is a miracle because in the seven years preceding her birth I learned firsthand all about how many children are born unblessed with those qualities. In fact, because I learned that particular lesson so well, Marina's very existence on this planet is a miracle.

Marina's older sister, Katya, was born with a veritable catalog of physical birth defects and with Down syndrome. Today, eleven years and half-a-million dollars worth of medical attention later, Katya is a polite, sociable, happy little girl who is well known and well loved by an enormous number of people within and beyond her family. She is the first child with Down syndrome to be placed by our school system in its "mildly disabled" special education track. At age six she learned to read much as I learned to read, by which I mean that it just happened. (Yes, we read to her constantly from the time she was big enough to take an interest in pictures.) Katya even had a major effect on the passage of P.L. 99-457, IDEA, the federal legislation which has extended educational opportunities to very young children with disabilities.

Katya is a miracle herself — a miracle of medical technology, a triumph of our hope and will over our initial despair, a victory wrenched from the defeatism of outdated thinking. I have often written about her struggle to live and thrive and about my family's struggle to survive the economic, emotional and physical battles brought about by her birth (which threatened to do us in). Someday I may write more — because some battles never end, they only change form.

But the miracle of Marina, although her existence is also due to medical technology, is a triumph over hope and fear and a victory over defeatist thought. Born to me at the age of 42, Marina exists almost despite me.

A few years after Katya's birth, my husband and I decided to try to have another child. To state that more truthfully, my husband Peter wanted to have another child and I agreed to try while inwardly rejecting the idea with every fiber of my being. Aside from the fact that we were dealing with a couple of medical problems that continued to physically and financially exhaust us in regard to Katya's care, I had come to know more than anyone should ever be forced to know about the things that can go wrong from the moment sperm meets ovum. Anyone who has ever spent much time in newborn and pediatric intensive care units tends to learn those things. It's not a matter of choice — it "just happens."

For more than three years, Peter tried to conceive and my body refused. It was perplexing to us because Katya's conception had been almost instantaneous; within two months of deciding to do it, there she was, swimming around inside me. But while Peter became more and more concerned about the lack of conception as the months passed, I felt nothing but great relief. A friend of ours told another friend, "The reason Kate's not getting pregnant is that she doesn't want to."

And I didn't; I knew too much. Even though I knew I could go through amniocentesis and thereby gain the option of choosing to prevent having a child with obvious chromosomal problems, I knew about all the problems that amniocentesis can't diagnose. I knew about all the problems newborns can present due to environmental factors or a "messy" birth. I knew and I didn't want to be responsible for any of it. Had Peter had the biological capacity to become pregnant, I'd have turned the job over to him without a moment's hesitation or a single pang of regret. I'd seen friends of mine go through pregnancy after having a child with birth defects and I knew the emotional agony they'd felt. Nine months is a long time to undergo that kind of stress. Any pregnant woman in a similar situation who says she didn't give it a second thought is, in my opinion, either a saint or was lobotomized prior to the pregnancy.

When we learned that an acquaintance's teenaged daughter was pregnant and planning to give up the baby for adoption, it sounded like the perfect solution to me; we could have a baby without having to have a pregnancy. Peter wasn't excited by the idea at first, but he came around. We sent a message through an intermediary that we would be interested in adopting the child. Because we spent time with the girl's parents at the intermediary's home at least once a year, we worried that a direct approach might make them feel uncomfortable.

We waited and waited, but never heard a thing from them, learning only much later that the intermediary never approached them. And I still didn't get pregnant.

Peter wanted us to get medical help. After one discussion of the subject with my gynecologist, Steve, who gave me the goods and directions for taking a sperm sample, I bailed out. "Either it happens or it doesn't," I told Peter. "I just can't go through this. It's too much pressure when I already feel so ambivalent."

At age 41 and after more than three years of trying, I decided that I probably was simply unable to get pregnant again. It felt terrific. "Man proposes, God disposes," I told my gynecologist. "See you around for Pap smears."

Two months later, I missed my period. I tried to convince myself that it was a case of early menopause, but one morning after Peter had gone to work, I made myself go out and buy a home pregnancy test kit. According to the kit, I was definitely pregnant.

I sat down and cried in the bathroom. I thought about the local abortion clinic, where I knew I could have an abortion without telling Peter because a friend of mine had done so after her husband's post-fifth-child vasectomy had failed. Then I got up, went to work and called Peter to tell him we were pregnant; he was thrilled. I knew that if I hadn't called him then, I might never have called.

And so began my pregnancy with Marina. At the very beginning of Peter's attempt to conceive, I had told my gynecologist that if I got pregnant I wanted to undergo chorion villi sampling (CVS). I didn't want to wait the extra time for amniocentesis because I didn't want to have to explain to anyone about terminating a pregnancy, if it came to that. Since CVS testing is done between the ninth and eleventh weeks of pregnancy, with results available soon after, an abortion could be performed without friends or co-workers ever knowing I'd been pregnant.

When I had discussed this with Steve, the closest places where CVS testing was available were in San Francisco and Chicago. Now that I was pregnant, he told me testing was available only 200 miles away. He set me up for a sonogram to make sure that the pregnancy was at the stage we thought it was, and then made an appointment for my test.

The day before the test I drove the 200 miles to Bozeman and stayed overnight with a friend who had agreed to see me through it. Peter couldn't come because someone had to stay with Katya, who still needed medical supervision 24 hours a day and couldn't be left overnight with an untrained adult. The test the next morning was quick and painless. The doctor, whose presence made CVS miraculously available in Montana when it wasn't yet available in any of the states surrounding us, was wonderful. I was back on the road and headed home by 10 a.m. Headed home to wait. And wait, and wait.

The lab tests took longer than expected, and when they came back they told me I was having a girl. Because I wanted another girl, this was good news. However, because it was a girl and because the lab had a few problems when it was set up a couple of years before, I was asked to come back to Bozeman for amniocentesis in order to prove that the cells that had been checked were the baby's cells and not my own. The extra test was needed only for the lab's own documentation and certification, I was told. The amniocentesis would be done at no extra cost to me. They were "99 percent sure" that everything was just fine with the baby.

To those of us who have been through the statistical mills, percentages mean little or nothing. Just as one knows that the odds of winning millions in the lottery are less than slim, nevertheless we read about lottery winners on a daily basis. When you get right down to it on an individual basis, in both lotteries and pregnancies either you win or you don't. As far as I was concerned, the lab's 99-percent certainty translated into a 50/50 proposition. I agreed to have the additional test. I loathe needles.

I made the 400-mile round trip to Bozeman again, this time accompanied by a friend who'd tried to have amniocentesis during her last pregnancy. They'd stuck the needle in nine times without penetrating the amniotic sac before she called it off and left. It was not encouraging. In Bozeman they put the needle into me twice, deciding after much discussion following the second attempt that they had enough cells to make the test possible, which was good because I had decided at some time during the discussion that they weren't going to put it in again. Even so, I noticed after Marina's birth that she had a little "amnio dimple" on her side. It's not disfiguring, but it's never gone away and I have thought about it more than a few times and shivered each time.

I went home to wait again. Did I think about abortion at this point? Yes. Did I have any idea what I would actually do if the test results brought bad news? No. What I wanted to know was that all of the baby's chromosomes were the right numbers in the right places.

I don't honestly know why that was so important to me because Down syndrome, which the test could tell me about, was not my greatest fear. My greatest fear was a repetition of all the physical defects Katya had suffered, which the test could not tell me about and which I had by now seen in a whole raft of children who had no chromosomal problems whatsoever. Go figure.

Eventually the results came back. All was well — at least all that could be tested for was well — and we settled into a holding pattern. Peter happily, me blocking out the entire idea as much as possible. I wanted to feel Marina — we had named her by then — kicking up a storm because Katya never had, but Marina was just as restrained as her sister had been. I tried to ignore it.

The onset of gestational diabetes and the process of sticking myself for blood-sugar tests four times a day forced me to think about the pregnancy, which I resented even more than having to keep track of everything I ate and when I had to eat it. It didn't help that it was diagnosed two days before Thanksgiving. I came away from the situation, which thankfully disappeared after Marina's birth, with great admiration for long-term diabetics who function cheerfully and normally.

Marina was due at the end of January. By mid-December I knew more about the problems associated with a diabetic pregnancy and I didn't like it. I became obsessed with the idea of having a Caesarean section. By Christmas I was having major problems with my eyes and had to stop working since the major part of my job involved editing reams of printed material on a computer terminal. Steve, who'd gotten me through a lot with Katya, told me that babies whose moms are diabetic tended to be bigger yet less developed and tended to be born later. Later? I already didn't think I could take another week of this! I brought up the idea of a Caesarean and he deflected it.

More waiting. It was an interminable waiting period, and I didn't even want another baby. Peter was very supportive. Marina seemed perfectly content to just stay in the womb until it was time to go to college.

Three days before Marina's original due date, I flipped out. I woke Peter up in the middle of the night sobbing because all I could think about was something going wrong during labor and anoxia and cerebral palsy. I spewed out a long list of rational reasons for wanting a Caesarean, but the real reason was pure, mind-permeating, uncontrollable terror. Peter said he didn't care if I had rational or irrational reasons for wanting a Caesarean, he just wanted me to not be so scared. "Talk to Steve about it at your appointment tomorrow," he said.

I walked into Steve's office the next day with a written list of reasons for wanting a Caesarean. I got about two lines into it before he smiled and said, "Well, I've only done two Caesareans on request before, but this seems like a good time to do a third. I'm going to be out of town Friday, but we can do it tomorrow or Monday."

I was stunned. I chose Monday because throughout the pregnancy I had refused to get ready for the birth. Peter had hauled out the crib and put it together, but we had no diapers on hand and Katya's baby clothes were still in boxes in the attic. There was a lot to do before Monday. And I suddenly realized that if Marina wanted to stay in the womb until it was time for college, maybe that wasn't such a bad idea. I could put off facing the outcome of this pregnancy for 18 more years. I was happy with our family just the way it was. I was used to Katya and we functioned well the way we were. I didn't like surprises. Katya had provided us with enough surprises for a lifetime, for several lifetimes. Why were we doing this?

We presented ourselves at the hospital Monday. Peter held my hand throughout the Caesarean and held Marina while Steve tied off my fallopian tubes. "Last chance to reconsider," he said, standing over me with a smile. "No problem," I said, "We're never doing this again."

When I woke up in my room later that afternoon there was a big chocolate cake sitting on the bed table. Peter had had the baker decorate it with the words "Goodbye Diabetes!" The baker had asked how to spell the name and commented that it must be Greek, Peter said.

Now Marina is four. She sings, she dances, she runs like the wind. She draws rainbows — arced rainbows, round rainbows, square rainbows, rainbows with eyelashes, tree rainbows, fire rainbows, water rainbows, huge rainbows, tiny rainbows. She brings us a new rainbow almost every day. They decorate the room she shares with Katya and cover our refrigerator. I have a folder stuffed with them. I have a heart stuffed with them.

Katya, used to being an only child with major adult attention, took a while getting used to the idea of being a sister, but now takes great pride in being able to read stories to Marina and in the fact that she's taller and can reach things Marina can't. On the other hand, Marina, who would rather stay up and play cards than go to bed any night of the year, told me the other night that when she's a grownup she's going to "take Katya to the park every day because that will make her happy." They have become sisters, and I, who grew up as an only child, am almost envious of them.

A few months after Marina's birth, Peter confessed that he had called Steve the morning after I'd flipped out and told him that if there was any way he could possibly see his way clear to performing a Caesarean, Peter would be eternally grateful. I am eternally grateful to Peter for calling and to Steve for listening.

So, we won the lottery with both Marina and Katya. I love each of them fiercely. And you couldn't pay me 47 million dollars to go through it again.

CHAPTER 15: JOSHUA

"Are You Super Mom, or What?"

Jan Spiegle

Carly McClure, author of the following manuscript, and I met when our children were very young, at our local support group for parents of children with special needs. As four or five mothers sat around a table over coffee, I took my turn introducing myself and telling about my family's situation. As I told my story, Carly pointed a finger at me and said, "You're the one! I've been hearing about you and resenting you for months. Are you Super Mom, or what?"

As the conversation progressed, I discovered that Carly's son and my daughter shared the same early intervention home teacher. I was obsessed in those days with doing everything possible for Sara, and had dived headlong into the tasks of home-based early intervention. I ran more learning programs and took more data than I care to remember. That behavior was, I think, my way of coping with the diagnosis, my way of finding out if I could make Sara "normal." (This kind of reaction appears to be typical of many parents in the "bargaining" stage of the grieving process referred to in Ethan Russo's manuscript, *To Know Them As People*, Chapter 11.) Our home trainer praised me enthusiastically for my efforts, and had evidently told Carly what a "model" mother of a child with a disability I was.

While the progress Sara made was remarkable, in actuality my obsession was the cause of many problems in our home. My husband (who would, in time, become my former husband) and I had lost track of one another, and Sara's two older sisters were adrift for much of the day as I focused my efforts almost entirely on teaching Sara the tasks at hand. I routinely neglected my own personal need for down time, to say nothing about the laundry!

When I began to tell Carly about the reality of life in the Mariska household, she began to relax with me. She and I would eventually become best friends — compatriots — who compared notes and fought battles for our children side by side. We listened to each other with the empathy that only someone who has been there can possess.

Late in the summer of 1986, Carly moved away to a distant state. Her departure left a void in my life that was nearly impossible to fill. We have maintained our friendship since then with a sporadic flow of letters and phone calls, and with two brief face-to-face meetings that we managed to arrange. Carly's letters are newsy, lengthy accounts which chart the evolution of a family through a tremendous number of life changes in a comparatively short time span (five years).

The letters are sometimes angry diatribes against recalcitrant service delivery systems, and sometimes poignant glances inside the heart of a family with special needs. They offer other families a unique and rare chance to identify with and experience what life is like for another parent of a child with disabilities. To helping professionals, they present an unrestricted mosaic of the problems, issues, and triumphs that families may share, and of the ways that quality (or lack of quality) service delivery impacts families.

Though I am not in the habit of keeping correspondence, I had kept all of Carly's letters. Tucked away in bedside tables and pigeonholes of desks, I searched them out, put them in order, and edited them. The experience was much like looking through the pages of an old photograph album, reaquainting me with humor, compassion, and insight. I was hesitant to ask Carly whether she would allow the use of her letters in *Changes*. Much of what I have included is of a very personal nature, yet it is directly applicable to the lives of almost all parents of children like ours. Her positive reply was an affirmation to me that parents who have been there have much to learn from one another, and that such families gain a unique validation through that sharing process.

There are several places in the following manuscript which required an "editor's note" to clarify the context of the letters. I have added those, denoting their presence with brackets. I briefly considered deleting the use of expletives in these letters, but I decided that type of editorial modification would tamper with reality. With a few very rare exceptions, I've yet to meet many parents of a child with disabilities who don't swear like linebackers in the company of other parents of children with disabilities.

Happily Ever After?

Carly McClure

Carly is a Registered Nurse and the mother of three children, Joshua, Rachel, and Mark. Joshua has a pervasive developmental delay.

July, 1986

Just before Carly moved she gave me an American Greetings card which carried this verse on the front:

Hope
is not pretending
that troubles don't exist . . .
It is the trust
that they will not last forever,
that hurts will be healed
and difficulties overcome . . .
It is faith
that a source of strength
and renewal lies within
to lead us through the dark
to the sunshine . . .

Inside the card, Carly wrote:

My dear friend Jan,

I will miss you so much. You helped me put some normalcy in my life. You helped me laugh. You helped me learn to fight. I love you and I *will* keep in touch.

P.S. How do you eat an elephant?

One bite at a time. (My life's motto!)

Always, Carly

August, 1986
Hi Jan,

Thank you for the card from the support group. I have read and reread it — I am drawing strength from you all. I wish you were here right now — you know how the "fears" can get to you. It's going to be hard to start all over.

I feel pretty good, other than tired and emotional, and occasionally morning sick. [Carly had discovered she was pregnant just before she moved.] I haven't found a doctor yet — maybe when I do they'll be able to find a heartbeat — I was so excited with Joshua, I think this time I'm mixed with fear, dread, and excitement. This being pregnant again is a toughie! Knowing you've made a decision, knowing you're going to stick with it, and being scared shitless all at the same time! C'est la vie.

Will get Joshua in a preschool August 27th. There is only one class for all the 3-year-olds. I hope it's OK. If it's not, we'll tackle it later. Want to hold off on job-hunting til Joshua is settled into the new program.

Always, Carly

Later August, 1986

So, here it is three weeks. It seems like we've been here an eternity. I'm not working yet. It's so funny. I should be enjoying being home, but I am so restless. I play less with Joshua than I did working 4 days a week.

Joshua starts school tomorrow. We'll see. I have my reservations — if it doesn't work out we'll figure something else out.

I saw a doctor, and he seems nice enough. I know he has good skills. We'll see about his bedside manner. They are always taken aback by "us" [mothers who have a child with a disability], aren't they? They expect some dumb cluck — he didn't believe me that chorion-villious biopsy (CVS) or amniocentesis would *not* be appropriate in my case. While I was there, he called genetics people who indeed thought it would be a waste of time, since Joshua's disability cannot be genetically identified. Then he tried the old "if I could tell you this child has what your first child has, would you still want to continue the pregnancy?" routine. He backed down off the pulpit when I said, "If you had a child with a disability, then you would understand why I answer 'yes.'" He did loosen up some, told some jokes and seemed pretty nice. He gets another chance.

Love, Carly

September, 1986

Well, just another shitty day in paradise, right? I think I just have too many expectations for Joshua. You'd think I'd learn.

I'm sure Sara has not hit a plateau. As you said in your letter, sometimes when we aren't studying them so close they don't seem to change, but the truth is, they most certainly do. Chin up, lady, she's my "brag" kid! Thanks for pointing out that you see progress in Josh. I'm the opposite. I look at him under a microscope and can't see him move. It works both ways, I guess. He's had a cold (sinus infection, I'm sure) for two weeks now. He's handling it fine and I am too, sort of. He needs to be off the prophylactic antibiotics, I think, so they'll work when he's really sick. I'm trying not to panic. [Children with disabilities are often placed on preventative antibiotics during cold and flu season, to ward off complications from such infections. Carly speaks of panicking because Josh had been through so many life-threatening pneumonias and hospitalizations due to "complications" arising from the common cold.]

In his first year of teaching, Brian [Joshua's dad] is discouraged with the educational system. We live, it appears, in a very backward world here. I still reserve judgment about Josh's school. At least he gets speech and physical therapy there. The PT [Physical Therapist] put him behind a walker (the granny kind with wheels). He does pretty well, so we are practicing. I like the speech lady . . . Josh's schedule is fairly light, but it seems like enough.

Brian's folks are driving me nutty. It's not interference anymore, but lack of consistency. They promised to keep Joshua one week after school until I got home from work at 4 p.m. The day before I was to go to work, they called to say they couldn't. I was pissed! I ended up taking him to my mom, a twenty-minute drive away. She had to take the time off work to keep him. My mom is my sole supporter. Brian's mom doesn't work, but had a party to get ready for in the following few days. Needless to say, I will not and have not asked them to help out with babysitting, and when they've offered, I had "already made arrangements." Their idea of interacting with Josh consists of a 5-minute visit — "Hello, champ!" — a pat on the head, and back out the door. And yet they keep the other grandchildren for weeks at a time. It hurts a little. Although they'd deny it, it is because Josh is disabled. I think they really believe "these people" are "happiest," and it would be the "best for all concerned," if they were all placed in institutions. I hate it here sometimes. Truly, my only regret in leaving here would or will be leaving *my* family. My mother loves Josh and I love her support.

Josh's school wants us to have his eyes examined, since he seems to have little or no eye-hand coordination. So, off to the eye doctor we go. We wouldn't want all the medical bills to be caught up, now, would we?

Need to attend to Josh. He's playing with his See and Say, but wants some attention. He slept through school today, so I am the entertainment committee this afternoon. We are going to play "vacuum the cookie crumbs" — exciting, huh?

I've spent a fortune on toys for this Christmas. It's funny, if he were "average" I'd give him a pot and spoon, but he gets electronic gadgets. I think its a toy company plot! But truly, if you don't have imagination skills, how can you play with something unless it *does* something? Do you have any ideas? I'd guess we need things in the 12-24 month range. I'd appreciate anything.

Take care of yourself, my friend. And tell me that the two Irish Creams we drank together the night before I left didn't hurt this baby. I can't get rid of this one. I need a pep talk.

Love you, Carly

November, 1986

Hi, Jan,

Your letter was a confirmation that I have been doing what I should be doing. I needed the reassurance that my type of parenting was indeed effective. No, I don't want any "learning programs" — thanks for reminding me how it takes the fun out of playing with our kids. I wish we were back there and had him in those programs. Not that they are perfect, I know, but at least I'd know whose butt to chew if I were unhappy. They apparently *do* have a program here for children who are "mildly disabled," that is in the school system itself. The one child Joshua seemed to be learning from at his school graduated into it. [The new public school that Josh attended was segregated — no "average" children were present in his learning environment.] I was happy for his parents but disappointed for Josh. He does well around more "average" kids. He tries. He's pretty much the big guy at his school now. There are much older children who are verbal, but none of the little ones except Joshua are. Most are very multiply disabled. We're on a waiting list for a private school that's supposed to be better — maybe it won't take a year.

We can't afford to have private physical therapy or speech therapy after January. Joshua's deductible is $1000. Before we had two insurance companies, so it wasn't a problem. Now it is, so I suppose what he gets from school will have to do for now. Bummer! I'm basically feeling good about him, not that he's changed. I have the feeling, at least for today, that I'm just glad he *is*.

Talked with another mom from back there today. She sounds very defeated, you know what I mean, "I'm tired of evals, tired of evaluating everything she does, of clarifying and defining. I just want my daughter to be whatever she can be." She needs to vent and not feel she's inadequate. I guess their home teacher gave them a pile of programs to work on when they left the early intervention program. That went over like a lead balloon! They left because they didn't *want* to work on any more programs. I suppose when burn-out hits, it hits hard. I feel less and less resentment toward our former home teacher. I suppose it's because I feel good about what I've been able to do with Josh. Even though the things she did made us feel like "less than good parents," we think that we've been damn good ones. At least *today* I'm feeling confident and more secure.

A new little girl with Down syndrome started at Josh's school. She's just a one-year-old, not talking yet, but *walking*. Can you believe it? Her fine motor skills look good too, from a brief observation, of course. I haven't met any parents here — they're funny that way at this school.

My love to your crew, "hi" to support group.

Carly

December, 1986

Hi Jan,

It had to happen. Things were going too smoothly. I went and observed at Josh's school. I'm very disappointed. The teacher *tries*. She even split the preschool up into mornings and afternoons (Josh is in afternoons). That's not the problem. It's all the other kids. Jan, there are fourteen- and fifteen- year-olds, eight-year olds, mostly very severely developmentally delayed or autistic. They sit doing nothing, but certainly make a lot of noise. I couldn't believe it. They supposedly have two teachers, but I've only seen one in the classroom. There are nineteen kids ranging from age three to age fifteen. They include a child who is deaf (with an average IQ) and a fifteen-year-old (very loud) young man who has cerebral palsy and autism. It was overwhelming. I will spend a few days regrouping and try to decide what to do. I feel the teacher keeps the preschoolers the busiest, but still the time seems so wasted. Physical therapists can't see the kids in the afternoon program. The occupational therapist is worthless. The speech gal is great, but they only have her in the classroom on Tuesdays and Thursdays for half an hour. Josh needs to be with kids his own age. He seems fairly oblivious to the older ones, but it looked like chaos to me. I cannot stomach the idea of Joshua vegetating there. I miss the CO-TEACH classroom and their magic touch. I miss Kevin's music. Josh loved it so much. I feel compelled to start "home programming." Barf! Why can't it be like it needs to be? I know it's not just here. All programs have some flaws, but this one seems beyond repair. I am discouraged.

The baby is moving and kicking a lot. I'm nineteen weeks, but I started feeling flutters at sixteen. Movements are stronger and more aggressive than Joshua's were — I'll take that as a good sign.

Josh is doing OK other than school, pulling up by himself and becoming stronger. His words this week were "light" and "knee." There's a lot of jabber and senseless talk, but I will take his handful of words as another good sign. Without CO-TEACH people keeping me encouraged, I feel he isn't changing fast enough, but then again he would only be fast enough if he tested out at age level. He's climbing on things and curious. Attention span is increasing and he must attend before he'll learn, so . . .

I miss you, miss having the directions to take with Josh. You and Susan [another support group mom] always seemed to know who I should talk to or who I should chew on. I need that right now. I don't really know where to start. Guess I'll start on Monday — at least I have a *when*.

"Hi" to support group people. Miss you all.

Love, Carly

January, 1987

. . . I'm feeling good now (29 weeks). Had a few scary weeks. Was having lots of false contractions and having to see the doctor weekly. I would not have a 26-week-baby if I could help it; I know what the risks are. So I prayed and I sweated a lot and it turns out I was not going into labor after all.

It was positive, all the scariness, in one way. It confirmed in my mind that I want this child and that's a nice feeling. It's funny how different #2 is — with Joshua I wanted a matching, cutsie nursery, all the latest developmental toys, the best stroller, etc. This time we're using the crib that was mine. No darling cradles or baskets or swings or other "essential baby equipment." It's nice to know that "average" kids grow up all by themselves. And, if this child *is* disabled all the cutsiepooh accessories will not cure him or her. Guess I feel more secure about motherhood.

Josh is doing OK, or rather mom is feeling OK about Josh. He is trying so hard to communicate — goes through his repertoire of words — I know they're not always appropriate, but he gets a reaction and some conversation. Over Christmas, he learned "puppy" and "meow" for kitty. He's at least headed in the right direction.

Took him to the eye doctor — really a good and kind pediatric man and Josh is "quite farsighted." Just another label to add to the list. We are going to try some glasses especially/only/mostly (depending on his tolerance) during fine motor tasks. The doctor says all kids are a little farsighted, but Josh is *a lot* farsighted. So . . . we have to try, it won't cause miracles, but maybe it will help some.

Just received your letter today. I miss you so much and miss my Wednesday fix. [Wednesday was when the evening support group met.] Haven't bothered with parent groups here — too far to drive and don't feel the need. I want my old parent group back!

Sorry to hear about Sara's eyes, I know you're disappointed. Chin up!

They've had Josh in a standing frame at school (I know his physical therapist back there would be mortified!). I really haven't protested. I figure it can't hurt, right? Well, it *is* helping to strengthen his legs, but today he apparently fell out of it — hard. He didn't get anything but a goose egg, but now he's afraid to stand up at all. Thanks, guys! We'll work on coaxing and supporting now. The old one-step-forward and two-steps-back routine. Take care.

Love, Carly

March, 1987

Hi Jan,

It was so good to hear your voice, even if you did have a rotten cold. Pretty much told you all the news on the phone — am 34 weeks and hope to hold on another two. The doctor wants to do an amnio at 36 weeks, if I go that far, and if the baby's lungs are mature, we'll do a C-section. [Amniocentesis results can help doctors assess many things, among them the lung maturity of an unborn baby.] Seems to me like cheating the baby out of picking his or her own time. Besides, I'm scared to death of an amnio! Maybe I won't have to make the decision. I really don't feel emotionally ready to have this child in two weeks. Other than being tired of being fat, I think I would leave him or her "inside" forever. Then I wouldn't have to know. Having a preemie is scary enough without bringing the fears *we* get to bring into a birthing room. The doctor doesn't want me to go into labor — thinks I'd rupture [Carly had a Caesarean section when Joshua was born] — so I suppose reality will be thrust on me, ready or not. Brian's folks have hired help two hours a day for me. They *have* been supportive in some ways. It's nice to have a clean house if you have to lie and look at it all day. [Carly was confined to bed rest for the last few weeks of this pregnancy.] They never mention "the baby" — I know everyone is holding their breath — "average" or disabled? Hell, how do I know?

Brian still harbors a lot of resentment deep down about this baby. It comes out every once in a while. He'll tell me I should have aborted, that he didn't want it, etc. . . . so much baggage for a new baby to carry in with him or her. I ignore what he says, knowing I had no other choice (for me) — if we could turn time back, we could change "now", but that's not the way it works, is it?

Joshua does grow stronger. I do see strength changes when I'm not being so critical. He can confidently "cruise" short distances and can stand alone a second or two. He coughs hard now, so I foresee that our "pneumonia-death" days may be behind us. I absolutely loathe the idea of him turning four. I know it's not until July, but the gap is getting wider year by year. He's a big kid, and that's even worse, I think. He may be fun with the baby. Even though he doesn't understand many things, he knows what a baby is and can say it. He laughs at them and seems very inquisitive. He's a bit out of sorts with my being immobile; maybe he understands more than we give him credit for? Who knows? Doesn't really mind his glasses for short periods — I hope my feelings about them aren't getting to him. It's so hard to see those coke bottles on his pretty face.

My mom is great. She feels no excuses or explanations are necessary and takes him every and anywhere. The pride I cannot feel, she does. I hate that in me and have always admired people who took their kids with disabilities out and about. I do go. I force myself to do it for both of us, but it's safer in your own home. No stares and no explanations. You love them and it's comfortable. You go out the door and your vulnerability is there for the world to see. At home, I'm so proud of his speech attempts. In public, I'm awkward and would like him to remain quiet. Maybe no one would know if he just sat by me and didn't open his mouth! I hate it Jan! I hate myself for feeling it. Maybe some of it is just my screwy pregnancy hormones, but the root of it isn't, I fear. Love to you and your girls.

Carly

[Carly's second child, Rachel, was born healthy and sound in March, 1987.]

April, 1987

. . . Rachel seems to change so fast. She is a joy. Tiring, but such a blessing. She helps me feel better about Joshua. He's going to turn four soon. God, each birthday is a killer. He has gotten *very* tall. I wish he wouldn't, but Brian is 6'5" — it's in his genes. We'll start back with private physical therapy this summer; no summer school to be found, bargained for, etc.! It makes me so sad for what he's not receiving. Oh, well, you do what you can, right? He is making more and more attempts at communication — now he is using his words more meaningfully — he says "bye" when he wants to go somewhere. It's nice to see him be less passive. He'll push you away if he's been scolded and is mad at you. He's trying to imitate most every word we say to him — "beep, beep" goes the car, "morning," "hi, puppy," "hi, baby" — are some new additions. He still flunks the Bayley [a developmental assessment test] though. He won't put cubes in a cup or stack blocks or do most anything on that damn test. By far, fine motor and gross motor skills do him in. I'm sure they don't work much with him on fine motor skills at school. We're going to try to spend 15 minutes a day either doing stretching exercises or playing some games this summer. I refuse to call it "home programming."

Sometimes I feel so good about him, but someone always manages to ruin it. The big Fourth of July picnic our in-laws have will be unattended by us. There are usually at least 100 friends and relatives, most of whom "can't deal with" Joshua. Screw 'em! I will *not* leave him home, nor will I spend five hours in 100 degree weather feeling uneasy if he "stims out." [Self-stimulation behaviors such as arm-flapping and ear-pulling are common in children with developmental disabilities.] I'm not far enough down the road to just go and ignore them. We'll probably go for the fireworks. It's hard to try to "take him out of the box" when people are nailing the lid shut. Brian has become particularly aware of this phenomenon and has started taking Josh with him to the store or fishing or wherever.

It seems to me Joshua learns more "just being." When I was on bedrest, I'd sing "If you're happy and you know it." Well, Joshua goes around saying "happy, happy" and clapping to start the song. He's also gotten "happy boy" just from that stupid song. Seems the less directed and the more fun something is, the better he learns.

There's an eight-year-old girl with Down syndrome at Joshua's school. She's there only because she's a "trouble-maker," talks too much at regular school! I remember you wondering if Sara would ever talk! Now this kid can't go to regular school because she talks *too much*? Can you believe it? She's tall, well not really tall, but she's thin and has blond braids. She's great, Jan. Does her reading and math. She reminds me of a grown-up Sara.

Brian is employed for next year. I'm taking one class this summer, so the work load will be light when I start nursing school in the fall. I hope I don't regret starting with the baby still so young. Yet, if I don't start sometime, I'll never get through. Compromise! Compromise!

Brian and I celebrate our ninth anniversary soon. You're never out of the woods in a marriage, are you?

Jan, I don't know how you do it with four kids. I'm worn out with two. Am still struggling with having to spend less and less time with Joshua as the baby's demands get louder. I know it's normal, just tough on me. I'm used to giving him all the attention; he's used to getting it. It'll probably be best for both of us. Well, the little princess calls — again! "Average" kids are more demanding, aren't they? Certainly louder!

Love, Carly

May, 1987

Miss you. I started back to work this weekend, only Friday and Saturday nights. [Carly was working as a Licensed Practical Nurse in the Labor and Delivery Unit of a local hospital.] I feel good about it since it forces Brian to nurture the kids. He hasn't really done anything since I was on bedrest in January. He is tickled with Rachel. It's amazing how social an "average" baby is *so early*. She is cooing and laughing, growing like a weed. She's three months already. I catch myself worrying now and again. I suppose I won't relax until she walks. Crazy, isn't it. She's smiling, laughing, cooing, and starting to bat at things and push up on her elbows. Yet, I still worry it will somehow stop and she won't keep progressing. I praise God for each milestone, but don't believe it's really for real. I wish the milestones were not ingrained in my mind. I don't check the book or look it up in the Early Lap [another assessment instrument], but I still hold my breath until she passes another one. I keep trying to stop, relax, enjoy, but often find it difficult. I hate myself for not relishing every moment. She's my last. [Carly thought that Rachel would be the "finish" to their family. Like many of us, she was wrong.] She's my average. Yet, her good nature lets me do all those things I have to get done like laundry and cleaning the bathroom. I know "average" kids grow up without parents in their face all the time. It's just an adjustment from parenting Joshua. I even feel guilty if I hold her too much because she should be "being programmed" by batting for eye-hand coordination, lying on her tummy and "scooting".

Joshua is back with private physical therapy and speech two times a week. Still no summer school — an adjustment for me! One of Brian's teacher friends in PE/ Special Ed wants to *maybe* do water therapy in her pool with him this summer. I hope it works out. Keep your fingers crossed.

Josh's "end of the school year" report arrived in the mail today . . . the usual bad news.

Love you. Give my love to your family and hello to everyone at support group. Miss you.

Love, Carly

[The letters seem to indicate that Carly and Brian's marriage began to fall apart soon after Rachel was born. Usually they were undated and as I edited, it was difficult for me to be certain of the correct sequence. I gave it my best guess, but the manuscript still reflects some inconsistencies. For the purposes of *Changes* it seemed more important to document what happened, rather than worry about when it occurred.]

June, 1987
Hello Jan.

At last school's out. Josh is supposed to go to some "developmental pediatrician" on August 15. I made the appointment last January. This guy's supposed to know what schools are best for what kids. I'm afraid, I haven't had to do this kind of evaluation crap in years. What if he says to put Josh in an institution? Or that he'd benefit from more consistent stimulation? What am I saying? Must be having Early Lap flashbacks. I'm not prepared to hear his prognosis. Would I ever be? I guess the counselor and I have a few sessions ahead of us on this one. I know Joshua is more developmentally delayed than I like to believe. I just can't look at it. I know that if he can feed himself, walk, dress himself somewhat, and talk some, that will be the best he can do. I just can't hear the label. He is so physically disabled. I guess I always saw the low tone, but as he gets bigger and heavier, the fine motor skills (at least the ones he has) also seem so crude.

Now he's even having constipation problems. I feel like an inadequate mother again. He hasn't used his walker in days. I haven't stretched his knees in weeks. I'm treating him like Rachel, but as evaluation time approaches, I panic. What have I done? I put off dental appointments, eye appointments! I'm having a "mad-at-God" week. Can you believe it? I still put my fist up and ask "Why?" Oh, hell. At least Joshua loves Rachel.

I miss you. I may throw the kids in my car and drive to your house! But thirty hours in the car doesn't exactly thrill me. I do feel like running away.

Brian's on his rafting trip to Europe. A friend he has there bought him the ticket. I feel so vulnerable; I miss him. I'm afraid of what can be, what was, what is.

I've been working extra hours. I really don't want to. Don't know why I do it. . . . Yes, I do. Because I'm afraid of having time to think. I'm going to cut this off here and pick it up when I don't feel so out of control. I miss you.

Hello, again, it's forty-eight hours later and I've had a full 8 hours of sleep. Those night shifts sure play havoc on my mind and body. Have forced myself to make Josh use his walker — even in public today. The stares bother me, but he really does seems to enjoy the independence and my back is saying "Halleluia." I suppose somewhere in my psyche I thought no one would *know* if he were in a stroller or being carried but . . . I'm going to try to do it more.

I have at least had time to put things in my house as I like them. Brian says we'll need a bigger place when/if we move back in together.

As a nurse, the country is mine to choose from if I want to go it alone. But three people on $20,000 might not make it everywhere. I suppose if Brian and I do permanently part, I will either 1) move closer to my mom for the financial and emotional support, 2) move to New England because that's my heritage and they're supposed to have good schools for *all* kinds of kids, or 3) come back out West.

Jan, is it time for me to be seriously investigating group homes? Brian's folks slay me. I finally talked to them and flat out said, "Yes, one day Josh will live in a different home than me — I'm sure by the time he's sixteen or eighteen or when I physically can't handle him. But at five, if that is what Brian and you have planned, then I *will* be a single mother of a son with a disability and a wonderfully 'average' daughter."

I don't relish the idea of working full-time and having a sitter with the kids all day. That's a plus for moving close to Mom. Damn, this sucks. Lose your independence and go home to Mom, so that the kids will be well-cared for while I work. Perhaps our generation will reinvent the extended family?

Love, Carly

August, 1987

Wonderful to see you in July. We needed so much time together and had so little!

On my return to the Midwest, I moved us away from Brian's parents; five miles to be exact. Being away helped me realize the subtle and not so subtle pressures and stresses they were exerting on me and my family. So we moved, to the country even. The house sits on two acres with 80 acres of pasture if we want a horse or a llama or just to look at the greenery. We have to drive Josh into town and pick him up from school. So far we have worked it out. We are now out of the school district, so we must keep a low profile in case he doesn't get into the private program next year. Yes, we're still on the waiting list.

There is a new teacher who seems to have some good ideas. She has him on a potty program and is having positive results. Hooray! She can be a little "put ten blocks in the cup 80% of the time-ish", but I think she realizes that Josh will fail at most everything if he's bored or frustrated. She is at least trying. Actually I feel pretty good about school this year. She has him on a walking program in addition to physical therapy, just so he can practice. I still wish there were some "average" kids around at school, but the nieces and nephews and two kids at the babysitters will have to fill that need. Now that Rachel is crawling and relatively safe with Joshua, she has helped draw him out too. I know she will be the best thing that ever happened to him. I worry that the reverse will not be so true. She *is* wonderful. I say thank you to the "powers that be" daily. She crawled right at six months and comes to a sit by herself. She eats bits of food off her tray by herself, squeals, and coos and is interested in *everything*. She's *so* aware. She helps ease the losses.

I'm struggling with my brothers. As Josh has gotten bigger, less babylike, and obviously disabled, they have withdrawn from him to the point of not even saying "hello" or "goodbye" to the child. Now that Rachel is here, I can see it is clearly Joshua's being disabled that causes this reaction, and not an inability to relate to kids. I'm angry with them. They say "cop out" things like "I just can't handle it." I want to say back to them "Tough, I've *had* to handle it. This is how it is." I haven't communicated with them for over a month. I'm regrouping and planning to write to them in a while. It never ends, does it? I feel OK about Josh, but have to prod the family to do the same. I expect strangers to have difficulty, I suppose I expected more from kin.

Always, Carly

September, 1987

Hello Jan,

Well, the dreaded evaluation for Josh came and was *wonderful*! The man was marvelous — spent three hours with us talking about every area of concern. He confirmed my fears of Josh's developing bowel problems and encouraged me to start a laxative regimen as you had described. I bought the Agoral [brand name] today. He's got some ideas, and wants to meet with Josh's teacher to work on his IEP [Individualized Education Program] this year. He thinks an adapted chair for fine motor tasks would be beneficial. As he described it, all of Josh's energy — physical and mental — goes into just keeping himself in a sitting position. He basically said what I've always felt: Josh is somewhere between what they used to call "trainable" and "severe." Not good news, but livable. I asked if he thought self-help skills, a group home, and a sheltered workshop placement are reasonable expectations for the future. He felt Josh would accomplish at least that much. Jan, it's crazy to be glad about that, but my intuition was right. The confirmation felt good. I'd have loved a miracle, but at least he had some ideas, something to try. I was so let down when the PT said, "I don't know what else to do for him," last year.

As for Brian and me, who knows? Too much work to think it through. He says he can't go back to having Josh tear his stuff up (he tears paper, breaks phonograph records, and has destroyed stereo equipment we can't afford to replace). I told him he'd need to keep his stuff in a locked room. I know that he was devastated that we may have a "two-year-old" for a long time. It may come down to my choosing Brian or "placement" (as his mother calls it) for Josh. I'm afraid Brian would lose. I think he knows it too. Someday, the time for group home placement will probably come, but it's not at five years old.

Counseling is hot and cold. Some days it's great, some days it seems like a waste. We haven't gone jointly yet. Brian's good when he's with the kids, but it's at his convenience. He's not watching them when I work, except when he feels like it. The babysitting's killing me financially. I suppose if this continues, I'll need to check into some other arrangements. This "single parent" stuff has been good for me I guess. I may need to get used to it permanently.

Miss you. If you happen to be within an eight-hour drive any time in your travels, please call. I'll come see you.

Love, Carly

October, 1987

My wonderful friend,

Well it's been five + months of separation and I think I have come to a decision. I will probably file for divorce after the first of the year. Brian's copped out essentially and will leave things status quo; I cannot. I suppose I have come to feel that life alone is preferable to a life with him. I don't know if the changes necessary to allow this marriage to survive can be made. I also see potential for us both being very viable, healthy adults if we're apart. He is doing some writing again. I am changing, I think, in positive ways also. I am feeling more in charge of myself. Brian simply cannot accept Josh; Josh's messes, Josh's lack of bowel and bladder control, Josh's severe developmental delay. I do know he loves him as much as he can, but he cannot live with him. I'm not sure how I know these things, but I do. He speaks of "placement" for Josh. Well, Jan, I'm at the crossroads. I will not "place" him, so if that means I will be alone, perhaps it needn't be lonely. I've met many people, been out with a few male friends, and even if I never have a marriage again, perhaps those contacts will fill that void.

I'm sad for Rachel. I'm sorry that she won't know a nuclear family. But the truth is I am a happier person without him and so is he. I've never been faced with such a difficult choice, except for carrying my pregnancy to term with Rachel and choosing to resuscitate Josh. How 'bout a break, God?!

So here I am writing songs on my guitar again. Bittersweet music, mostly. Toast with me, my friend. To **a** future, may we be true to ourselves, may we not grieve for the decisions we make.

Love, Carly

P.S. I *do* feel a little resentful toward Josh, bless his heart. But I remember something I wrote and it helps:

It hurts me to know what they say about you
It hurts me to know they laugh at you
It hurts me to see their curiosity,
Animosity.
Don't they know *they* have the disability
  through their hostility.

Brian is more disabled than I had ever thought *and* more disabled than Josh will ever be.

January, 1988
My friend,

A man had been blind from birth — people were asking "who sinned, this man or his parents, for him to be born blind?" Neither he nor his parents. He was born

blind so that the glory of God could be manifested in him.
John 9:1-4

Don't know why I wanted to share that with you. Perhaps because it is one of the few scriptures I know, perhaps because it has given me solace on occasion. Perhaps because it gives some reason to Josh's disability and my personal growth. Maybe I'm the kind of person who needs to believe there is a purpose.

Am mostly OK with him. Can finally separate that it is the actions that disgust or infuriate me, and not the child. I am frustrated by the developmental delay, but not the little being trying to do the best he can with his abilities. I get frustrated by his latent infancy sometimes, and then look at him the next day and am not so unhappy that he is who he is. Mostly, I'm physically exhausted with him. He's so big. He's more steady on his feet these days. Can walk holding on to my hand all the way to the car! Rachel passes through those developmental phases so much more quickly than he! She's proficient at walking, now. Says "cookie," "dada," "bye, bye," and "baby." Incredible! She loves her brother. He loves her.

There is, by the way, another reality Rachel's brought me. I get just as mad at her whining as his — at her turning the TV off and on. I feel less guilty about those negative feelings now that I realize they are part of "average" parenting, too. It is a healing beyond explanation! Brian adores her. He's always saying "Just look at her!" They dance, go shopping — and either out of guilt or healing — now he'll take Josh to "work out" or they read Dr. Seuss books together. It makes me glad to see.

Josh is making progress at school, too. His teacher is excellent this year. I do feel good about that — am finally realizing that given an enriching environment, it's mostly the kid and their "given" abilities.

Love you, my friend.

Carly

February, 1988
Hello friend,

Well, you asked about my life, so here goes. It's hectic and I often am so stressed that I feel close to the edge of flipping out. You know I work every Friday and Saturday night, from ll p.m. to 7 a.m. Work is actually my only free time — I look forward to it. At least it's *my* time. I try to sleep when I get home, but how much sleep I get is dependent on Brian's ability to cope with the kids. Sometimes I get five hours, often less. So, by Monday, I am pretty much a bitch. I hate my impatience with my kids! We can't afford to eat out, and with nursing school, that usually means making dinner under pressure of hungry kids. Brian's not much help with the kids. I guess he figures he does his share on the weekends. Yes, you sense some resentment. A lot of it, because we haven't made much progress in this area. He'll say, "*I* never wanted kids," etc. We've talked about this before, I know. So once the "kid-duties" are done, then I'm supposed to study. Ha! I find it hard to see my house such a disaster all the time, not to mention my nerves. I feel like I do a half-assed job at everything. When I do have a free day, I'm even more stressed out, because I can't seem to gear down. It's a mess, Jan. Always running, always late.

Josh is getting no other therapy than what he gets at school. The PT's don't think they can do any more and say, "He'll just walk all by himself one day." He's fourth in line for getting into the private school, so maybe next year. They have an aide for each kid. On the flip side, it's a 45-minute commute.

Rachel is a gas! She must have over a dozen words and she runs! She is a stinker, but what a joy.

Josh is now healthy. He ran up $8000 in January with epiglottitis (*bad* croup) and was intubated [a procedure to aid breathing] for four days. Smart, aggressive doctors saved him from a tracheotomy. It was from a virus, but hey, he didn't get pneumonia. He's made some developmental gains, I suppose — just hard to see. He's also in trouble all the time for messing with the TV, getting in the fridge, and hurting his sister. Oy, vey!

I miss you. I could always see the light when I saw you surviving four kids. I remember Jan's Taxi Service! I miss talking to you.

Love to the girls and Bud, Carly

March, 1988
Hello friend,

Your letter was a godsend — to know someone else has been that frustrated. I still haven't found the gumption to stand up to Brian and demand some more time for me. I am such a peacemaker, you know. Don't rock the boat, and all. The waters are so rough, we surely will sink . . .

I reread your letter often and forgive myself when I am impatient with the kids or the house is a mess. I'm having babysitter problems at the moment. I know "this, too, will pass." Just another headache.

I am saddened that Rachel had her first birthday. Silly, I know. I wanted her to walk and talk and be OK, but now she's not a baby. I feel I missed out on something.

Always busy doing something else. I can't seem to slow down. I'm going to schedule myself. Make little lists of what I will and won't do. Then maybe I'll feel like I'm accomplishing something. And I won't feel so guilty when I'm away from the kids at class most of the day. Sometimes it's like I'm avoiding them — "Just let me be!" And then, I turn around, and it's her birthday. Hell.

The good news is that my insurance picked up Josh's January hospital bill, so we won't owe them **any** dollars. Will miracles never cease? Now I can actually pay for day care! Aaargh!

Hope this finds all well.

Always, Carly

P.S. It's several days later. Thought that I'd add that I found a new sitter. Hope it works out. Feeling better today.

April, 1988
Jan,

Have lent your book to Josh's teacher. [The booklet I helped to write along with three other mothers, Susan Duffy, Kathy McGlynn, and Jeanie Murphy, called, "Acceptance is Only the First Battle".] She lent it to the Director of Special Services and they loved it! They have ordered copies to keep on hand for staff and parents. Your support group is touching us 2000 miles away!

Josh spends less and less time "self-stimming." He's generally here with the program. That is perhaps his biggest change — not *what* he can do, but that he is *aware*. He'll follow Rachel around into their room and play with toys. It's very basic 12-month-type play, but no prompts, no "good job," no "do this, Josh." Wow.

Still have no leads on a summer program. Wish again we were back there. Oh, well, guess he'll just play with his sister!

Brian's been somewhat better. Still no free time unless I schedule it, but I have started leaving the kids an extra hour with the sitter now and again — just so I can take a nap!

I love you, my friend. If you want to be warm and experience wonderful pecan pie and mint iced tea, my door is open. I miss you.

Carly

May, 1988
Hello Jan,

My future is uncertain. I've decided that if or when we divorce, I will keep the house. The commute is 20 + miles, but the kids are stable here, have a good sitter, and I don't want to disrupt them any more than necessary. Damn it, Jan! This week, Brian's done the things I would want from him. He's helped with the kids, split some housework, and stayed calm so we could talk. And yet his distance from me grows. He says he wants to be friends. I feel deserted. I sleep alone. I eat, I eat, I eat. Don't cry anymore. Brian leaves in three days for another rafting journey. Perhaps he'll come back "in love" with me, but "I doubt it," says Brian.

School's been OK. It's pediatric nursing. We're doing respiratory diseases in children! I think I could teach it. It's been a bad year for Josh. Epiglottitis in January, ear tubes in April, pneumonia earlier in May, three serious intensive care unit visits! (Those tensions made this struggle in our marriage surface even more.) We're going to keep him on antibiotics for an indefinite period of time and some bronchodilators. He acts like a cystic fibrosis kid, but tests negative. He's well today, but we've been told "he can't be so sick again so soon," whatever that means. We've been encouraged to decide how "far we want to go" to "save him." Crap, I'm not in any emotional position to make life or death decisions for anyone! Who is? So because he's developmentally delayed (read retarded), we don't try? I pray he remains well until the marital situation resolves one way or another. Rachel is my joy. Sorry to dump all this on you.

Love you, Carly

May, 1988

My wonderful friend,

. . . our marriage is quickly becoming a statistic, a casualty. Brain says he "will stay until you graduate. That's what I can promise. I think our problems are unresolvable." . . . So that is where I am. . . 29 years old, two kids, one disabled. . . me, Mormon Carly who expected the "happily ever after" scene. Ten-year anniversary soon. No celebration. He'll be rafting. Jan, I will be OK. Sorry such a heavy letter...

Always, Carly

Late May, 1988

I feel I am emerging from a cloud. Perhaps it's because Brian is gone for three weeks and I don't have to cope with "the decision." I go talk to a new counselor tomorrow. Can't afford to, but think I need to. I am so unsure of what I want. I don't know how I feel. But, maybe it's a step toward . . . toward something.

Josh is well today. I am so relieved. That would be the final straw, I'm afraid. I need to go percuss Josh [Carly refers to a percussion treatment that helps to keep

Joshua's lungs clear]. Back later.

Hi, again. Josh's latest word is "monkey." I guess because I call him that. I wonder if Brian and I would have worked out if he'd been "average." Oh, well, he's not and we haven't. I love you. You are a wonderful friend.

Always, Carly

P.S. I didn't even ask how you were! How are you?

June, 1988
[Carly had called me just days before this letter arrived, saying that she'd made a decision about her life. Brian was still on the rafting trip.]

. . . Well, I confronted Brian on the phone . . . my lines were well rehearsed . . . he was full of so many contradictions, my mind was spinning when we hung up . . ."I want Rachel to love me — I want to be part of her life . . ." *Nothing* about Josh's life?! I feel much less angry and more sad for the mess we've gotten ourselves into. I did say I wanted him out of this house right away. I cannot live as "house-mates" anymore. I need some reality therapy. My fantasies are replacing my anger — maybe if we took a vacation together, we'd fall in love and live happily ever after in perpetual orgasm? Then again, maybe not.

Thanks for the calls, the support, the shoulder.

Love, Carly

July, 1988

Just a note. Brian's back. We're trying yet again. We're not living together. The time alone is good for me. I never was on my own.

School [nursing school] ends tomorrow. I am glad and frightened. I use activity to keep from feeling, and now I will have a lot of time on my hands to feel. Brian was offered a job near you, teaching special education P.E. What a twist that would be! Wouldn't it be funny if that turned out to be the future? Happily married, two terrific kids, living where we've always wanted to, me with my nursing degree. Too wonderful, too hopeful to look at now. So much work to do . . .

Josh's birthday came and went. It was OK — finally — no pressure, no parties, no expectations. A victory of sorts.

Carly

October, 1988

. . . It's been so long . . . but not much has changed. Neither of us wants to file for a divorce, but neither will recommit. Without the kid factor, it would have happened long ago, I'm sure. He takes the kids every other weekend. Rachel even says, "Daddy's house" and "Mommy's house." I hate what she must perceive as "normal." Josh is doing fine.

Miss all of you there. Miss the unconditional friendships we all had in support group. Know how much you mean to me.

Carly

February, 1989

Hello, hello!

No, I didn't fall off the face of the earth. Yes, I have been busy. Graduation in May. State board exams in July. Got a job offer in Labor and Delivery at the hospital where I've been working all along!

The big D. [divorce] was final February 1st. I feel good, Jan. I am in a healthy place, finally. Calm with the kids. Broke, but peaceful.

OK, OK. His name is Matthew and he's wonderful! He loves my kids and has a very positive attitude toward Josh. He is divorced and has a son. We all get along well. He's a grownup, Jan! I am in love and so enjoying being treated like the greatest thing since sliced bread. He's even checking on some music therapy for Josh.

Brian takes the kids every other weekend. He looks so sad when I see him. I don't find love in my heart. Care and concern, but I can no longer imagine life with him. It feels good to have moved on. The kids are super. Rachel is so funny. Josh is well so far this winter. More later . . . don't give up on me . . . I promise I'll write.

March, 1989

. . . Things are still stable. Matthew's still wonderful. I wish I could write to you about all the work we're doing with Josh, but the fact is, we're coasting. We will be changing school districts for next year, and I haven't even gone to see the program. I'm told it is "the best," but . . . we've heard that before, huh? Focusing on making it to my graduation.

Josh is blossoming with Matthew, it seems. He said, "my book" to him several times as he grabbed it away. He is still so physically demanding, but so affectionate. The reality of his developmental delay becomes blatant now. In some ways, watching this relationship develop has been healing to me. I can't explain it, but Matthew's acceptance of Josh is a testimony. Maybe the world can accept my child?

Always, Carly

May, 1989
Hello friend,

Against all the odds, I made it. Boards in July and then I'll be an R.N.! Am working in Labor and Delivery, and, of course, I love it. I suppose I value life in a different way than most. Yes? I hear you answering me.

Glad to still be in a healthy *real*-ationship. Yes, it still works! I'm probably reckless loving so soon again. Oh, well. Suppose it's in my nature to walk a bit out of step.

Josh is well. People remark that his affect is changed for the better since the divorce. So much less stress. So much more acceptance. Rachel is my wonderful, awful firecracker. Can't keep up with her.

Just wanted to touch base. Let you know how much I still miss you.

Love, Carly

August, 1989

. . . had an experience this week that made me aware of a lot of unfinished business. We had a teenage babysitter scheduled to sit a few hours on Sunday. She'd sat for us before, never acted like anything was wrong or difficult. So why ask, right? Well, the night before, she called and canceled, saying that she didn't know what to do with Josh, he was too much for her to handle. More reality therapy. I had to call off work. I fell into a major funk and stayed home feeling guilty with my "handicapped" son. In effect, I became "handicapped" myself. Not even Matthew could reach me.

I moped with a headache the next day, too, just for good measure. There is so much healing left to do about Joshua. I felt angry at Brian all over again. If he couldn't accept Josh, then why should anyone else? So, this morning, I thought I'd let you hear my self-pitying, self-abusing rap. I really *am* OK, Jan. Just a case of "grieving revisited."

Matthew and I are looking seriously at April 7, 1990 as a nice day to get married. What do you think? There's this great old church and I'm having my Mom's wedding gown altered. It's over thirty years old and has a better history than my previous dress.

Josh has joined me at the table . . . guess it must be time for lunch. Rachel is hollering because "Josh is going to get my crayons!" Oy, vey. These three days off have sure been good for me...then again, maybe I'm glad I work.

Love, Carly

May, 1990
Hello, Hello my friend,

I am off this morning and am sitting on the deck of my house (I've never owned a house before) gazing down the valley. It is a good house. A strong house. A strong beginning. We married April 7. It was lovely.

[I read these words and felt great irony. April 7, 1990 was the day I moved out of my home with Bud — the day *my* marriage fell apart.]

The kids are settled in and seem adjusted. Matthew is "Daddy" as far back as Rachel's memory goes. He adores the kids and they him.

Brian has been silent for over a year. I receive cashier's checks for child support with no return address. Despite my bliss he sometimes comes to mind, sometimes in dreams. We left so many pieces undone, not even spoken. I can't imagine a life with Brian now, but I indeed had one. And it is in my psyche. Am still in therapy; I love it. Often it's tough, usually it's helpful. I am now on three 12-hour shifts a week at work. Allows me to be home more. I'm not quite used to it. In many ways, the demands of the kids are more taxing than my job. But the Mrs. Cleaver part in me needs to be home. If nothing else, so that I will write a letter, or intercede in the crises of my 3-year-old. My house is no cleaner and I haven't baked a single cookie. Oh, well. I was here to hear Rachel say, "I scared when Daddy [meaning Matthew] goes to work. He won't go away, will he?" Just when I think the wounds of divorce have been spared my children . . . she can't remember Brian or pick his picture out, but in her little soul he left an impression.

Yes, it's possible already . . . I might be pregnant. Go to the doctor in two weeks. Sometimes I think God's a stand-up comedian. So much so quickly. In two years I have graduated from nursing school, divorced, fallen in love, remarried, and now, I might have a Christmas baby. Matthew is overjoyed; old wounds promised of healing. I am relaxed, perhaps I need healing, too.

It's so foreign to be with a man who loves children and fatherhood. He gets the kids up and fed and off to school every morning I work. If I work nights, he picks them up from daycare so I can sleep "a few minutes longer." In some ways his psyche has more room for Rachel and Josh than mine does. He and Josh go to baseball practice for Joey [Matthew's son] and to the hardware store. Rachel often goes along, but her favorite is to go to the office or the park for a picnic. The pressure is off. No more being Super Mom! I can be an OK mom who some days can be a great June Cleaver. Matthew's not always perfect; he runs low on energy, too. But I know that usually at least one of us is in an energetic space. We have talked adoption and if Brian quits sending child support, we will pursue it. But right now we are saving the checks for college or a group home or whatever. It's almost like I stepped out of one life and into another. No — I worked damn hard to *break out* of one life.

Josh is good. He's had a tough spring with asthma, too much rain and mildew. But we have a doctor who is aggressive. He listens to me and doesn't stereotype. So Josh has a breathing machine that really seems to be helping. Rachel is busy, bossy, talkative, loving, happy, crisis-oriented, exasperating and demanding. Three years old, I guess.

I am good. We travel to another state this week for a job interview for Matthew; I am divided. I think the fresh start could be good, but I do like living an hour and a half away from mom. I like the comfort of my job, the kids' schools. We will have to go and check out schools and programs. I suppose if the pay were terrific, we would think harder. We'll see. Brian's parents live so close to us; it may be healthier to be gone. Have heard some positive things about the special education programs there. I can be employed anywhere. This area is notorious for crappy schools. We are fortunate to have Josh in a private school now, but it only goes to 11 years old. . . . Oh well, I will wait. If it's to be, it will be irresistible!

I'm doing my first constructive thing for special kids tomorrow. Am sitting on a parent panel that is addressing the need for qualified daycare for special kids. My kids' daycare is the only one in the area designed for both kids with disabilities and their siblings.

I love you and think of you often. If you're ever this way — even half way — let me know. I would love to see you.

Love always, Carly

June, 1990
My dear friend,

I am indeed saddened to hear of your separation and divorce. I understand your silence. I too was confused and angry and afraid to tell people when Brian and I separated. I hurt for you, Jan. I know the months ahead will be rough. But look at me now! You wrote this to me when I moved away:

"Sail on silver girl
Sail on by—
Your time has come to shine..."
"Bridge Over Troubled Water"
Simon & Garfunkel

Appropriate to you I think. We're survivors. You're bright and talented. The world is waiting for you.

I do know that kids are resilient. I am glad I had them to buffer the loss of the marriage. At least they were something good amongst the bitterness divorce becomes. And, food for thought: When you're on your feet, remember that Reeboks and designer jeans do not make one home a better place for kids, even if they can have more things there.

Subject change. Yes! Please use whatever you want for your book. I can't believe that 1) you saved all that stuff, and 2) that you want to publish it, but do — if it is helpful to anyone — write, write, write!

You are my inspiration — on the front lines for people with disabilities. I am only now having to deal with people being rude and staring because Josh is so obviously disabled. No more carrying him through the mall and pretending. Did I tell you we ordered his first wheelchair — $2000. Hopefully, insurance will pay for it. He needs one. My (and Matthew's) back needs one, too. Josh will be able to go more places, not restricted by his very limited walking ability. He also has a new walker ordered and his legs will probably be casted and braced this summer. All of which adds to the stress of moving out of state and a new baby due December 24th!

There seem to be good programs for Josh where we are going. Apparently, when the Homeward Bound folks here (a group which fought for and succeeded in closing the state institution) wanted experts to testify, they came from the university there. There was a speaker here 2 months ago from that university discussing rights for people who have developmental disabilities. Anyway, it must be better there than it is here! I'm half excited and half scared. Too many changes too soon: marriage, pregnancy, and a move in 3 months. Think my stress factors are high? Surprisingly, I don't feel stressed out. I think we'll be OK wherever we are led. My mom was disappointed, but has since decided it'll be a good place to visit. I think it'll be a good decision, eventually.

Take care of yourself, my friend.

Love, Carly

Late June, 1990

Hello Jan,

Can you believe it? Two letters in 6 months? Got a call from a friend back there this weekend. Made me miss everyone, so many bittersweet memories. Have been in a funk ever since.

Josh's creeping up on 7 years — July. Here I am brooding pre-birthday. Maybe I'll get it out of my system. Been a long time since I've been deeply saddened by his disabilities. Just when you think it's all behind you . . .

I miss my friends who shared the beginnings. I don't have the energy to get re-involved in a group of parents like us. I just want the old groupies who already know the stories.

I suppose this funk all started with my going to my step-son's little league baseball game. [Parents often speak of being reminded just how much their children are missing when they witness "average" kids doing everyday things.] Matthew tries to understand, but he doesn't have the biology or the history. That's good for Josh. He loves him as he is. He hears only that Josh (medically) shouldn't have lived at all, and to that he says "you had a miracle." I suppose he's right, but I'm grieving it all anyway. Must be my condition . . .

I admire your activism for kids like mine. Perhaps if I got mad enough to fight, the grief would leave. Nah, it lies dormant waiting for a trigger . . .

Other than my rainy mood, things are great here. Am well, the crew is happy! Matthew is wonderful! Maybe I'll go strum a note or two. Haven't played my guitar in over 6 months. Love you always.

Your friend, Carly

July, 1990

My dear friend,

And so another chapter closes — I just found out that Brian was killed in a rafting accident. I am devastated. The anger, hurt, disappointment, and frustration are gone. His family and I have made amends. They desperately need Josh and Rachel now. In lieu of flowers, they had donations sent to the Little Lighthouse (Josh's school); the gifts have been substantial.

It seems that from the hell of our divorce emerged the man I knew was there. Apparently he "found" himself and a niche and became at peace. He was working in a school for kids with severe disabilities. He apparently loved it and was terrific. Perhaps he never could come to terms with bearing a child of his own, but was able to transform his pain into action. He was engaged to be married and quite happy. I feel released. My only sadness is that 1) it couldn't be us, and 2) we never resolved our anger with each other. He died without us ever being kind or civil to each other as human beings.

Matthew has been terrific and supportive, of course. I can't imagine life without him. So we move on. To a new life without the bitterness and fear. The kids can have both names and have their grandparents back. Matthew wants to adopt them officially as soon as Brian's estate is settled. Perhaps, in his death, he will provide for them as he never would have done living. Such a turn of life.

I am grieving, Jan. When the anger was lifted I realized I still loved him and cared about him. I didn't want to be his wife, I didn't even like him most of the time, but for some reason, I did love him. I feel a loss, if nothing else he was a formidable enemy. So in the darkness and aloneness I weep, appropriate or not. I am mortal and may not sleep with anger in my heart again. Perhaps that lesson is left for those of us who survive.

God speed, my friend. I hope you are well.

Always. Love, Carly.

November, 1990
Hello friend,

The kids are both asleep — home with strep throat — I'm sipping a cup of raspberry tea and relishing the quiet. The wind is blowing, it's gray, and looks like snow's on the way. Thanksgiving is two days away and I don't feel hurried to make a feast. It'll be only "us." Feels wonderful.

I am savoring my part-time work status. At last, I feel rested. I'm not quite sure what I do with all my extra time. Perhaps the laundry is closer to being caught up, or the house a little neater, but I haven't found that I want to be obsessed with the house. It's trashed in 10 minutes, anyway. Haven't made homemade cookies except for once, and am not doing any crafts. Not being a Super Mom, no whirlwind adventure days with the kids. I'm happiest when they're off playing together and I'm sitting quietly, not doing much of anything. I suppose it's the freedom of grabbing lunch with Matthew, of thrift shop hopping, making appointments for the kids that don't have to be juggled around a full workday, and having the time to write a letter. This is a luxury I have never known.

I enjoy work, but it doesn't interfere with my *life*! We have less money but Rachel is home more. I'm not sure if that's better yet. She goes to preschool two times a week, and in some ways she's easier to deal with for only a few hours at a time. Now, I am weary of her questions by 1:00 p.m. I don't think I'm really that much more available to her, just present more in her life. I still use Sesame Street to babysit and have all my other bad habits. If anything, I am tougher on her now as she becomes more demanding (like any four-year-old).

Josh is blossoming. Well, perhaps that's an overstatement. He is still classified "severely/profoundly mentally retarded" for IEP purposes, but his spirit is so *alive*. He is so interactive, has minimal autistic behavior. Maybe I'm the one who's changed; my expectations of him are clearer. I can see him being productive in a small way. Matthew's dream of a working farm/ranch for people with disabilities may need to materialize. Do you know of any? Would like to find out how one starts up such an endeavor.

Today I said, "Josh, you are going to need a bath," just in passing him to go take my shower. A few minutes later, he's in the tub, fully dressed of course, but filling it up with water and laughing. Seems like such a simple task, but to me it says, "I *do* understand." He may not motorically be able to follow through on everything, but I *know* the understanding is there.

I've been having a hard time writing to you. I started several letters, mailed one that was returned (did you move again?) I've been waiting to find the right mood. I think it's hard for me because I want to give advice from a divorce survivor, but know how feeble it really sounds. I likened my divorce to my being told that Josh would die — so full of conflicting messages and feelings. The loss of the dream, the sense of "family," promises broken, and now, new hope for the future with Matthew. I was so angry. Then Brian died. I am still struggling with that. Not that we could have made it as a couple. I think he had a good ten years of maturing to do and I needed a mate and father for my kids — *now*. He and I never really resolved anything. I guess if we could have, we wouldn't have divorced. But how I wish that we could sit down and talk, hug, and say, "Once I loved you very much — perhaps too much — but we are incompatible life partners."

How nice it would be to have left the manure slinging and blame aside. From my friends who have divorced, I learn that day does often come, but it's years after the judge pounds his gavel. I am glad you are being reinforced and validated by your friends and a special male companion. It is so exciting and so scary — "You mean someone loves me for *me*? Stretch marks, crowsfeet, special needs child and all?"

I am reserved about this baby. Actually, I feel guilty for not being more excited. I suppose, somewhere deep down, I am worried about its health (of course), but mostly about its place in this family. It'll have to fight for a spot. Do I have the energy and love for another? I adore Rachel — can I give up her throne? How fair is this to

Josh and Rachel, to bring another in? I'm also afraid of labor. I know it's true I work with women in labor all the time, but now it's *me*. This child is a "maturing" child — making me re-examine my basic values. I also know the work ahead . . . Oy vey! Sometimes I wonder if we should have been more careful. Just last minute jitters I'm sure; am due 12/24. Could be any time!

I love you and hope you have a good Thanksgiving. Write when you can, but I truly understand when you can't. My prayers for strength and courage.

Love, Carly

January, 1991

Thanks for the postcard. Hope things are settling down — such a difficult time to endure.

Our waiting is over, and Mark is beautiful. The birth was vaginal. Complicated, of course, but an experience Matthew and I will both treasure. I've had a houseful of company until today, so I suppose I'm just now having time to feel the blues. Seems we waited and planned life by this event. I was tired of being pregnant and am glad to be done, but still sad. I don't remember this with the other two. Perhaps I didn't allow myself to feel it then. There is that sense of mystery and importance when you are pregnant. People talk to you and joke — your identity changes for that time — then you're delivered. Now, I'm just overweight and busy and tired. I need to restructure my ego. I am glad for my part-time job. I think it will help me gain control of Carly, the non-pregnant person. I don't feel totally depressed, but a little blue.

The kids, so far, are all doing good with the new member of the family. We are trying to find a routine we can all live with. Matthew's back at his job — he went back the day after I came home. Seems strange to share such an intimate, life-changing event, and then go back to regular life. I suppose I feel abandoned. I hope my energy level improves quickly. Rachel and Josh have been on auto-pilot for weeks now.

This was supposed to be a birth announcement! Full of cheer and excitement. I think they should be written at the hospital when life is still so euphoric and people offer you back rubs!

I love you and am keeping you in my thoughts and prayers. The date of my divorce still burns in my heart. It will soon be two years — since then, he's died, and I've remarried and had a baby. Life is full of so many tricks and turns!

Love you, Carly

February, 1991
My dear friend,

Thanks so much for the packet of materials. [I had sent Carly *Common Ground*, a collection of essays for parents and professionals who unite to serve the needs of young children with special needs.] I like your business card! You have taken the pain of our kids and made it not only constructive and helpful, but healing. Sounds like a miracle to me. I dare say you will do the same (when the wounds scab over) to help those divorcing and divorced. Your gift of word and pen is a blessing to me.

Matthew and I were pondering an interesting idea. We wondered if perhaps the deep, deep wounds of having children with disabilities or children who die, are simply too buried. Although parents intellectually may not blame each other, perhaps at an imperceptible level, we do. I know many second marriages that function so differently regarding the kids. Matthew said something about how these situations [having a child with a disability] produce shame. He feels that guilt harbored toward oneself *is* shame. Unwarranted, but nonetheless shame. I'm not sure. This is a whole new theory on shame to me. It's a little foreign. Thought I'd bounce it off of you. Then again, maybe we simply choose differently the second time, and that is the reason for harmony.

Mark has disrupted *our* harmony as all newborns do. I'm glad I've been here before. Matthew is thrilled with him, but is feeling jealous and left out. At least he's mature enough to verbalize it. So many changes.

I'm excited to hear that your travels will be bringing you so nearby. We can have a cup of coffee and hug and laugh and cry. I start back to work this Saturday, but I'm sure someone will trade shifts with me if it conflicts. I remember newly divorced finances, let me know. OK? OK! I am really excited about it. Even if all you do is brood and pout, I can *see* you! We can be present with each other.

Love you, Carly

July, 1991
Hi Jan,

How's it going. You've been silent; that means that things are either terrific or very difficult. How's David? [David is the "Matthew" in my life.] The girls? We're in a new house. I love it. It's really my first house. Matthew had owned the last one, but this is one we picked out for our family.

Kids are good. Rachel's been crossing her eyes so we got some glasses for her. I hate them. She picked out cute, expensive frames but I don't like seeing *my* daughter in glasses. I'm trying to keep those feelings to myself and so far she is positive about her glasses. I suppose it's an old wound of mine — I got specs at 13. I know I need to come to terms with it. When we first picked them up she asked me, "Will I still be pretty?" Out of the mouths of babes! I, of course, said, "Yes," but in my heart . . .

Josh is good. Summer school here is a farce — I'm disappointed. He'll be out next week. They have a day camp in town, but I've heard so many bad things about it that he's not going. Oh, well! Baby is super, 6 1/2 months and all develops well. Been working too much, but then will be off for 10 days and I'm going to Mom's. Love you.

Take care, Carly

September, 1991
Hello Jan!

Been thinking about you so much lately! How are you? David? Am debating whether to study, clean house, make a dessert for our parent meeting tonight, go garage sale-ing or write you. All the other options seemed so demanding! Have gotten a group of parents of kids like ours together! We're meeting bimonthly.

Josh is now in Cub Scouts (with other boys with varying disabilities). Not sure yet if it's for him or me. Want to take him horseback riding and start him in swimming lessons, too, but can't quite swing the time yet. I know he'll love that!

Rachel's good. Always my challenge. Can't imagine four girls to challenge the feminine spirit! She started wearing glasses for a lazy eye. Trauma for me — she's fine. Can't believe I would equate her "being" with my self-worth. Thought I gave that up with Josh. Also, can't believe how shallow I can be — to value looks over person or health. Girls certainly force a woman to examine her definition of female and feminine.

Mark's great! He weaned this week — his idea. I'm bittersweet. I love the freedom, but feel rejected.

I am taking two night classes, Chemistry and Ethics. Going to put some more letters behind my name. This is causing some internal conflict over the good mother/student/employee/wife business. I read a wonderful statement: "We only have to be 'good enough' parents. Not Super Moms!"

Miss you, wonder how it's going. Are you planning any trips our way? Love always...

God speed, Carly

P.S. Matthew is, as always, wonderful.

November, 1991

Hello dear friend,

How goes the battle? It's snowing today. I love it. An excuse to stay in, cancel appointments, and rock the baby. Mark is now 11 months old. He is taking steps and jabbers up a storm. I can't help but worry about him. Seems the Denver Developmental [yet another assessment test] is so ingrained in my being that if one step seems to "lag a day or two" I can't let it go. Rachel was so quick — 9 months to walk and say words. Mark has the sounds, but no words yet. He's happy and easy going. I, of course, want him to be waving bye-bye, shaking his head no-no, saying "mama," "kitty," "dadda," and "baby." Those damn milestones — Matthew just laughs. I know there is a large span of normality, but that is in my head, not in my always vigilant, wounded heart. Matthew is a wonderful father, but he does not know the pain of those early years. He can't. He can hear it and have empathy, but that memory's journey is now only mine.

So Mark is fine. Developing at his own pace and keeping me in mine. He is a charmer and a delight, always into something. Like most third-born children, he points and grunts, and Rachel gets! I have heard this story before!

Rachel's good; she keeps me off balance when Mark doesn't. I swear they work in shifts. She's got a million and one questions. She's enjoying preschool and dance. I'm glad she can have those kinds of activities.

Josh is healthy. We have a loving, conscientious teacher, so he will have another good year.

Did I tell you I got a parent's support group moving here? It's going — slow, but going. Have made some good contacts and feel it's a cause I am willing to put some effort into.

This semester is almost over and it looks like I'll make out with good scores. I guess the time away from the kids is worth it. Who knows? I'm sure some day only their therapist will know!

So how's your love life? The girls? The official adoption went through. We had a house-blessing and family-blessing party. It felt complete. The kids have enormously long names, but what the hey!

Matthew is good, busy at work. I work just 4 shifts every 2 weeks, so we can have more time together. He is fun to be married to. I suppose I thought we'd live happily ever after without any strife, but we fight and fuss sometimes. It's different though because deep down I have the feeling that we'll be OK, no matter what.

Well, suppose I should get doing something, like studying or cleaning, but I think I might choose napping! I think of you often and hope we can stay up until 4:00 a.m. again soon.

[I was traveling for work in February of 1991, close enough to rent a car and make a long drive that would allow me to see Carly, if only for a few hours. We did just what you might expect. We asked Matthew — he really *is* as wonderful as she says! — to take the kids. Then we proceeded to talk non-stop for about eight hours. Only total exhaustion kept us from going on. It was fantastic!]

Am sending your Christmas card now, because you know me — it'll be January if I don't!

Love always, Carly

Epilogue

Jan Spiegle

February 14, 1992

The Civil Rights movement in the United States progressed from the actions of one tired and courageous black lady, Rosa Parks, who refused to move to the back of the bus, to legislation which mandated the acceptance of equality and cultural diversity in this nation.

Led by visionary parents, professionals, legislators and persons who themselves have special life challenges, the movement toward full integration of persons with disabilities is happening. The laws, including the Americans with Disabilities Act and the Individuals with Disabilities Education Act, are, for the most part, in place. As with the Civil Rights movement, the attitudinal changes are slower to occur and seem to evolve over time, even, perhaps, over generations. Yet, day by day (as my friend, Virginia, says "one bite at a time,"), and on a national scope, constructive changes are occurring in the way society views the rights and the potential of people with disabilities.

I am impatient. Since 9:15 a.m. on March 31, 1983 — the moment that I was told that my daughter had the genetic anomaly known as Down syndrome — I have wanted the rest of the world to view her through my eyes, to see her simply as the wonderfully complete human being she is in her own right. *Changes* has grown to completion out of that basic maternal desire. To credit the book's completion to any other motive would be less than honest. So, for all people with disabilities (and, of course, for Sara), may those who read *Changes* learn a little, grow a lot, and make positive change happen all around them.

Where to Get More Information. . .

A national reference list of agencies who provide patient/family oriented publications on a wide variety of disabilities and diseases is available free of charge from:

> The Division of Educational Research and Service
> School of Education
> The University of Montana
> Missoula, Montana 59812
> (406) 243-5344

APPENDIX 1

Topical Index

This index will provide university course instructors and family support group members and leaders with a listing of stories from *Changes* which are appropriate and helpful reading for 12 specific topical issues. When grouped by focus area, the readings are useful as the basis for class or group discussion and for many other applications such as the reflective writing assignments detailed in the Instructor's Guide, Appendix 2. Topical issues are underlined with a list of related readings following each.

<u>The power of positive thinking</u>
"Insisting on the Positive Possibility"
"Let Her Do It"
"Hope and the Ability to Dream"
"Twenty-Eight Years Later"
"Letter to a Friend"
"The Birthday Invitation"
"Skyriding"
"To Know Them as People"
"Kids and Labels"
"Happily Ever After?"
"Decisions and Objectivity"
"Daddy, Phone's Busy"
"From a Classroom Teacher's Perspective"

<u>Perspectives from people who have disabilities</u>
"Hope and the Ability to Dream"
"Twenty-Eight Years Later"
"Conversation with Lisa & Virginia Deland"

<u>Fathers' perspectives</u>
"Daddy, Phone's Busy"
"Isn't Testosterone Wonderful?"
"Happily Ever After?"

<u>Mothers' perspectives</u>
"Prologue"
"Insisting on the Positive Possibility"
"Letter to a Friend"
"Untold Diagnosis"
"It's OK Because She's Sara"
"The Birthday Invitation"
"Dispensing More Than Drugs"
"One Bite at a Time"
"The Decision for Out-of-Home Placement"
"An Eye in the Storm"
"Are You Super Mom, or What?"
"Happily Ever After?"
"Skyriding"
"And the Winner of the Rainbow Lottery is..."
"Epilogue"

<u>Siblings' perspectives</u>
"Let Her Do It"
"Sara's Lamp"
"Sister of the Heart"
"Dear Mom and Dad"
"From a Sibling and Physical Therapist's Perspective"

<u>Impact of diagnosis/disability</u>
"Foreword"
"Insisting on the Positive Possibility"
"Let Her Do It"
"Letter to a Friend"
"It's OK Because She's Sara"
"Daddy, Phone's Busy"
"One Bite at a Time"

"An Eye in the Storm"
"To Know Them as People"
"Through the Door"
"With Respect and Thoughtfulness"
"From a Sibling and Physical Therapist's Perspective"
"On Miranda"
"Happily Ever After"
"Feelings in a Manila Folder"
"Decisions and Objectivity"
"And the Winner of the Rainbow Lottery is..."
"From Provider to Consumer: An Involuntary Transition"
"Halloween and Hamburgers"
"Epilogue"

Impact of no diagnosis or "late" diagnosis
"Untold Diagnosis"
"Isn't Testosterone Wonderful?"
"Dispensing More Than Drugs"
"The Decision for Out-of-Home Placement"
"To Know Them as People"
"Pharmacists Helping Families: An Unique and Untapped Resource"

The necessity of respite care
"Respite Care, A Most Necessary Choice"
"The Decision for Out-of-Home Placement"
"It's OK, Because She's Sara"
"Happily Ever After?"

Full inclusion/integration in least restrictive classrooms
"Preface"
"The Birthday Invitation"
"An Eye in the Storm"
"Kids and Labels"
"From a Classroom Teacher's Perspective"
"Happily Ever After?"

Life transitions and fears of risk
"Insisting on the Positive Possibility"
"Twenty-Eight Years Later"
"Let Her Do It"
"The Birthday Invitation"
"Conversation with Lisa & Virginia Deland"
"One Bite at a Time"
"The Decision for Out-of-Home Placement"
"From a Classroom Teacher's Perspective"
"From Provider to Consumer: An Involuntary Transition"
"Happily Ever After?"

Professionals and families in partnership — advice from people in the trenches
"Twenty-Eight Years Later"
"Letter to a Friend"
"Pharmacists Helping Families: An Unique and Untapped Resource"
"One Bite at a Time"
"Respite Care, A Most Necessary Choice"
"An Eye in the Storm"
"To Know Them as People"
"Decisions and Objectivity"
"From A Classroom Teacher's Perspective"
"From Provider to Consumer: An Involuntary Transition"
"Are you Super Mom or What?"
"Happily Ever After?"

Personal impact on professionals
"Foreword"
"Respite Care, A Most Necessary Choice"
"On Miranda"
"To Know Them as People"
"Through the Door"
"Kids and Labels"
"Feelings in a Manila Folder"
"From Provider to Consumer: An Involuntary Transition"
"Halloween and Hamburgers"
"Epilogue"

APPENDIX 2

Instructor's Guide

During the summer of 1991, selected readings from *Changes* formed the foundation for an undergraduate/graduate class in education at The University of Montana entitled "Families and Disability: Diverse Strategies for Growth." The response from the students using *Changes* as a textbook was overwhelmingly positive. In anonymous evaluations completed as the class ended, students spoke of its value as a teaching/learning resource for anyone preparing for a profession in human service delivery. We hope that the university students who read *Changes* will find it, as one student put it, "an assignment in life."

The following discussion questions and writing assignment suggestions are grouped around the subject areas found in the Topical Index. We believe that they will be of value to instructors who choose to use *Changes* as the main or supplemental text for preparatory classes in social work, education, psychology, medicine, nursing, sociology and other human service occupation areas.

Topical area — The power of positive thinking

Discussion Questions

1. What common themes emerge from the readings grouped under this heading?
2. What concerns and fears do parents/guardians exhibit about allowing children with disabilities to take the risks common to the "average" person's life experience? For example, starting preschool, moving to a new town, or going off to college.
3. What feelings seem common to people with disabilities when confronted with life's normal events and transitions? For example, taking a vacation, moving away from parents, starting a new job.
4. Why do medical and educational professionals often feel it is their duty to inform families of the worst case scenario or prognosis? Is it? How might such professionals make telling such information "easier" on families?
5. How do attitudinal differences among professionals have an effect on people with disabilities and their families? For example, what might have happened differently with Jon had Mary Pielaet not pushed for a diagnosis?

Reflective Writing Assignment

In terms of family impact, discuss negativism, positivism, in the light of one of the following quotations:

Don't walk away from negative people. Run! — *Anonymous*

Most people live, whether physically, intellectually, or morally, in a very restricted circle of their potential being. They make use of a very small portion of their consciousness, and of their soul's resources in general, much like a man who, out of his whole bodily organism, should get into the habit of using and moving only his little finger. Great emergencies and crises show us how much greater our vital resources are than we had supposed. — *William James*

If he could speak to us he would say, "Love me with smiles and laughter...if you can only love me with tears, do not bother to love me at all." — *T. DeVries in the book* The Story of Jan

We are wide-eyed in contemplating the possibility that life may exist elsewhere in the universe, but we wear blinders when contemplating the possibilities of life on earth. — *Norman Cousins*

People are always blaming their circumstances for what they are. I don't believe in circumstances. The people who get on in this world are the people who get up and look for the circumstances they want, and if they can't find them, they make them. — *George Bernard Shaw*

He who has a "why" to live can bear almost any "how." — *Nietzsche*

You gain strength, courage, and confidence by every experience in which you really stop to look fear in the face . . . you must do the thing you think you cannot do. — *Eleanor Roosevelt*

Healing is a matter of time, but it is sometimes also a matter of seizing opportunity. — *Hippocrates*

Topical area — Perspectives from people with disabilities

Discussion Questions

1. Besides the fact that they have a disability, what do Bruce Blattner, Martha Hansen, and Lisa DeLand have in common?

2. Martha Hansen speaks of trying to be "the affirming strength" to her students that her family was/is to her. What does she mean? How can professionals be an affirming strength in the life of a person with disabilities?

3. How did the death of Bruce Blattner's good friend Jon Paul become an affirming strength in his life?

4. Bruce Blattner and Lisa DeLand discuss sexuality in different ways within their manuscripts. Are there common threads? Do you generally view people with disabilities as asexual? How do societal attitudes foster that viewpoint?

Reflective Writing Assignment

Define "affirmation" and discuss it in terms of what it (or the lack of it) means to people with disabilities and their families.

Topical area — Fathers' perspectives

Discussion Questions

1. "I was just looking for an end to something that seemed impossible for my family to face," Bud Mariska says of his initial response to a professional's comment that his daughter, Sara, wouldn't live very long. In terms of the grieving process common to all people experiencing a significant loss, how is this comment relevant?

2. From outside research or personal knowledge, discuss the financial impact of having a child with a disability in America today. Discuss why this particular impact is one which research indicates is most stressful on fathers.

3. How might it be that a person or family dealing with disability might have the "rare ability to focus on the really important things in life" better than the average person on the street. (Bud Mariska says this about his daughter Sara.)

4. How did Fred McGlynn become an affirming strength for his family as they dealt with Sean's problems?

5. Discuss the "medical technology blindness syndrome" (as described by Fred McGlynn in "Isn't Testosterone Wonderful?") and its effects on families searching for a diagnosis.

6. Discuss the ways that Brian's ("Happily Ever After?") response to having a child with a disability affected his family. Also, focus on the positive affirmation that Brian was able to finally create for himself concerning this issue.

Reflective Writing Assignment

Research and discuss the special reactions, needs, and concerns of fathers of children with disabilities.

Topical area — Mothers' perspectives

Discussion Questions

1. After reading the mothers' perspectives in *Changes*, discuss whether you believe the grieving process for parents of children with disabilities is cyclical or finite.

2. Describe common maternal responses to having a child with a disability. Translated to behavioral terms, how might these responses have both positive and negative effects on

family functioning, health, and stability?

3. What does it mean when professionals, speaking of the mother of a child with a disability, say "She's come to acceptance"? Is there a difference between acceptance and resignation?

Reflective Writing Assignment

Research the impact of raising a child with disabilities on mothers. What reactions, needs, and concerns seem to be specific to moms?

Topical area — Siblings' perspectives

Discussion Questions

1. David Hansen speaks of his experiences as a sibling of a sister with disabilities making him more introspective. What evidence is there in the writings of Sara Wilson, Jamie Mariska, Joel McGlynn, and Elizabeth Couch that this impact may be a common experience among siblings?
2. Discuss the impact of being a sibling in "real world" examples. What might a sibling face that would be different from the average kid? Give both negative and positive examples of situations and outcomes which might occur.
3. David Hansen and Elizabeth Couch both wrote from the perspective of adults looking back on their experiences as young siblings. Discuss commonalities and differences in their experiences and in the ways that their families handled their life situations.
4. Discuss the ambivalence which comes through in Joel McGlynn's letter to his mom and dad and in Sara Wilson's piece on Sammi. Do you think that this ambivalence is a healthy/normal reaction to having *any* sibling? To having a sibling with a disability?
5. Identify and discuss what you consider to be some special reactions, needs, and concerns of siblings of children with disabilities.

Reflective Writing Assignment

Discuss how growing up as a sibling of a child with a disability might be a "terrible, wonderful experience."

Topical area — Impact of diagnosis

Discussion Questions

1. Discuss how a diagnosis of permanent disability might affect the person involved. Discuss how it might affect the family. Identify and discuss common family reactions, feelings, and healing mechanisms.

2. From the readings, identify how it is that unforeseen events may have the power to trigger the grieving process in family members even years after the fact of the diagnosis.
3. Read "On Miranda" again or read it out loud to someone. What does the poem reveal about the impact a child's diagnosis may have on even casual friends of the family?
4. "Feelings in a Manila Folder" and "Through the Door" discuss the issue of "acceptance" in a different light . . . from the perspective of the professional. Is acceptance an issue for professionals, too? How might a professional have to come to terms with the limitations and/or complications imposed by a person's disability? Discuss concrete examples.
5. How might the impact of an acquired disability like Bruce Blattner's or John Freeman's be different than the impact of a disability that a person is born with?
6. Discuss the impact of the decision a mother/family might make to become pregnant again subsequent to the experience of parenting a child with a disability, especially when the disability is one known to be genetic in origin.
7. What might be some special concerns for a single parent raising a child with a disability?
8. What does Sue Wilson mean when she says that her family chose not to accept the neurologist's prognosis (*not* diagnosis) for Sammi's condition? What's the difference? Discuss the impact of a "gloom and doom" prognosis on a family. Is there a time when it is important for a professional to give the worst case scenario to a family? Under what circumstances?
9. What might be some special concerns for adoptive parents raising a child with a disability? How might their responses to disability and their needs and concerns differ from those of birth parents?

Reflective Writing Assignment

If you had to be told that you or a family member had a permanent disability, how would you want the news delivered? Set the scene. Write the script.

Topical area — The impact of no diagnosis or late diagnosis

Discussion Questions

1. What problems are common to parents/families who are unable, for some reason, to obtain an accurate diagnosis in a timely manner for their child?
2. How might ancillary health care professionals (such as pharmacist Byron Dodd and the physical therapist who worked with Jon Pielaet) facilitate a family's search for accurate diagnosis and/or treatment?
3. Sue Wilson says in "Letter to a Friend" that the "if onlys" will make you crazy, but for the sake of discussion, consider what might have been different for Austin Baker and his family "if only" they'd had an early and accurate diagnosis.

4. An underlying theme that seems to surface in these readings is the claim by families that professionals often fail to hear or place credence in their observational information. Why should all professionals be active listeners? How might "professionalism" sometimes get in the way of this happening?

5. Do people with disabilities and their families have a right to know all the possibilities being explored when a diagnosis is uncertain?

Reflective Writing Assignment

Discuss Sue Wilson's statement that, "The neurologist was so afraid of giving us false hope that he left us no hope at all." Compare and contrast Sue's experience with that of Mary Pielaet in "Untold Diagnosis."

Topical area — The necessity of respite care

Discussion Questions

1. Families of children without disabilities probably wish they had respite care available to them. Is it so much more important for families of children with disabilities?

2. Tim and Tane Walmsley describe their experiences as respite care providers for Austin. How did their experiences change their perceptions of parenting a child with a disability? How is being a respite care provider or parent different from being a teacher or health care professional? Which perspective provides a more holistic view of disability?

3. How might Delanie Baker's life and that of her family been different if she'd been able to acquire respite care services from the time Austin was very young?

Reflective Writing

Write a dialogue between a health care provider or teacher and a mother who literally does not leave her child's side because the child has life-threatening, chronic health problems. Through the dialogue's progress, gently impress upon the mother the reasons why "taking a break" is so important. Find out the reasons why it is so hard for this mom to leave her child. Find out how you can help.

Topical area — Full inclusion/integration in least restrictive classrooms

Discussion Questions

1. Why do parents and people with disabilities believe that full inclusion in society is so important?

2. "They need to be there, if for no other reason than to teach the rest of them humility." What is the point of this comment from Catherine Schuck, a teacher in an integrated classroom? What might inclusion of children with disabilities teach the other kids besides humility?

3. What benefits might occur to children with disabilities in a fully integrated school? What disadvantages might occur?

4. Full inclusion for people with disabilities has now become federal law under several acts. As a professional, how will you respond to the prejudice that still exists attitudinally? For example, what will you do as a teacher if your building principal directs you to keep a student who uses a wheelchair off the playground because "the child may be hurt, and the school could get sued, and the chair is a safety hazard for the other children . . ."

Reflective Writing Assignment

Assume that the child in question #4 above has no ability to communicate orally to the building principal. Speak for her. Tell the principal why you need to be on the playground and why the other children need you there.

Topical area — Life transitions and fears of risk

Discussion Questions

1. Discuss the dignity of risk (and failure) as it pertains to any human being.

2. How might overprotective feelings toward people with disabilities be counterproductive for a professional to hold?

3. In "From Provider to Consumer: An Involuntary Transition" Rick van den Pol speaks of looking for nursing home placements as his father pursues singles volleyball. Does each attitude seem to serve a purpose? Was Nic wrong to deny the inevitable? Was Rick wrong to investigate the options? Discuss how family members might respond differently to any given situation.

4. Rick van den Pol speaks of "following the prescription of a different expert." What does he mean?

5. Bruce Blattner and Martha Hansen have achieved more than many of us with able bodies. Identify the risks which they and their families took to make those things happen.

Reflective Writing Assignment

Discuss a risk that you or someone close to you took that seemed doomed to fail from an outsider's perspective. Even if the venture did end in failure in some way, describe why it was still important to take the risk.

Topical area — Professionals and families in partnership

Discussion Questions

1. Based on the readings, discuss how an unaccepting or prejudicial professional attitude toward a child with a disability can hinder effective service delivery.

2. A family has reacted to your professional advice concerning their child with challenges and noncompliance with your recommendations. How will you respond?

3. A professional has told a family that their son's accident will "likely" leave him with quadriplegia. You are the hospital's social worker and the first person to talk to the family after the diagnosis is given. Discuss what you will say and do.

4. The school's principal calls you at work to say that your son has been cruelly teasing a child with Down syndrome who is in his first grade class. Today at recess he talked her into "mooning" the other kids on the playground and they both got in trouble. You are a professional who works with people with disabilities daily. You talk about your work with your son. You thought your son had an accepting attitude toward people with disabilities. How will you handle this situation?

5. You are a classroom teacher. A child with cerebral palsy who uses a wheelchair is in your class this fall. Just after school starts, several parents of the other children call you to complain that they are worried that their children will get less attention because you'll spend all your time with the child with a disability. How will you respond?

6. Rick van den Pol says that "experts and consumers may be one and the same individual." What does he mean?

7. Define and discuss "professionalism."

8. Research completed in collaboration with families of children with disabilities indicates that there are several basic qualities which a family / professional relationship must have in order for it to "work" for the family. The top three qualities which families identified as essential are mutual respect, trust in the professional's commitment to their child, and honesty. Discuss what actions a professional might take in his/her initial contact with a family which would lay the foundation for the development of these qualities. Discuss what ongoing actions a professional might take to ensure that those interpersonal relationship qualities remain intact.

Reflective Writing Assignment

Identify and provide a rationale for each of your personal "Ten Commandments for Working with People with Disabilities and their Families," *or* identify and discuss at least ten strategies through which families may empower themselves to form effective alliances with education and medical professionals.

Topical area — Personal impact on professionals

Discussion Questions

1. There are very high turnover rates for almost all professionals in the human service field — special education teachers, social workers, etc. Many families will tell you that "the good ones don't last very long." Why might that be the case? How can a professional avoid "burnout" without compromising quality of service to the people he or she assists?

2. Discuss Rick van den Pol's change in perspective as he went "from provider to consumer." How might his personal experiences affect his job performance as the director of several programs serving young children with disabilities and their families?

3. Though people with disabilities are healthier and living longer than ever before because of medical advances, if you work for any length of time with this group of people, you will likely face the death of one or more of them. A physical therapist once told me that she expected to lose about one of the people she works with each year; that is how it has "averaged out" in her experience. Discuss (or maybe just take time to think about) the fact that this will probably happen to you. Enough said.

4. Many selections speak eloquently of the ways in which contact with children with disabilities has impacted their lives. Talk about *your* contact with people with disabilities and how it has impacted your personal perspective and your professional commitment.

5. Many of the people writing as professionals in *Changes* have been impacted directly by disability in their personal lives. Discuss why they may be better equipped to do their jobs given their personal experiences. Then discuss how their personal experiences may hinder their professional effectiveness.

Reflective Writing Assignment

It is unlikely you chose your particular professional focus because you expected to become wealthy as a human service provider. If money was not your reason, then examine your personal motivations for choosing your career goals. Discuss your motivation in terms of how it may affect your style of service delivery to people with disabilities and their families.

APPENDIX 3

Support Group Discussion Guide

We include this appendix in the hope that it may be a catalyst for families of children with special needs to begin sharing their common experiences and knowledge in support group settings. However, from my attendance at the meetings of several different support groups for parents of children with special needs, it is my impression that rarely do these people have trouble talking openly to one another. They usually have more to say than there is time for in an evening meeting. Far from being a directory of rigid discussion topics, this guide is meant to be only a starting point from which sharing can begin.

The discussion suggestions which follow are grouped by the 12 focus areas in the Topical Index. To support group members or leaders they offer focus areas which may address issues relevant to the experiences of members of the group. They center primarily on issues which would be most relevant to support groups for families of children who have disabilities. They may be of some help, also, for individuals who want to further reflect about the many complications and joys of life with disability.

Topical area — The power of positive thinking or "We laughed at all the "wrong" places during *Rain Man*"

The families who wrote for *Changes* have many things in common: they have lived through what, for most people, would be considered nightmarish events and circumstances. Yet an emphasis on keeping a positive outlook and recognizing the *good* things that have happened to their families as a result of dealing with disability seems prevalent among them.

As your family has dealt with disability, have you found that there are "positives" to the experience? If so, identify one of the best things that's happened and share it with the others in your group.

There are times for all of us when focusing on the "positives" is difficult, if not impossible. Sometimes we need to acknowledge that our situations *are* extraordinary and stressful, that we're not super-human, that we get tired, angry and depressed. Talking with other people who live with similar circumstances helps a lot. In fact, one of the best things that's happened to me because I'm Sara's mom is that I've met a wonderful group of people that I'd never have met if Sara hadn't come into my life. I have cried with those people sometimes, but amazingly enough, I have laughed with them much more often. Keeping a sense of humor is a powerful coping mechanism. (Sometimes our humor might seem offensive to a lot of people; it's often a kind of ironic, "black" humor that people might have trouble understanding unless they've "been there.")

One of the best things we do at support group is share the funny things that happen to us because we're parents of kids with disabilities. Below, I've written one of our group's favorite stories. Sharing your own stories with each other would probably be a lot of fun!

A GENIAL GENETIC GIGGLE

There was a mom who had a little girl with Down syndrome. She found a great preschool program when her daughter was about four. In fact, she heard about the program (a "regular" preschool where kids with disabilities were fully included) from another mom of another (slightly older) little girl with Down syndrome. Soon the moms were car-pooling so that they had less driving to do and more time for themselves. As the first mom exited the preschool with both children one day, another preschooler's mother (obviously one who was unfamiliar with Down syndrome) gushed forth the following comment:

"I just *knew* they had to be sisters! I've never seen two kids who look more alike. They don't look like you, though. Do they take after your husband's side of the family?"

Topical area — Perspectives from people with disabilities or Over Hill, Over Dale, Where *was* that Accessible Trail?

As a parent, I have learned a lot about what it actually feels like to live with a disability from listening to my friends Bruce Blattner, Lisa DeLand, and Martha Hansen. People with disabilities have an incredible knowledge base and usually they are more than happy to share that knowledge. They can help us help our children.

Why not ask some people with disabilities in your community to share their stories and life perspectives with your group?

Topical area — Father's perspectives or "The Surgery's Going to Cost *How* Much?"

Bud Mariska, Fred McGlynn, Peter Carlyle, and Matthew McClure are exemplary of fathers who are fully involved in the lives of their children who have disabilities. Yet research literature is full of references to fathers who disengage emotionally from their child (and sometimes their family) when a disability is diagnosed.

Have fathers been given a "bad rap" What experiences in your life might help to answer that question?

Some fathers speak of feeling left out of the family picture when it comes to dealing with a child with a disability. One father in our local support group complained that he didn't know how to help his wife with their son because she never let him do anything, or if he tried, it wasn't done *right*.

Does the scenario above sound familiar to you? How can families come to share the tasks and responsibilities that are part of our lives?

Fathers who have written or spoken about their lives with children who are disabled often say that they feel they must be strong and let their families lean on them. Many say they never reveal the true depths of their sorrow about what has happened to anyone, not even their wives. (Perhaps that is why fathers have been seen by researchers as detached?)

How are fathers' reactions to life with a child who has a disability different than those of other family members?

How might this circumstance cause friction in a family?

One issue which looms prevalently in discussions of fathers of children with disabilities is the one of financial stress. Fathers seem to feel this impact in stronger and more long-term ways than do other family members. Some fathers are accused of retreating to the workplace for longer hours to escape the situation at home, but many respond that they are simply trying to make enough money to pay for what their child needs.

Why might fathers respond so much more strongly to the stressor of greatly increased financial strain than do others in the family?

How might all the above situations become marital stressors?

Topical area — Mothers' perspectives or "But I Can't Hear the Heart Monitor from the Bathtub"

It seems to be a typical circumstance for mothers to carry the major role in caring for a child with a disability. They schedule and attend appointments with doctors, therapists, school personnel, and the hoards of other professionals whose assistance is required. Mothers also seem to take on the largest role in providing home-based learning experiences for their child, and in advocating for needed services. Needless to say, there is little time left for anything else. Moms at our support group and in the research literature frequently speak of the physical and emotional exhaustion which invariably accompanies those roles.

Do you think the "super mom" response to the presence of a child with a disability is a common phenomenon? Do you see evidence of this happening in your life?

How might the "super mom" response be a positive one in the short term? How might it carry negative repercussions in the long run? How might it become a marital stressor?

As a mother, do you find ways of doing something for yourself each day (even if it's just to take a bubble bath, read a book, or fix your hair)?

Moms typically worry a lot about not having enough (any?) quality time with their husbands, significant others, etc. They sometimes speak of feeling as if they lead parallel lives with the person they love; they live in the same house, eat at the same table, sleep in the same bed, but rarely "connect." One mom who has a medically fragile child routinely sleeps in the same room with her child to make sure she hears his heart monitor if it sounds an alarm. Her recent comment at support group was, "My husband doesn't even have a warm body next to him in bed at night anymore."

Obviously these circumstances can place extraordinary stress on our most significant relationship. How might mothers and fathers avoid, or at least lessen, this impact?

Many mothers quit working outside the home when a child with disabilities comes into their lives. For many, there is no option. Often they speak of feeling like they have lost their identity to the disability (to say nothing of the income their family loses). I know that for a very long time in my life many people did not think of me as Jan; they simply thought of me as "Sara's mom." In reality, taking care of Sara was about all I did . . . and it was more than a full time job.

As a mother, does the situation above ring a bell? How do you retain some sense of self within the circumstances of your life?

In "And the Winner of the Rainbow Lottery is...", Kate Carlyle writes with stark honesty about her fears of another pregnancy following her experiences with her daughter, Katya. Carly McClure also discusses this issue within the context of her letters to me. It is also no coincidence that my fourth daughter's name is *Hope*. She got her name because that's what I did for nine months!

One of the most valuable supports the mothers in our group have offered each other has come during the months of waiting for a new baby to be born subsequent to our experiences with our children who have disabilities. Mostly, it simply helped to know that *someone* understood how frightened we were.

Discuss fears common to moms in this situation. Think about how you might help one another if someone in your group faces this scenario.

Topical area — Sibling perspectives or "Yeah, he's my brother. I'm just lucky I guess."

Like David Hansen, Jamie Mariska, Sara Wilson, Joel McGlynn, and Elizabeth Couch, siblings often speak of being enriched in many ways by their experiences with disability. They also talk about the negative side of the story.

Identify some of the positive outcomes that come from being the brother or sister of a child with disabilities.

What common concerns/problems might siblings face day-to-day?

How can families help siblings to adjust and cope with the extraordinary circumstances in their lives?

Parents often struggle with the fact of simply not having enough time/energy to go around. Siblings often feel they've "lost out," especially in families where the care of a child who is medically fragile or physically disabled simply must come first.

How does your family mesh the needs of all family members with the demands of your life circumstances? Share common strategies for giving siblings quality time when there is no way to give them enough time.

Topical area — Impact of diagnosis/disability or "No, she can't talk, but she smiles."

Carly McClure talks frequently about feeling constrained and angry about her extended family's reaction to Joshua. The comment she made which strikes a chord with many parents was "It's hard to take him out of the box when people keep trying to nail the lid shut."

Have extended members of your family (grandparents, aunts, cousins, etc.) or close friends had difficulty accepting the fact of your child's disability? How

have you handled the situation?

Carly also talks about how difficult it became for her to take Joshua out in public as he became older. Lots of times parents feel very uncomfortable with the reactions their children often receive in public. (Once a lady stared so long at Sara that I eventually asked if she'd like a photo!)

How might families deal effectively with their own "uncomfortableness" about having their child out in the real world?

How might families deal effectively with the situation when public response to our children is not what we would wish?

In "The Birthday Invitation," I talk about how scary it was for me to place Sara in a situation where she had to compete with same-age, nondisabled peers. It often seems much harder for parents to allow natural risks to be taken by our kids than it is for the kids themselves.

Do you have fears and concerns about your child being included in everyday situations with kids who do not have disabilities (daycare, school, sports, etc.)? How do you handle those personal feelings? Have you ever let these feelings keep you from allowing your child to do things other kids do?

Single-parent families of children with disabilities face the same demands on time, energy, and money that other families do, except they do it alone.

If your group includes single moms and dads, talk about some of the issues which are particular to their life situation.

Some of the coping techniques which single parents develop out of necessity can be very helpful to two-parent families. Have the single parents in your group share some practical coping strategies, for example, how do you go to a laundromat with a child in a wheelchair and keep your sanity?

Finding competent childcare for our kids with providers who have accepting attitudes is frequently a problem.

Have the members of your group share strategies for finding and keeping good childcare providers.

Topic area — Impact of no diagnosis or late diagnosis or "The doctor said he's got *what*? How do you spell it?"

In terms of long-term stress, inability to qualify for services and/or financial assistance, and many other related consequences, the impact of not having a diagnosis or receiving one long after the fact is traumatic and frustrating. While all of us cringe at the labels that are placed on our children, the fact is that in most places, without a label there is very little help available.

If there are families in your group who have experienced the lack of a diagnosis or a late diagnosis, share those stories. How is the impact different for them and their children? How might we help other families who are experiencing those problems right now?

Topic area — Full inclusion/integration in least restricted classrooms or "Bruce, can you show us how to do a wheelie?"

Federal law mandates the inclusion of our children in least restrictive environments. The law is in place because families, professionals, and the Congress agreed that it was the way things ought to be. The intent of the law is easy to understand; implementing it is a whole lot more difficult. Complications arise on every front:

Some parents may not want their kids fully included or included at all in "mainstream" classrooms.

Some parents confront ambivalent feelings as they work toward inclusion for their children — they feel scared about their child competing in the real world, but they know, for the children, it's the right thing to do.

In school districts which have resisted integration parents, often do not want their children to be the "trail blazers" of integration. Parents themselves are often too weary to fight that battle.

Some families are simply unaware that it is their child's right to be included in a least restrictive environment. And even though, by law, it is the school's responsibility that parents be informed of those rights, it doesn't always happen.

Out of prejudice, fear, or simple lack of exposure to people with disabilities, sometimes parents of kids without disabilities object loudly to the inclusion of our children in their child's classroom. Sometimes those attitudes are carried over by their children.

Sometimes mainstream classroom teachers are very frightened and resistant to the inclusion of children in their classroom whom they do not feel qualified to teach. Often, lack of exposure is again the reason. In addition, school districts have been accused of complying with the law by "dumping" kids with disabilities into mainstream classrooms without adequate (or *any*) support services for the teachers and the children.

As a group, brainstorm solutions for your particular area and situation to each of the inhibiting issues presented above.

Topical area — Life transitions and fears of risk or "I can do it, Mom and Dad, really I can!"

From reading *Changes* and living your lives, you know that all parents in some ways resist the "letting go" process which allows all children to grow up. For families of kids with special needs, the fears are a lot bigger. One mother from our support group says it helps to keep reminding herself that "our children have just as much right to fail as any other kid."

Share examples of ways that your family has overcome (a little bit at a time) the fears common to parents of kids with special needs. Talk about risks you have allowed your child to take, and whether they ended in failure or success, talk about what was learned from the experience.

Topical area — Professionals and families in partnership or "You mean I'm an expert, too?"

Changes offers ample reading and advice on family/professional partnerships. But often the most effective counsel may come from people who are dealing with the same doctors, the same teachers, the same school systems, or community with which you are dealing.

Share within your group personal knowledge and expertise of how to build effective partnerships with the unique people and situations in your community. Strategies which have worked for you will be particularly helpful to others in the group.

Topical area — Personal impact on professionals or "Stuffing feelings in a folder isn't always easy."

One of the nicest things about being a parent of a child with disabilities is getting to know professionals who become friends as well as people who help your child/family in some capacity. All of our lives have probably been enriched in some way by a caring professional whom we would never have met without the fact of our child's disability.

Share your stories of "the professional who made a wonderful difference in our lives."

INDEX

ability to dream, 11
Acceptance Is Only the First Battle, xvi, xvii
agencies, national referral list, 214
Alcoholics Anonymous, 120
alternative therapy program, 27
volunteers, 27
responsibilities toward, 30
Americans with Disabilities Act, 214
amniocentesis, 156 (see also, Marina and Katya)
amyotrophic lateral sclerosis (ALS), 120
anencephaly, 25
Applied Behavior Analysis, 149
positive reinforcement, 149
Austin, 96, 106
autism, 101, 102, 106
childhood onset pervasive developmental disorder, 102
respite care, 106

balance between necessary and optional treatment, 123
Bayley Developmental Assessment Test, 169
breaking bad news, 125
Bruce, 12, 14
C-5 Quadriplegia, 14, 204
perspectives and risk, 15
sexuality, 16
societal acceptance, 15
stigma of disability, 23
who's the expert, 20

Carnegie, Dale, 149
catheters, use of, 21
cerebral palsy, 38, 40, 204 (see also, Jon)
change necessary to meet needs, xvi
children with emotional disorders, suggestions for coping, 113, 114
choreoathetoid cerebral palsy, 116
chorion villi sampling (CVS), 155
chromosomal abnormality, 4 (see Down syndrome)
Civil Rights movement, 214 (see Rosa Parks)
classroom teacher's perspective, 137
early childhood and special educators working together, 139 Clinitron bed, 21 (see also, Bruce) Common Ground, 190
communication among parent, child, and physician, ongoing, 124
Comprehensive Developmental Center (CDC), 34, 35 (see also, Jon)
congenital heart defect, 49 consumer assertiveness, 131
communication with pharmacist and physician, 131
CO-TEACH Preschool Programs, xi, xii, xvi, 106, 139, 166
mainstreaming children with disabilities, 139
Cousins, Norman, 198

Department of Social and Rehabilitative Services, Developmental Disabilities Division, Montana, xiii
DeVries, T., 198
diagnosis of disability, impact of, 200, 210
none or late, 201, 211
Dilantin, 66
Dispensing More Than Drugs, 65, 131, 133
implications for consumers and health care professionals, 132, 133, 134
Division of Educational Research and Services, Montana, 149
Down syndrome, 15, 42, 135, 141, 153, 156, 165, 204, 207
Duchenne muscular dystrophy, 116

Early Education Program for Children with Disabilities, xiv, xv
early intervention, 27, 42, 53, 159
Education of the Handicapped Act Amendments of 1986 (P.L. 99-457), viii, x
epiglottis, 179

"Families and Disability: Diverse Strategies for Growth," 127
families of children with disabilities, 50
feelings of therapist who fails, 144-45
Food and Drug Administration, 130
Friedreich ataxia (spinocerebellar degeneration), 117

genetic bias for disabling conditions, 119
family's need to know, 119
gestational diabetes, 157

health care providers, 115
Hippocrates, 198

home-based therapy, 26
questions to consider, 29-30
House Subcommittee on Select Education, ix, x

independence, striving for, 19
Individualized Habilitation Plan (IHP), 89
Individuals with Disabilities Education Act, 214

James, William, 198
John, 111
difficulty with anger, 112
relationships with teachers, 112
traumatic head injury, 111
loss of athletic ability, 112
Jon, 33
physical therapy, 36
spastic diplegic cerebral palsy, 38
Joshua, 159, 161
developmentally delayed, 176, 179
evaluation, 174
group home placement, 174

Kazdin, A., 150
Klonopin, 68, 69
Kubler-Ross, Elisabeth, 119

Least Restrictive Environments, 135
full inclusion, integration, 202, 212
life expectancy with quadriplegia, 16
life transitions, fears of risk, 203, 213
Lisa, 71
Child Study Team, 84
Kiwanis Club, Herdsman Award, 77
self-determination, 93
self-sufficiency trust bill, 86
sterilization, 86, 93

Magnetic Resonance Image (MRS) Scan, 39
mainstreaming children with disabilities, 139-43
communicating with parents, 141
Marina and Katya, 153
chorion villi sampling (CVS), 155
Down syndrome, 153
Martha, 1, 5, 9
attitudes and choices, 1
mainstreaming, 3
positive possibilities, 1, 4
spinal fusion, 3

medical advice in crises, importance of, 22, 23
medical technology blindness syndrome, 63, 199
Miranda, 109
wholeness, 109
Montana Early Intervention Outreach Program, 106
Mycostatin, 65
myoclonic seizures, 119
Mysoline, 66

National Association for the Education of Young Children, 138
Nietzsche, 198
nocturnal epilepsy, 60, 63, 67
nystagmus, 61

Office of Special Education Programs, Division of Personnel Preparation, xv
out-of-home placement, 96

package inserts, medication, 130, 132
parenting special needs child, Hvi
commonalities, xviii
optimal service delivery, xx
Parent's Let's Unite for Kids (PLUK), 90
Parkinson's disease, 150, 151
consumer as expert, 150
parks, Rosa, 214
partnership, professionals and families, 204, 213
Pediatric Developmental Questionnaire, 35
pediatric neurology, 115
perspective for reader, 16
perspectives
of fathers, 199, 208
financial stress, 208
of mothers, 199, 208-209
of people with disabilities, 198, 199, 207
of siblings, 200, 210
perspectives and risks, changing, 15
perspectives of sibling/physical therapist, 147, 148
pharmacists, 127
adverse reactions to medications, knowledge of, 130
ally and advocate, 131
partnership with families and physicians, 128
qualifications of, 127
services offered, 127, 129

pharmacology vs. etiology, 127
physician's most effective role, 122
Pitocin, 60
  drug to strengthen uterine contractions during delivery, 60
porencephaly, bilateral, 25
positive possibilities, 1,4 (see also, Martha)
power of positive thinking, 197, 206
professionals, personal impact on, 205
Public Law 94-142, 79, 84, 87
Public Law 99-457 (IDEA), viii, x, 153
purpose of project, xvii

quadriplegia C-5, 14, 204

resolving the abnormality, 6
respite care, 106
  need for, 107, 108, 202
Reye syndrome, 118
Roosevelt, Eleanor, 198
Russo, E., 159

Sammi, 25
  alternative therapy program, 27
    volunteers, 27
  bilateral porencephaly, 25
  cerebral palsy, 28
  early intervention, 26
  home-based therapy, 26
  spastic quadriplegia, 28
  trusting one's instincts, 26
Sara, 31, 42, 46
  congenital heart defect, 49
  Down syndrome, 42, 47
  mainstreaming, 53
Sara's Lamp, 31
Sean, 60
  "Dispensing More Than Drugs," 65 (see also, 129)
  medical technology blindness syndrome, 63
  nocturnal epilepsy, 60, 63
  nystagmus, 61
seizure disorder, 64, 66
sexuality, 16
  male/female relationships between persons with disabilities, difficulty of, 19
Shaw, George Bernard, 198
significant emotional event, 42
Sister of the Heart, 56-57
Skinner, B.F., 149
  behavioral assessment, 149
societal acceptance, 15
spastic diplegic cerebral palsy, 38
Specialized Foster Family Care, 104
Special Olympics, 15, 136
stigma associated with disability, 23
  attitude toward by person with disability, 24
Supplemental Security Income (SSI), 96, 102
support group settings, 206

thoughts for professionals, 41
trusting one's instincts, 26

"Untold Diagnosis," by Mary Pielaet, 118
utilizing book's structure, how to, xix
  Instructor's Guide, xx
  Reflective Writing Assignment, xx

VIDEOSHARE, 106

Werdig-Hoffman disease, 1, 5, 9
Wolf, M., Social Validity, 150